AmICA

D1440598

University of the
West of England

**ST MATTHIAS
LIBRARY**

This book should be returned by the last date
stamped below.

Telephone Renewals (24 hours): 0117 32 82092

Library Web Address: http://www.uwe.ac.uk/library/

American Cold War Culture

Edited by Douglas Field

Edinburgh University Press

Editorial matter and organisation © Douglas Field, 2005.
Copyright in the chapters is retained by the individual contributors.

Edinburgh University Press Ltd
22 George Square, Edinburgh

Typeset in Goudy Old Style by
Hewer Text Ltd, Edinburgh, and
printed and bound in Great Britain by
Antony Rowe Ltd, Chippenham, Wilts

A CIP record for this book is available from the British Library

ISBN 0 7486 1922 4 (hardback)
ISBN 0 7486 1923 2 (paperback)

Contents

PART TWO: CULTURAL FORMS

Acknowledgements

Many of the contributors themselves provided resources, encouragement and suggestions. In particular I would like to thank Robert Corber for his initial support of the collection. Thanks to the team at Edinburgh University Press. Nicola Carr's support and insight have been invaluable, as well as Eddie Clark's cheerful efficiency. I would also like to express my gratitude to Ben Harker and Hugh Stevens for reading sections of the book and for their sharp and thoughtful observations. Thanks also to Duke University Press and Rowman & Littlefield Publishers, Inc., for supplying me with books when I was down and out. Finally, a big thank you to Harry Morgan for his acute comments and sense of humour and, above all, to Marie Crook, for her sharp eye, incisive suggestions and relentless support.

Notes on the Contributors

Robert J. Corber is Professor of Queer Studies, Trinity College, Conneticut.

Douglas Field is an independent scholar who has taught at the University of York and Staffordshire University.

Jacqueline Foertsch is Assistant Professor of English at the University of North Texas.

Catherine Gunther Kodat is Associate Professor of English and American Studies at Hamilton College.

Scott Lucas is Professor of American Studies at the University of Birmingham.

Alan Nadel is Professor of Literature and Film in the Department of Language, Literature and Communication at Rensselaer Polytechnic Institute.

David Ryan is a Principal Lecturer in the School of Historical and International Studies, Faculty of Humanities, at De Montfort University.

Dina Smith is Assistant Professor of Film Studies in the Department of English at Drake University.

Hugh Stevens lectures in nineteenth- and twentieth-century literature in the Department of English Language and Literature at University College London.

I wus lookin' high an' low for them Reds everywhere,
I wus lookin' in the sink an' underneath the chair

.   .   .   .

Then I changed my name to Sherlock Holmes.
Followed some clues from my detective bag
And discovered they wus red stripes on the American
   flag!
(Bob Dylan, 'Talkin' John Birch Paranoid Blues', 1962)

Introduction

When the Cold War ended, some predicted that the era of direct threats
to our nation was over . . . They were wrong. While the threats to
America have changed, the need for victory has not. We are fighting
shadowy, entrenched enemies – enemies using the tools of terror and
guerrilla war.

(George W. Bush, 'Speech to Citadel Cadets', 2001)[1]

In these conflicts . . . the force of world Communism operates in a
twilight zone between political subversion and quasi-military action.
Their military tactics are those of the sniper, the ambush, and the raid.
Their political tactics are terror, extortion, and assassination.

(Secretary of Defense Robert McNamara, 1962)[2]

In Chandler Davis's story 'The Nightmare', an FBI agent discovers a laboratory
for manufacturing bombs in New York City. Contemplating the devastation of
these violent devices, he imagines, 'A pillar of multi-colored smoke rising from
the city, erasing the Bronx and Manhattan down to Central Park . . . A
nightmare, a familiar and a very real nightmare, an accepted part of modern life,
something you couldn't get away from.'[3] Four years on from 11 September 2001,
Davis's story, which was published in 1946, has an eerie and prophetic quality.
The Cold War has ended but the 'age of anxiety' remains.[4] The spectre of
communism has been eradicated, but the spectre of terrorism looms.

In his presidential address to the American nation on 6 June 2002, George
W. Bush announced the formation of a permanent Department of Homeland Security. Nine months after the events of 11 September 2001, Bush
proposed 'the most extensive reorganization of the federal government since
the 1940s':

During his presidency, Harry Truman recognized that our nation's fragmented defenses had to be reorganized to win the Cold War. He proposed uniting our military forces under a single Department of Defense, and creating the National Security Council to bring together defense, intelligence, and diplomacy. Truman's reforms are still helping us to fight terror abroad, and now we need similar dramatic reforms to secure our people at home.[5]

Bush's decision to create the Department of Homeland Security (uniting, among other agencies, the Coast Guard, the Border Patrol and Immigration officials) was hastened, as the President makes explicit, by the shifting nature of threats to America. 'This is a conflict without battlefields or beachheads,' Bush declared to the American public in 2001, 'a conflict with opponents who believe they are invisible'.[6]

More than half a century after the height of the Cold War, there is a startling return to a rhetoric of anxiety: a renewed concern to fortify national boundaries; a drive to combat and contain an international threat to America; and a continuing struggle to identify and detain these 'shadowy, entrenched enemies'.[7] In contrast to the brutal beginnings of this present 'war on terror', indelibly inscribed by the events of 11 September 2001, historians and cultural analysts have long debated the origins of the Cold War.[8] As Alan Nadel notes in his influential book on Cold War culture, *Containment Culture: American Narratives, Postmodernism, and the Atomic Age*, 'some date the beginnings of the cold war to Churchill's iron curtain speech, and others to US–Soviet relations that antedate even World War II', while for Nadel, 'the crucial factor . . . that gives the cold war its unique qualities is the atomic bomb'.[9]

Despite differing views on the genesis of the Cold War, the political and cultural period from *c.* 1947 to the mid-1960s is characterised by a rhetoric of containment, a doctrine that sought to stem the 'red flow' of communism. In 1947 George Kennan, director of Secretary of State George Marshall's policy planning staff, drew attention to the rising geopolitical threat of the Soviet Union. Unlike the clearly demarcated battles of the Second World War, communism, Kennan iterated, 'cannot be easily defeated or discouraged by a single victory on the part of its opponents'. Instead, Kennan proposed that America must respond, not with 'threats or blustering or superfluous gestures of outward "toughness"', but through a policy of 'long-term, patient but firm and vigilant containment of Russian expansive tendencies'.[10]

Although Kennan would later disassociate himself from the political strategy of 'containment', his famous article (published under the pseudonym

Mr X in *Foreign Affairs*) quickly became the defining political and military strategy to confront and resist the encroaching spread of communism. The direct impact of Kennan's article ('The Sources of Soviet Conduct') on American diplomacy is difficult to gauge: it is not clear whether Kennan initiated a shift towards containment, or whether he voiced a growing consensus in the Truman administration. What is clear, however, is that containment increasingly became a defining narrative of the Cold War era, spurred on by the 'steady ooze' of communism. By 1949, as Ronnie D. Lipschutz points out, 'Soviet-backed governments had gained power in all of the countries of Central and Eastern Europe except Austria'.[11] Even more alarming was the eruption of communism beyond the borders of Europe and the Soviet Union. The victory of communism in China (1949) was swift and unexpected, and news on 25 June 1950 that Communist North Korea had invaded South Korea made it clear that the containment of communism was a global, not just a European struggle.

In contrast to the clearly identifiable enemies of Second World War (Italy, Germany and Japan), communism transcended geographical borders, including hastily erected boundaries, such as the Iron Curtain, a Bamboo Curtain in the East and 'parallels' in Korea.[12] If the 'disease' of communism emanated from the Soviet Union, then other countries were quickly 'infected'. To contain one country was difficult, but to quarantine a growing number of infected states questioned the very foundations of this policy. On the one hand, as Scott Lucas has pointed out, 'the objective of the US government from 1948 was not to contain Soviet Communism but to vanquish it'.[13] And yet the very difficulty that American strategists faced was extinguishing the source of communism. As critics of containment, such as James Burnham, quickly pointed out in the early 1950s, 'in a profound sense . . . there is no Soviet border'.[14]

The growing awareness of communism's ability to seduce and infiltrate disparate countries (including former allies) was a crucial turning point in American Cold War politics. From the late 1940s there was a growing concern that communism, this 'hydra-headed super-enemy', could take root in America itself.[15] By the early 1950s, communism was increasingly seen as a threat, not only from without, but also from within the American body politic. In 1950, American policymakers set out a long-term strategy, NSC-68, that emphasised the Soviet Union's aims to 'contaminate' the Western world with its communist ideology: 'The Soviet Union, unlike previous aspirants to hegemony, is animated by a new fanatic faith, antithetical to our own, and seeks to impose its absolute authority over the rest of the world.'[16] Crucially, the authors of NSC-68 pointed not only to Soviet threats abroad, but to how their 'preferred technique is to subvert by infiltration and intimidation'. America, the report warned, must be on its guard against the corruption of 'labor unions, civic enterprises, schools, churches, and all media for influencing opinion'.[17]

The NSC-68 report highlighted (and also reproduced) two crucial shifts in the perception of communism. The first was that communists operated covertly, with the implication that, since they preferred 'infiltration and intimidation', they were not easily identifiable. And the second was that labour unions, schools and churches – important organs of the American body politic – were open to corruption. While the US government had deployed tactics to detect communism in national organisations from the 1930s (most evident in the House Un-American Activities Committee (HUAC)), there were increasing concerns that this Soviet 'disease' would spread to the entire American body politic. From the early 1950s, attempts to contain the threat of communism from within were repeatedly illustrated by sharply drawn rhetorical boundaries, acutely illustrated by Eisenhower's inaugural speech in 1953: 'The Forces of good and evil are massed and armed and opposed as rarely before in history – Freedom is pitted against slavery; lightness against the dark.'[18]

Crucially, this Manichean view of a word divided between bad and good, darkness and light, communist and capitalist, was increasingly adopted at a time when the very divisions were constantly threatening to collapse and elide. While an Iron Curtain rhetoric in America made rigid distinctions between 'Us' and 'Them', the very source of Cold War anxiety lay precisely in identifying these oppositions.[19] Nowhere is this division made more apparent than by the HUAC, where the very name of the organisation made clear distinctions between American and non-American behaviour. And yet, as I show below, during the Cold War era in America this very distinction threatened to fall apart. There was, as Tom Engelhardt writes, 'confusion over the location of the real enemy. Was the enemy out there, or was it some aspect of the American self?'[20]

Us and Them: McCarthy

It starts with upholding doctrine. The doctrine which says either you're with us, or you're with the enemy.

(George W. Bush, 'Speech at Massachusetts Victory Reception', 2002)[21]

The allusion by President Bush's speech-makers to Truman's creation of the Defense Department points to the radical post-war reorganisation and expansion of federal government employment. Not only did Pentagon expenditures quadruple between 1948 and 1953, but the number of government employees rose from 953,891 in 1939 to almost three million shortly after the war.[22] Not surprisingly, the increase in federal employees fuelled national security concerns. In 1947 the FBI's J. Edgar Hoover testified before the HUAC, pointing to the threat of domestic communism. While Hoover acknowledged that the Communist Party of the United States consisted of less than 1 per cent of American voters, he was quick to point out their 'ability to infiltrate'. Crucially, Hoover also drew attention to what he saw as the thin line between socialism and communism, a point discussed below: 'I do fear for the liberal and progressive who has been hoodwinked and duped into joining hands with the Communists.'[23]

Hoover's call to turn attention to domestic communism gave one man in particular, Senator Joseph McCarthy, a political direction that had proved hitherto elusive (in 1950 he had been voted 'worst US Senator').[24] Much has been written on the devastating effects of McCarthy's much-loathed political career to the extent that myth has merged with fact. As one of McCarthy's biographers, Arthur Herman has noted: 'most of what people ordinarily mean when they talk about the 'red scare' – the House Un-American Activities Committee; anti-Communist probes into Hollywood, labor unions, and America's schools and universities; the Rosenberg trial . . . had nothing to do with McCarthy.'[25] Herman's biography teeters between clarifying statistics ('Exactly 560 persons, out of more than 2 million employees, were dismissed or denied a federal job between November 1947 and the end of April 1953') and exonerating McCarthy ('no one went to jail [in the McCarthy era] without a legal warrant, no one was convicted without a trial').[26] While Herman is surely right to clarify recalcitrant myths about McCarthy, McCarthysism contributed to a crucial aspect of Cold War America. According to David Caute, McCarthy

> was the first right-wing demagogue in American history who denounced no specific racial, ethnic or religious group . . . one of the appeals of McCarthyism was that it offered every American, however precarious his ancestry, the chance of being taken for a good American, simply by demonstrating a gut hatred for Commies.[27]

Caute's striking observation points to ways in which McCarthyism sought to define a homogeneous American identity, one united in opposition to communist practice. And yet this deceptively simple division lies at the heart of Cold War anxiety. Magazines in the 1950s confidentially published articles on how to spot a communist (according to an article in *Life* magazine

'Even his sex life [was] synchronized with the obligations of The Cause').[28] Films such as *I Was a Communist for the FBI* (1951), *My Son John* (1952) and *Pickup on South Street* (1953) were obsessed with the ways in which communists could be identified, offering differing and confusing advice.[29] In politics, there were important disagreements about the boundaries between socialism and communism: according to hardliners such as Robert Taft, the position was clear: 'Those who accept the principle of socialism . . . have a hard time battling against the ideology of Communism', yet for others it was acceptable that communism and liberalism shared certain ideological goals.[30] Even more worrying was the notion that Americans 'became communist' without realising it, illustrated by the 1956 film *Invasion of the Bodysnatchers*, where people are taken over by alien forces without their knowledge.[31] The extent (and the failure) of these relentless investigations did, however, prove one thing beyond doubt: that communism could not be easily identified. And if 'They' could not be identified, what did this say about 'Us'?

BOUNDARIES AND ANXIETY

> Obviously we were afraid of something more than the Communists. Dread has been loose in the twentieth century, and America has shivered in its horror since the Depression and the Second War.
>
> (Norman Mailer, *The Presidential Papers*, 1964)[32]

Recent Cold War scholars have urged for a re-examination of the narrative of containment during the Cold War. In 'Considering Cultures: How to Make Sense of our Cold War', Scott Lucas is mindful of the need to question the overuse of the term 'containment': 'A term like "domestic containment" can be bandied about so often that analysis has little significance. Who was being contained? By what means? And, most significantly, to what end?'[33] Lucas's essay usefully points to the ways in which terms associated with Cold War culture have become embedded in recent scholarship, reminding scholars of the need to question and re-examine established narratives.

American Cold War Culture explores the relationship between politics and culture in the period of c. 1947 to the mid-1960s. While the book engages with the theme of containment, the chapters critique and expand on recent Cold War scholarship. Central to the book is the claim that this period was characterised by an anxiety over boundaries. Thus, while *American Cold War Culture* explores the impact of communism on American political life, it explores the ways in which this period witnessed an increasing anxiety over manifold boundaries, whether racial, sexual, political or cultural. In particular, the collection is attentive to the need to re-examine American Cold War culture; to take a new look at the relationship between politics and culture, but also at how discussions of Cold War 'culture' in America need to consider a wide range of phenomena. Too often Cold War American culture is presented as white, male and monolithic, overlooking the impact of race, homosexuality and feminist cultures.

Nadel's discussion of the bomb in relation to the Cold War serves as a pertinent reminder that atomic warfare not only marked the beginning of the Cold War but also had the capability to finish it. On the one hand, the very real threat of nuclear war during this age led to a profound sense of anxiety: the fear that all national boundaries could be obliterated. And yet this new kind of warfare, launched from one country to another, also redrew the boundaries across the world. Much as advances in technology led to the idea of a 'global village', the long ranges of atomic and nuclear warfare led to a 'nuclear village', paradoxically drawing countries closer at a time when boundaries were hurriedly sought. While magazines and films testified to the devastating destruction of atomic bombs, radiation, unlike conventional weapons, had the ability to contaminate and destroy invisibly. From politics to culture, seeped an unstoppable rhetoric of contamination, illustrated by Kennan, who, in a rhetoric analogous to sci-fi films of unstoppable ooze, referred to communism as 'a fluid stream which moves constantly, wherever it is permitted to move . . . Its main concern is to make sure it has filled every nook and cranny available to it in the basin of world power.'[34]

During the 1950s, the Truman 'Loyalty Program' defined disloyalty not only through membership of communist organisations, but also through association. As Jacqueline Foertsch has shown: 'This introduced the idea that one could be and not be a communist at the same time, that one could "contract" the ideology without even knowing it.' The difficulties in identifying communists precipitated what Foertsch calls 'fears of widespread "contamination", a red plague'.[35]

This fear of contamination, whether from radiation or communism, was manifest, as numerous cultural critics have noted, in the plethora of invasion and horror films of the 1950s.[36] The boundaries between science, culture and politics also blurred in the post-war years, as advances in virology and immunology drew attention, not to the city or house, but to the ways to safeguard the body from unwanted germs. As Emily Martin has observed, the 'notion that the immune system maintains a clear boundary between self and nonself is often accompanied by a conception of the nonself world as foreign and hostile'.[37]

In *Enemies Within*, Jacqueline Foertsch convincingly argues that the Cold War era in America was like a plague, 'not of communism or of bomb-related illness, but of paranoia, xenophobia, and red-baiting that took on witch-hunt proportions'.[38] In an era that saw the collapse of the racial order (and in particular the desegregation of the army and the education system in 1948 and 1954 respectively), there were increasing references to the 'contamination' of miscegenation, the blurring of boundaries between white and black culture.

A rhetoric of contamination also dominated discussions of deviant sexuality. Homosexuality, as Robert Corber has argued, was directly linked to national security concerns: more government employees were dismissed under the suspicion of homosexuality than for communism.[39] Influential post-war studies (notably the Kinsey Reports of 1948 and 1953) argued, not only that homosexuality was widespread, but that it was difficult to identify.[40] As George Chauncey has noted, 'The specter of the invisible homosexual, like that of the invisible communist, haunted Cold War America.'[41] 'Not All Homos Are Easy to Spot', warns a March 1958 issue of the men's magazine *Sir!*, in a language reminiscent of the concerns to spot communists.[42] Homosexuality, like communism, was frequently referred to as a disease and invasion; both were seen as infections that were not locatable under the boundaries of ethnicity, dress, language or religion. In the words of Norman Mailer, writing in 1962, 'we have presented the Russians to the American public as implacable, insane, and corrupting. We could have been talking equally of the plague or some exotic variety of sex.'[43] Even the language of cultural criticism was not 'immune' to the language of disease and pollution. While critics such as Lionel Trilling wrote of the novel's sickness and death, Dwight McDonald warned of the spread of mass culture: 'there is slowly emerging a tepid, flaccid middlebrow culture that threatens to engulf everything in its spreading ooze.'[44]

The rhetoric of contamination and anxiety from the late 1940s to the 1960s illustrates the ways in which the Cold War impacted on American life, from politics to high and low culture. With the looming threat of communism, American culture became, as Stephen Whitfield has argued, 'politicized'.[45] And yet, in a profound sense, American politics was becoming increasingly acculturated, just as American culture became politicised. As the chapters in *American Cold War Culture* iterate, not only was US culture far from monolithic, but the boundaries between politics and culture are shadowy and blurred.

Part One of this book, 'Cultural Themes', begins with Jacqueline Foertsch's chapter, '"A Battle of Silence": Women's Magazines and the Polio Crisis in Post-war UK and USA'. Analogous to other Cold War scares, the dangers of polio, Foertsch contends, were 'contained' by (and within) contemporary popular magazines that 'silenced' the very real threat of contamination to children. Foertsch examines how polio-themed articles present the role of the mother during this crisis, exploring contradictory portraits of the mother as inspirational 'protector', but also as lax housewife in 'need' of advice and guidance.

Foertsch's chapter is followed by Robert Corber's, 'All about the Sub-versive Femme: Cold War Homophobia in *All about Eve*'. Arguing that Cold War discussions of same-sex practice have often conflated (male) homosexual and lesbian discourses, Corber explores the figure of the femme in relation to *All about Eve*. Unlike the butch, the femme, as Corber notes, in her ability to pass as straight, posed a greater threat to national security, while at the same time revealing the artificial constructions of 'normative' sexual behaviour.

David Ryan's chapter, 'Mapping Containment: The Cultural Construc-tion of the Cold War', argues that the cultural construction of the Cold War was imperative not just to mobilise US culture and society but also to facilitate the ideological construction of the 'West' and the integration of Western Europe into the US political, economic and ideological order. Given the diverse experiences between Western Europe and the United States, the Soviets provided a unique opportunity and object to contrast the Western identity against. As Ryan demonstrates, such a Manichaean construction and the creation of the West displaced several transatlantic divisions that had the potential to undermine the teleological US vision of the post-war order.

Dina Smith's chapter, 'Movable Containers: Cold War Trailers and Trailer Parks', explores the materialisation of Cold War containment culture through the trailer, connecting it to Cold War discourses on mobility, suburbanisation, domesticity and military escalation as they connect to modern design theories. Linking early Cold War trailer images to late and nostalgic Cold War narratives, Smith discusses the relationship between the trailer as a site for Cold War surveillance and how it shapes/unshapes various political discourses.

My own chapter focuses on the reception of James Baldwin's *Giovanni's Room*. While Baldwin's second novel is lauded as a seminal work of homo-sexual literature, its relationship to the Cold War is often overlooked. Set in Paris, with no black characters, Baldwin's novel, this chapter contends, reflects and critiques Cold War anxieties, both about racial integration, and also the spectre of 'invisible' homosexuality.

Part Two of the collection, 'Cultural Forms', begins with Catherine Gunther Kodat's chapter, 'Disney's *Song of the South* and the Birth of the

White Negro'. Focusing on the 1946 Disney film (an adaptation of Joel Chandler Harris's 'Uncle Remus' tales), Kodat examines the widespread popularity of this controversial picture. Moving beyond a discussion of the film's overt racism (the film has since been withdrawn), Kodat examines *Song of the South* in relation to a complex Cold War dialectic between 'Negrophilia' and 'Negrophobia', drawing on writing from Norman Mailer and Bernard Wolfe.

Scott Lucas's chapter, 'Policing Disssent: "Orwell" and Cold War Culture, 1945–2004', examines the ways that Orwell was claimed and mobilised by the UK and USA as a pawn in the cultural battle against Soviet Communism. Countering widely held views of Orwell as an anti-establishment voice of dissent, Lucas unravels entrenched views on this quintessentially British author whose writings and sentiments were increasingly adopted as 'the voice of an American-defined freedom to be spread around the world'.

Alan Nadel's chapter, 'Cold War Television and the Technology of Brainwashing', examines the significance and impact of television's entrance into American cultural life during the Cold War. Television, Nadel argues, had an unprecedented hold on American life. While it was heavily censored, it increasingly became 'the apparatus of umediated reality', a medium, it was believed, that could put Americans in touch with everything. At the same time, television was inextricably linked to the technology of the surveillance state, an invisible force that both facilitated and controlled personal freedom, a concern that Nadel links to the phenomenon of brainwashing.

In the final chapter, 'Confession, Autobiography and Resistance: Robert Lowell and the Politics of Privacy', Hugh Stevens looks at the career of Robert Lowell in the late 1950s and 1960s, exploring the poet's involvement in the development of 'confessional poetry'. Stevens argues that, even if confessional poetry represented the private and intimate self, it is also highly self-conscious about the political implications of representations of privacy in the public domain. Not only did the confessional poets develop an accessible poetic language, but they also registered the invasion of the political into everyday life. Stevens shows how key poems in the collections *Life Studies* and *For the Union Dead* register the complex emotional experiences of the Cold War, and represent the individual's relation to national politics in ways that provide incisive critiques of American imperialism.

NOTES

1. George W. Bush, 'Excerpted Remarks by the President from Speech to Citadel Cadets', Charleston, South Carolina, 11 December 2001, in Bush, *We Will Prevail: George Bush on War, Terrorism, and Freedom*, foreword by Pegg Noonan, introduction by Jay Nordlinger (New York and London: Continuum International Publishing Group, 2003), p. 91.
2. Robert McNamara, February 1962, quoted by Tom Engelhardt, *The End of Victory Culture: Cold War America and the Disillusioning of a Generation*, 2nd edn (Amherst, MA: University of Massachusetts Press, 1995), p. 154.
3. Quoted by David Seed, *American Science Fiction and the Cold War* (Edinburgh: Edinburgh University Press, 1999) p. 19.
4. See Warren Susman (with the assistance of Edward Griffin), 'Did Success Spoil the United States? Dual Representations in Postwar America', in Lary May (ed.), *Recasting America: Culture and Politics in the Age of the Cold War* (Chicago: University of Chicago Press, 1989), pp. 19–37.
5. George W. Bush, 'Presidential Address to the Nation', 6 June 2002, in Bush, *We Will Prevail*, p. 166.
6. George W. Bush, 'Presidential Radio Address to the Nation', 15 September 2001, in ibid. p. 8.
7. While I am not equating the war on terror with communism during the Cold War, there is a startling dialogue between the two eras, not only in the rhetoric of anxiety but in Bush's references to the Cold War in relation to the political climate following 11 September 2001. See for example Bush, 'Excerpted Remarks from the President's State of the Union Address 28 January 2003', in Bush, *We Will Prevail*: 'Before September the 11th, many in the world believed that Saddam Hussein could be contained. But chemical agents, lethal viruses, and shadowy terrorist networks are not easily contained' (p. 219).
8. See Engelhardt, *The End of Victory Culture*, who analyses the impact of Pearl Harbor in terms that are reminiscent of 11 September 2001: 'a savage, nonwhite enemy had launched a barbaric attack on Americans going about their lives . . . and that enemy would be repaid in brutal combat . . .' (p. 5.) See also Bush, who described Pearl Harbor as 'a decisive day that changed our nation forever . . . And the four years that followed transformed the American way of war' ('Excerpted Remarks by the President from Speech to Citadel Cadets', in Bush, *We Will Prevail*, p. 89).
9. Alan Nadel, *Containment Culture: American Narratives, Postmodernism, and the Atomic Age* (Durham, NC, and London: Duke University Press, 1995), p. 13. For a useful overview of Cold War developments, see anon., *Cold War Chronology* (1939–55), http://www.people.memphis.edu/sherman/chronoColdWar.htm
10. George F. Kennan, 'The Sources of Soviet Conduct', in Kennan, *American Diplomacy, 1900–1950* (Chicago: University of Chicago Press, 1951), pp. 98, 99.
11. Ronnie D. Lipschutz, *Cold War Fantasies: Film, Fiction, and Foreign Policy* (Lanham, MD: Rowman and Littlefield Publishers, 2001), p. 19.
12. Engelhardt, *The End of Victory Culture*, p. 95.
13. Scott Lucas, 'Afterword: Considering Cultures: How to Make Sense of our Cold War', in Nathan Abrams and Julie Hughes (eds), *Containing America: Cultural Production and Consumption in 50s America* (Birmingham: Birmingham University Press, 2000), p. 191.
14. Quoted by Arthur Herman, *Joseph McCarthy: Reexamining the Life and Legacy of America's Most Hated Senator* (New York: Free Press, 2000), p. 147.
15. Engelhardt, *The End of Victory Culture*, p. 6.
16. Quoted by Lipschutz, *Cold War Fantasies*, p. 43.

17. Quoted in ibid. p. 44.
18. Quoted by Herman, *Joseph McCarthy*, p. 208.
19. As numerous cultural critics have noted, since 11 September 2001 Bush has increasingly used a rhetoric of 'us' and 'them' and 'good' and 'evil'. See, for example, 'Presidential Address to the Nation', 11 September 2001, in Bush, *We Will Prevail*. The third sentence is as follows: 'Thousands of lives were suddenly ended by evil, despicable acts of terror' (p. 2.) (The word 'evil' is used three times in this very brief address.)
20. Engelhardt, *The End of Victory Culture*, p. 65.
21. George W. Bush, 'Excerpted Remarks by the President from Speech at Massachusetts Victory 2002 Reception', 4 October 2002, in Bush, *We Will Prevail*, p. 187.
22. Englehardt, *The End of Victory Culture*, p. 75; Herman, *Joseph McCarthy*, p. 42.
23. Herman, *Joseph McCarthy*, p. 57.
24. Ibid. p. 51.
25. Ibid. p. 4.
26. Ibid. pp. 108, 62–3.
27. David Caute, *The Great Fear: The Anti-Communist Purge under Truman and Eisenhower* (New York: Simon and Schuster, 1978), p. 21. See Chip Berlet and Matthew N. Lyons, *Right-Wing Populism in America: Too Close For Comfort* (New York and London: Guilford Press, 2000), who note that McCarthy avoided 'open ethnic bigotry', but that he 'helped initiate a broad rightwing move from open biological racism toward subtler cultural racism' (p. 161).
28. Engelhardt, *The End of Victory Culture*, p. 116. Recent events have seen a resurgence in surveillance operations that are reminiscent of the Cold War, including attempts at identifying terrorists by scrutinising shopping lists and employing a radar-based device that spots the way terrorists walk. On shopping lists, see Erik Baard, 'Buying Trouble', *Village Voice*, 24–30 July 2002, http://villagevoice.com/issues/0230/baard.php; on radar devices to identify individual walking patterns, see http://charleston.net.stories/052003/ter 20 pentagon.shtml
29. For a brief but incisive account of these films, see Lipschutz, *Cold War Fantasies*, pp. 35–53.
30. Herman, *Joseph McCarthy*, p. 59.
31. See Lary May, 'Movie Star Politics: The Screen Actors' Guild, Cultural Conversion, and the Hollywood Red Scare', in May (ed.), *Recasting America*, p. 142. Ronald Reagan, who acted as an undercover agent for the FBI, concluded: 'the bulk of communist work is done by people who are sucked into carrying out red policy without knowing what they are doing' (p. 142).
32. Norman Mailer, 'The Eighth Presidential Paper – Red Dread', in Mailer, *The Presidential Papers* (London: André Deutsch, 1964), p. 161.
33. Lucas, 'Afterword: Considering Cultures', p. 190.
34. Kennan, 'The Sources of Soviet Conduct', p. 98.
35. Jacqueline Foertsch, *Enemies Within: The Cold War and the AIDS Crisis in Literature, Film, and Culture* (Urbana and Chicago: University of Illinois Press, 2001), p. 19.
36. See, for example, Seed, *American Science Fiction and the Cold War*.
37. Emily Martin, *Flexible Bodies: Tracking Immunity in American Culture – From the Days of Polio to the Age of AIDS* (Boston: Beacon Press, 1994), p. 53.
38. Foertsch, *Enemies Within*, p. 9.
39. Robert J. Corber, *In the Name of National Security: Hitchcock, Homophobia, and the Political Construction of Gender in Postwar America* (Durham, NC, and London: Duke University Press, 1993), especially p. 8.
40. For a useful discussion of the impact of the Kinsey reports on male and female sexual behaviour, see ibid., especially pp. 8–9, 63–5.
41. George Chauncey, *Gay New York: Gender, Urban Culture, and the Making of the Gay Male Underworld, 1890–1940* (New York: Basic Books, 1994), p. 360.

42. Quoted by Harry M. Benshoff, *Monsters in the Closet: Homosexuality and the Horror Film* (Manchester and New York: Manchester University Press, 1997), p. 131.
43. Mailer, 'The Eighth Presidential Paper – Red Dread', in Mailer, *The Presidential Papers*, p. 161.
44. Quoted by Jackson Lears, 'A Matter of Taste: Corporate Cultural Hegemony in a Mass-Consumption Society', in May (ed.), *Recasting America*, p. 47.
45. Stephen J. Whitfield, *The Culture of the Cold War* (1991), 2nd edn (Baltimore and London: Johns Hopkins University Press, 1996), p. 10.

Part One

Cultural Themes

CHAPTER ONE

Family

'A Battle of Silence': Women's Magazines and the Polio Crisis in Post-war UK and USA

Jacqueline Foertsch

Sociologists isolate three topics of discussion with respect to families at mid-twentieth century – the role of women in the workplace during and after the Second World War; the birth-rate 'boom' in this same interval that resulted in new, 'child-centred' modes of family making; and the anxieties generated by the Cold War (specifically about communism and the bomb). This last undermined the prosperous, celebratory mood otherwise prevailing as soldiers returned from war and settled into suburban homes, college degree programmes and/or well-paying jobs and their wives became contented mothers, skilled hostesses and avid consumers of once-again plentiful or newly devised household goods. Elaine Tyler May argues that the war emergency in the workplace opened the doors to women's 'emancipation', yet more recent studies indicate that 'the overwhelming majority of mothers stayed home between 1942 and 1945' and were happy to do so.[1] Judith Sealander contrasts the strict discipline of 1930s-era childrearing practices with the more open, caring methods espoused by post-war experts like Dr Spock, and 'togetherness' was a byword that not only benefited children but potentially challenged men's traditional roles as strong, distant fathers.[2] May deals incisively with the sexual, social and atomic anxieties that drove men and women together in an orgy of marriage, reproduction and domesticity, yet created power struggles between the sexes as well; and in her study as well as Sealander's and Skolnick's, traditional gender roles, conformity-inducing suburbs and frustrated men's and women's 'hidden lives' speak of a striking amalgam of 'dis/content' for families in the post-war/Cold War era.[3]

Significantly, each of these issues and the complex contradictions defining them figure substantially in our understanding of a sometimes overlooked chapter in this story – the polio crisis of the 1940s and 1950s, during which time record infection rates struck terror into the heart of every family member in America. Polio is instructively analogous to the other 'scares' of this period, specifically in the ways in which, for instance, both polio and communism were feared to 'infect' American families in their supposedly safest havens – the school, the home, the neighbour's backyard; like the bomb, whose biological aftermath (burns, cancers, radiation sickness) would 'spread' through surrounding populations like rampant contagion, polio could move like wildfire during the hot summer months, visiting its deadly symptoms upon the guilty and the innocent with equal fervour. While polio predates by centuries the bomb and communist threat, it, like the other bogeys of the Cold War period, was a disturbing enough prospect to be contained by (and within) popular textual forms in deeply ideological fashion.

As polio was very much a child's disease, it was equally importantly a mother's crisis, and the multiple women's magazines surveyed for this chapter show how these texts did their utmost to contain (soften, distort, avoid) the issue of polio for their readership. In this discussion, I consider how polio-themed articles framed (that is, relegated to the frame or margin) the 'bad news' of polio as gracefully as possible, and how they often remained silent with regard to the disease's most frightening aspects. I then study textual examples of a different kind of silence – stories of illnesses, children or mothering dilemmas suggestive of polio but, finally, emphatically *not* polio-related. I contend that the 'false-alarm' subtext of these alarmist pieces ultimately provides therapeutic value for their maternal audience – a 'picturing exercise' that simulates the horrors of polio but brings readers through a less serious crisis with reassuring success. Here I focus on summertime as treated in fiction, features and cover art, as summer was the peak polio season and therefore an even more anxiety-filled time for mothers. In the final section I locate a latent feminist discourse in these serials, which gives women the 'job' of protecting children from harmful illness and credits their ability to do so through maintenance of a hygienic household and a healthy lifestyle. Such writings, however, are ultimately undermined by the wealth of material questioning Mother's lax or inept ways – in 'lifestyle' features that interrogate women's housekeeping idiosyncrasies and in 'advice' columns that berate mothers or spell out the obvious with respect to health care or hygienic homekeeping.

In the July 1950 issue of *Redbook*, 'The Town that Fought for its Kids' (Fontaine 1950) chronicles the polio epidemic that struck Muncie, Indiana, in the summer of 1949. The focus is on the nurses and doctors of Ball Hospital who treated that summer's 120 polio cases, and on the mechanics and industrial workers who fashioned several iron lungs on extremely short order, all demonstrating the sort of heroism and selflessness typical for the inspiring tales found in women's magazines of this period. But the language in the article that is devoted to the actual victims of this epidemic is remarkable for its depressing candour. Here author André Fontaine describes the fear and desperation of parents and spouses trapped behind glass walls, smoking on the lawn outside and pacing the gallery, while loved ones 'fought for their lives' within; in the opening moments of the article the first polio victim, an adult woman from the working classes, dies five days after becoming ill (ibid: 46), and mid-story a charming eight-year-old boy who struggles bravely to survive in an iron lung also succumbs (ibid: 77).

While poliomyelitis, a paralysing viral syndrome that struck children and young adults in record numbers in the UK and especially the USA throughout the immediate post-war period,[4] might have been a topic of chief interest in a magazine for mothers, in fact the direct confrontation of this crisis as represented in Fontaine's article constitutes a rare instance in top women's publications from the late 1940s to the mid-1950s, when the Salk and Sabin vaccines were finally perfected.[5] Strikingly, these magazines' chief purpose seem to have been to guide women in the process of ignoring, denying or forgetting the anxieties that attended motherhood during this period, especially during the dreaded summer months when polio incidence rates almost always dramatically increased. While such fears were everywhere in waking existence – and were referred to frequently in 'mainstream' media such as *Time*, *Newsweek* and *Life* magazines, *The Times* of London and the London *Observer* – women's popular media insisted upon stories of progress and triumph in polio, when they made mention of the issue at all.[6] The silence emanating from these publications was surely a containment strategy designed to quarantine fears of polio, to minimise the horror of its epidemic effects, while the virus itself remained unstoppable.

While polio's history dates back to the pyramids, its burgeoning during the Cold War may have been, as was the Cold War itself, an outcropping of the Second World War, after which American and British soldiers fighting far-flung battles may have returned home with new mutations of the germ. Likewise it functions as a striking parallel to and exacerbation of the anxieties surrounding the Cold War, when fears of communist invasion and atomic contamination threatened national and individual boundaries and them-selves reached epidemic (hysterical) proportions. The media did their best to present a profile of national unity, vitality and strength to a home-based audience (as well as any eavesdroppers from the Eastern bloc). But while accentuating the positive certainly encouraged optimism during the fright-ening days of nuclear brinkmanship, the worldwide spread of communism and record infection rates for infantile paralysis, the sugar-coated truths presented to readers resembled disturbingly those disseminated in Soviet societies, so frequently criticised by the 'free world'.

Interestingly, *Redbook*, subtitled *A Magazine for Young Adults*, stands apart from more motherly offerings in its aim toward a younger, more sophisticated, mixed audience. While the advertising targets women in a manner typical of this period (young women exclaiming over new ovens, missing out on parties because of bad breath), its hard-hitting exposés on 'quack' doctors, tainted produce and the Kinsey report could have drawn male as well as female readers. Anti-momist ideologue Philip Wylie was a regular contributor who kept world issues such as communism and the bomb before his audience when traditional women's magazines dealt only fitfully with the issue of communism and carried on as if the bomb had never been invented. While the title seems purely coincidental, *Redbook* was the serial that brought the 'red' menace – and a host of other concerning political issues – as close to its female readership as the editors (the readers themselves may have tolerated much more) could bear.

Indeed, we may in part attribute these silences to the gender politics characteristic of that period: not surprisingly, the editorial boards of these women's publications were at least half male, with men occupying many of the top editorial positions, and the assumption that women simply could not 'handle' realistic treatment of fearful topics is not surprising. Additionally, the example of the most famous polio survivor in the USA, Franklin D. Roosevelt, who enjoyed a richly productive presidency by largely ignoring his disability, may have set the example of genteel circumspection that publishers of 'ladies' magazines sought to emulate. In UK serials, the exceeding discomforts of the war's aftermath occupied the discursive centre stage instead: stories, letters to advice columnists and news articles described the crisis of the father, brother or son who never came home, and references to paper, soap and electricity shortages crop up in ads and announcements from the mid-1940s until the early 1950s. The number-one health concern was not polio but coughs, colds and catarrh, blamed on the UK's cold and rainy winter season with its heavy fog. Thus, while summertime was in fact the danger period for increased polio infection, and a theme of relevance in American women's magazines, summer was in fact the 'healthy' period for British families, and its warming, drying, healing qualities are celebrated in several *Woman* and *Woman's Own* articles in this period (see e.g. Williams 1954, 1955). The longest, most realistic treatment of the polio issue discovered in my search of British periodicals, the two-part feature 'Our Daughter had Polio' (Reiten 1954a, b), tells the story of a girl *from Minnesota*, indicating that this topic was so removed from the British cultural terrain that its polio stories had to be imported for public consumption.

Meanwhile, it has been well documented that women during the polio era were more than aware of the magnitude of the problem and were markedly effective against it. Jane S. Smith details the multi-level structure of the National Foundation for Infantile Paralysis, whose battalions of volunteers in every city were 'manned' in large part by women. Mothers were especially famous for their house-to-house search for donors to the annual March of Dimes campaign and came from all races and social classes to gather and disseminate information, collect funds for the Foundation, staff offices and provide humanitarian comfort to families in need.[7] In the UK, women functioned at every level of the British Polio Fellowship (BPF), from co-founders to branch secretaries to staffers at the Fellowship's Christmas card production facilities. Indeed, these women 'mobilised', as does any army against its enemy, and as they did so productively during the Second World War, when factories lost their male workforce and women rushed to fill the need. For all its horrors, the polio crisis gave women a new and equally vital role to play, and women contributed tremendously to the alleviation of the difficulties in the years before the vaccine.

Thus these texts' many silences regarding the polio problem are striking for the several ways that they in fact spoke of the polio crisis to their readers anyway: in their rare moments of actual reference to the issue, in their striking omissions in language and images that should have been – and thus in fact were – about polio in the first place, and in the latent feminism locatable throughout these publications, which averred while denying women's remarkable ability to handle adverse circumstances. Whether directly treated, identifiable only subtextually, or factoring into the general context of 'family relations' during this era, polio, I contend, enabled these popular publications to consider new configurations of family structure: the 'innocent victims' in this scenario – the children – were newly vested with power – to keep themselves healthy (clean, rested, well fed, removed from sick peers) and/or to 'forgive' their parents when polio struck them, their siblings, or even the parents themselves; meanwhile traditionally superior Father, now powerless to protect his loved ones from a dreaded disease, turned to Mother for her expertise in the matters of home health and hygiene, and shared with her his sorrow and guilt in the event of polio infection.

Certainly direct references to polio are found now and then in the pages of these largely escapist publications. 'The Girl who Never Gave up' (White 1952) offers the typically optimistic story of a beautiful polio victim, wheel-chair-bound but skilful enough with a paintbrush (held precariously in her enfeebled hand) to look forward to a successful art career. The *Woman's Own* piece mentioned above, 'Our Daughter had Polio' (Reiten 1954a, b), reassures readers with its first verb ('Had', not 'Has') that this is a story whose crisis moments have been successfully surmounted. Elsewhere, infection, prevention and treatment of the disease received treatment in lengthy, well-researched articles.[8] Yet each of these either carefully frames its bad news with insistent optimism regarding medical progress or relegates what is most disturbing about its story *to* the framing apparatus, to the margins where it can be bracketed from central focus. Despite her warm reassurance, for instance, that 'Polio is Being Defeated', all author Margaret Clark (1953) can do is provide an overview of research trials and errors to date, as the vaccine was still several years away. Richard Frey (1950) promises that summer camp – always a fraught proposition, since it involved the potential mixing of immune and non-immune populations of children – is 'safe', although later he indicates that 'safety' may mean nothing more than 'safely cared for', once infection has struck. Elsewhere such framing is so bizarrely employed that journalistic irresponsibility simply must be our ruling. In one, a 'Polio Pledge' (*Redbook* 1952) occupies the upper right quadrant of a page continuing the fiction supplement 'It's Always Some Man!', and the tiny insert 'If Polio Strikes My Home' (*Ladies Home Journal* 1952) floats incongruously in a sea of soup recipes from 'Our Young Marrieds'. Do these grossly inappropriate juxtapositions indicate a readership so 'at home' with polio that references found anywhere were expected, thus appropriate? Or do they bespeak an editorial discomfort so acute that efforts to hide, disguise and sugar-coat the medicine spoon of polio discourse resulted inevitably in such erratic and bad-taste presentations?

Even Fontaine's forthright piece for *Redbook* (1950) engages with and indulges in the issue of silence in polio narrative. It is Fontaine in fact who coined the phrase that titles this chapter as he described the town's dawning understanding that the epidemic was upon them: 'it was a battle against panic as much as polio. And it was a battle of silence, save for the occasional screaming of a siren through the streets, of waiting, of self-control, and of courage repeatedly renewed' (ibid.: 76). The stoicism modelled by the townsfolk is mirrored in the article's title – 'The Town that Fought for its Kids' – which lacks any specific reference to polio, postponing its disturbing theme to the small print of the story proper. If even 'radical' *Redbook* was ultimately incapable of a sustained realistic treatment of the disease in its most difficult ramifications, more traditional women's serials fared much worse. Their skirtings around this issue took two primary forms: first, 'loaded' language that fizzled into less serious, even frivolous, themes; and, second, fixations on subject matter distinctly proximal to the polio crisis itself – medicine, children (and the combined issue of sick or imperilled children) and summertime (a theme that also almost always suggested children).

In both US and UK serials, sensationalised, attention-grabbing titles draw the readers in, while benign, even frivolous subject matter reassures them that a 'false alarm' has been successfully quelled. The article 'Mother, Beware' (*McCall's* 1952) is about upsetting one's daughter during hair braiding; 'After that Cold' (Temple 1955) describes applying make-up to cover a red nose and puffy eyes, and 'Chilblain Cheaters' (Temple 1954) is a brief fashion layout for women's stylish boots. When topics of sickness and health are addressed (copiously, in every issue), these ailments are almost always of a mild, treatable kind, and sick youth featured in articles and columns – even those laid up in bed, wearing braces, using crutches, or confined to a wheelchair – have, with only rare exceptions, 'anything but' polio.[9] As these texts move as closely as possible to referring directly to the issue of fatal illness, specifically polio, without ever actually naming it, polio's profound ability to infect the cultural imagination ensures their supplemental status as 'about polio' nevertheless. The 'false-alarm' subtext of such alarmist features may have had therapeutic value for mothers who lived in fear of realised or unrealised medical catastrophe. Indeed, picturing oneself surviving a devastating experience is an exercise suggested by grief and trauma counsellors even today; these panicky headlines that 'turn out to be nothing' may have led women through just such a therapeutic enactment.

The seen-but-not-heard generation of children born during this period was in fact seen and heard in the pages of these magazines – the US ones especially but even those from the UK after 1950 – as they rarely are in contemporary issues of these same publications. The 'Mother, Beware' article referred to above was one of several features surveyed *on* children's hairstyles, while clothing and shoes for children and juniors received multi-page layouts at least once or twice a year. Children's pages with puzzles, rhymes, and cartoons were provided in many US issues; the regular 'Children's Corner' of *Woman's Own* featured drawings to colour, poetry and humour. And of course cute babies and small children were a staple in countless advertisements in both UK and US publications. If the cover art of the UK serials consistently depicted a young, pretty woman with her man hovering admiringly in the background, the American covers provided yet another context for youth images; *Good Housekeeping* depicted children exclusively on its covers throughout the years surveyed, while the 'surprised baby' offered a whimsical touch periodically – especially at holiday time – on the covers of *McCall's* and *Ladies Home Journal*. Most striking of all are the children's covers for the summer issues of these magazines, which almost inevitably picture the child beside a body of water. Of course the swimming pool and public beach were both feared hotbeds of infection during the summers of epidemic years, when mothers anguished daily over whether to keep their children at home or let them enjoy their freedom. Can images of pools and beach fronts, however idyllically rendered, have failed to strike a frightening chord in the subconscious or conscious understanding of these maternal readers? The editorial decision to position so many children blithely poised at the edge of the abyss is read by this researcher at any rate as remarkably insensitive.

The year 1952 holds the record for polio cases in the USA, yet this did not prevent *Good Housekeeping* from offering, for instance, a chilling July cover. Here a small blonde girl, hands folded prayer-style, arcs from a diving board into a pool. The child's prayerful attitude may suggest her fervent wish to be spared the scourge of polio this year, while of course the notion that prayers would be enough to protect children in this tremendously dangerous season reinforces the charge of irresponsible journalism I impose above. If we presume her relative safety because she is pictured *alone* in this setting, the solitude itself suggests a series of disturbing questions: are the other children missing because their mothers know better? because they fear the pictured child's potential infectiousness? because they have already succumbed to illness, leaving this last little survivor to spend the summer by herself? From a sufficiently aware perspective – one, I argue, that all mothers would have had access to, whether they engaged it or not – this pleasant, cheering image is grimly undermined. That such covers appeared dependably for many summers indicates that their potential offensiveness did *not* ever hit home; even in this period summer's traditional 'escapist' associations evidently encouraged mothers to escape from their summertime anxieties through these images, and enabled publishers to escape the charge of unethical journalism.

Interestingly, summertime, socially unconventional adults and children narrowly avoiding physical or emotional disaster are a recurring thematic combination in many fiction offerings throughout the pages of the US serials. As I noted above, the theme of summer suggests the presence of children engaged in warm-weather leisure activities, and likewise invites adult figures to indulge in escapist 'vacations' from the ordinary rules of spousal and parental behaviour. In these stories, the adult characters threaten the emotional or physical well-being of those around them with their selfish acts, and function as neglectful parent figures whether they have biological offspring or not. In short, they act up, misbehave, run away from home and carry on *like children* – a situation that summer probably inspires in all grownups at some point. Conversely, the children often display remarkably mature behaviours, caring for the adults in the midst of (and in spite of) their childish midlife crises, bearing the burden of the adults' mistakes and even taking the blame for these.

Of course I am reading these suggestive themes for their pertinence to the 'real' story that may be seen to lurk beneath – of failed parenting, familial betrayal and threatened or lost lives attending the polio crisis at this time. While certainly little to nothing could have been done to ensure a child's (or young adult's) health, parents – especially mothers? – no doubt felt crushed by feelings of guilt and remorse at a child's positive diagnosis. Ruminations about what might have been done differently and recriminations between adult family members were surely the topics of anguished dialogues (or internal monologues), and the urge to 'make up' to the afflicted family member – for lost time, lost happiness, lost chances to love better – would have been clearly spoken to by these stories of parents who get second chances and children who emerge from danger unscathed and well adjusted. In addition, these children function, in their spirited, generous ability to rebound from any situation, as the ideal polio patients – as 'brave little soldiers' who tolerate fear and pain with smiles on their faces and join with Mom and Dad in the charade that the excruciating infection, treatment and recovery processes are all just a 'little game' the family is playing. The reversals of juvenile and adult roles that constitute the conflicts and resolutions in these stories all comment importantly on the issue of sick and saved families.

In a comic tale, 'The Fair-Weather Kind' (Miller February 1952), parents Brad and Jody move their kids from urban to suburban LA and are then hounded by city friends who monopolise the pool and ruin the kids' sleep schedule; pathos is generated by the many selfish errors committed by the adults before they realise that 'our kids are people, too' (ibid.: 102). As they are shunted from the pleasant poolside back indoors or ignored during long weekends, little Ricky and Linda bravely agree to put up with the inconvenience, helpfully offering at one point to play in the sandbox instead. The children's maturity and generosity embarrass the adults; Jody 'wished that [her children] had had a tantrum. Anything but that painfully adult acceptance of [Brad's] rejection' (ibid.: 102). The story treats the issue of displaced children – again, a situation that could endanger non-immune children in new settings – when Jody and Brad move to a far-flung LA suburb for the sake of the kids, then regret the isolation from old friends that leaves them vulnerable to these friends' invasion as soon as summer comes. Interestingly, the parents see their error and recoup their kids' loss by *preventing* them from going near the water. They devise a plot to give their selfish friends a taste of their own medicine, and the reader presumes this will involve the children finally having access to their own swimming pool. But, in fact, the parents drive them back to the city, where in their various friends' cramped apartments they break vases and order large breakfasts at early hours until the light dawns on each offending couple. In a straight close reading, we might argue that something is missing here – that Brad and Jody use their kids to send a message to their city friends but fail to deliver on what the kids yearn for all hot summer long – free rein in their own swimming pool. From the 'polio' perspective, however, these parents act in the children's best interest – by resolving the larger privacy issue but protecting the little ones from the unsaid dangers that pools may have posed specifically to them at the time.

Two stories discovered in this search provide a striking aggregation of themes discussed in this study. Beginning with its plainly suggestive title, 'Dangerous Summer' (Miller May 1952) moves immediately to references to two characters with physical disabilities – Professor Charles Neill, who is 'lame', and Aunt Sophy, who sprains her ankle and cannot accompany niece Eve to tea with the professor, clearing the way for their eventual falling in love. Eve follows a limb-threatening 'rough footpath' up to the professor's home, and after the tea she watches in alarm as the professor's son Chip threatens his own life and limb 'traversing a tree branch [or limb] like a cat' (ibid.: 80). Charles's limp is in fact a result of polio in his childhood, and for me the direct reference infects with virulent strength multiple related elements in the story. Aunt Sophy, therefore, seems to have 'caught' her sprained ankle from the professor's contagious polio condition; in the early moments of the narrative, no sooner does she mention his game leg, than she 'comes down' with one herself, while both Eve and Chip come into harm's way but never show visible signs of 'infection', resembling the countless polio cases in this period, believed by doctors to have subsided after initial flulike symptoms.

In the 'polio' reading of this story, Chip's moment of acrobatics on the tree branch is its most resonant event. The act provokes in Eve a look of accusation towards permissive Father, who defends against the charge of possibly 'infecting' his son with his own lame condition by arguing, 'but I want him to be happy and free of fear' (ibid.: 80). His desire to see Chip active and fearless indicates his generous willingness to let his son outstrip him physically, yet also points to the distance separating the energetic boy and his middle-aged, disabled father. For, while the professor is dashing and distinguished, dances divinely, and turns out to be quite the romantic after all, his busy schedule at the university and reserved external manner mark him as distinctly unsuited for the raising of a small boy. He is in fact too busy to take Chip to the circus he is longing to see, whose high-wire act he had been imitating on the branch. If Chip is to gratify his free-spiritedness with a visit to the aerialist Madam Raj, Eve will have to enmesh herself in family politics by escorting the boy herself: 'she had come to the country to find peace and escape from the demands of other people. Yet now here she was, involved' (ibid.: 74). This initial 'involvement', contiguous with the path of 'infection' I have been tracing thus far, foreshadows her later dilemma regarding whether to return to her career as globe-trotting photojournalist or to trade in this physical mobility for a settled family life with Charles and Chip. Significantly, the 'danger' Chip is in – if not of falling from a tree branch then of being parented solely by a middle-aged man with insufficient time for him – causes Eve to realise both motherly and wifely instincts. Her decision to be 'on vacation' permanently at the story's end – to transform the seasonal 'dangers' of summer into a permanent condition for herself and her limping family – is effectively countered by the reading that in fact Eve saves her new son from 'polio' – from his father's disabled post-polio condition that would clearly have spelled a sadder, more limited life for him.

I was drawn to the story 'Summer Bachelor' (Kaufman September 1950) because the story's title and illustration (a grey-templed man leaning over a steamy young blonde) suggested immediately yet another enlargement of the adults-making-mischief theme I have explored throughout this discussion. Sure enough, Cowan Matthews summers alone at the country club while his wife Anne is away; the 'kid' he takes up with in her absence has a 'little boarding-school voice' and turns out to be 'Ed Durston's daughter' (ibid.: 28) but is primarily the homewrecking siren in this characterological triangle, while Cowan's father role is realised in the figure of his absent son Donny. Importantly, Anne and Donny have left Cowan on his own because 'there had been a frightening increase in the polio epidemic [near the country club] in the last few weeks' (ibid.: 28); if Cowan's failure to join his family did not reflect negatively enough upon his character, his indulgence in lazy after-noons at the beach, flirtations with young women, and card games with the club's notorious wife-swapping set, while Anne and Donny sweat it out in the 'even hotter' (ibid.: 90) summer camp setting, suggests his thorough un-worthiness as a parent. In fact, it is this level of negligence that might be held to blame in the case of an infected child, and this midlife-crisis romance that turns out also to be a story about polio raises fascinating questions about the issue of parental culpability in an epidemic moment.

Of course the lovers' beach setting is affected by the story's pervasive polio theme; recall that Cowan's love interest, Betty, is still a 'kid', a young adult almost equally likely to be infected with polio in the mid-1950s (when the virus tended to strike older children and adolescents), and thus endangered by her beach exposure, again by Cowan, who draws her to the water's edge day after day. Finally he suffers guilt feelings and summons Anne and Donny to join him. However, his effort to resume the role of respectable spouse and father is not only questionable for its basic inertia – why, in fact, does he not leave the country club to join his family instead? – but also for its being rooted in a dangerous lie. 'What about the epidemic?' Anne asks when he calls. 'Wasn't there a case in the village just last week?' 'Oh, *that*,' is Cowan's unconscionable brush-off. 'There's no epidemic here. Just talk' (ibid.: 98). At this most remarkable of cultural intersections, the story presents its readership with what at that time was a true moral dilemma: is the extramarital affair so morally depraved an act that it is acceptable to risk a child's health to avoid it?

In fact, the story's final movements play daringly with the potential seriousness of Cowan's lie. After his call to Anne, he hears of the 'County Judge's kid' who died of polio two days after coming down with it. Anne and Donny both arrive 'exhausted', with Anne complaining of the heat and refusing to go near the beach, and Donny 'collapsing slackly' into a rocking chair (ibid.: 98). That evening, Donny comes down with a headache and fatigue – the classic early warning signs of a polio infection – and his parents are terrified. But in a move that returns us to the comforting distance of polio metaphors and analogues, Cowan leaves Anne to wait for Donny's doctor while he himself goes to the country-club dance to break things off with Betty. At the party, he is 'sickened by' the revelling wife-swappers (ibid.: 100), seeming to take on his son's illness in a gesture of healing atonement, and overcomes his desire for Betty in a final leave-taking that confirms for the reader his moral soundness. This clean break is evidently all that is needed to redeem himself and his son; upon his return, Donny's symptoms have been diagnosed as a 'slight summer cold' (ibid.: 101), and Cowan's child-imperilling selfishness can be forgotten by the sympathetic reader. While this final text is remarkably 'about' polio, the entire time it tries to be about something else, I argue here that all three of these stories comment importantly on the effect of dutiful or negligent parents on their child's health, especially during those 'dangerous summer' months. In these works, both Mom and Dad are depicted as potential sources of infection, but in all cases, the family's return to moral order either fittingly substitutes for – or, in the last example, successfully fends off – the (polio) threat to the child character's physical health.

As mentioned above, world events came 'down' to the American readership through the narrowest filter ('Meet the Next First Lady', and 'Stalin and his Three Wives' being representative political topics), while the 'political' issue occupying the minds of British readers (seemingly to the point of obsession), when the discomforts of war finally abated, was the coronation of Elizabeth in 1953 and the doings of her royal relatives. Yet in fact a range of subject matter in both UK and US publications that tested – and thus testified to – women's ability to face serious social problems indicates the proto-feminist dynamic, however inadvertently mobilised, at work in these texts. The heavy coverage of war's hardships featured in the British publications (discussed above) and US- and UK-based stories of financial, emotional and physical travails of real women and their families indicated the extent of 'bad news' these readerships were able to tolerate – and no doubt turn to productive use in their own lives.[10] Thus women's interest in such narratives of personal disaster, and editors' willingness to open these worlds to their seemingly sheltered middle-class readership, make the diffident silence on polio, the most urgent family crisis of the era, an even greater curiosity. In addition, these magazines (especially the American ones) depicted the home during this period as in fact a fertile medium for the readjustment of power structures regulating gender codes. While ultimately the novel roles these magazines offered readers are recouped by the prevailing sex-based imbalances of the period, new territory opens up nevertheless – in part, I argue, because fears of polio (in addition to other scares of that time related to the bomb and communism) caused fathers to turn to mothers for advice and strength and to share in the guilt and sorrow in times of frightening illness.

Emily Martin has demonstrated how housekeeping was made into a science in these post-war publications, in an effort to sanitise and thus immunise the home environment against polio and other invisible invaders. While the pressure to eliminate invisible and potentially deadly germs from the home probably produced profound anxiety in mothers fearing the prospect of children becoming ill because of negligence, the scientised/ technologised home environment positioned the mother as chief scientist and the mastermind behind 'germ warfare' in every home, empowering women in new ways and at last crediting her long hours spent behind a vacuum cleaner or duster, if not financially at least ideologically.[11]

Yet the potentially liberating effects of scientised cleaning products and technologised home appliances caused a lingering concern during the polio epidemic. If women were 'breezing through' housework because of labour-saving gadgets, and using the 'spare time' to have fun with the kids or relax with friends, were they in fact failing standards of cleanliness guaranteed with traditional methods, endangering their family's well-being? How did the mother/homemaker balance her roles as light-hearted friend and activity coordinator to her children and no-nonsense dirt buster with little time for play? A 'This is How I Keep House' instalment from a July 1952 *McCall's* (Herbert 1952) – and recall that the summer of 1952 saw the greatest number of polio infections in American history – presents this striking mother's dilemma. On the surface of this story, homemaker Dorothy Hartley's play-now/pay-later philosophy is roundly endorsed by the text and attractively composed photos; the apologetics of this make-no-apologies credo must be located largely subtextually.

'Family fun comes first,' says Dorothy in the epigraph to the story. 'Work comes later,' adds author Elizabeth Herbert approvingly, then writes supportively of Dorothy's family-first mentality. Especially since the Hartleys live in a resort area of Massachusetts where outdoor life in the summer is especially pleasant, she congratulates this housewife's efficient, no-frills approach to chores that 'makes summer living pleasant for her family' (ibid.: 69). Herbert crows about the Hartleys' multiple time-saving appliances, especially the automatic washing machine, yet, despite the confidence exuded in these several remarks, elsewhere the article betrays a striking defensiveness of Dorothy's seemingly lax lifestyle. 'Dorothy Hartley's reversal of housekeeping procedures in summer . . . does not imply poor homemaking,' insists Herbert at one point. 'Just the opposite' (ibid.: 70). Clearly, the need Herbert feels to fend off such a criticism indicates its presence in the minds of her readers, who may look with suspicion on this shirking mother. Later, Herbert's comment that 'Dorothy doesn't believe in letting *everything* slide in summer' has recast the previously efficient measures as 'sliding' and rescues this lost sheep by assuring readers that even she has some scruples about home upkeep. Finally, a picture caption reveals that 'before they set out, all four girls have work to do' (ibid.: 68). So much for the play-first philosophy so proudly touted by mother and magazine in the headline of the piece. Even the most do-nothing of the photo compositions – the 'four girls' relaxing on the Padanarum beach – is underlined by a reassuring list of their many activities: 'While the three girls beachcomb, dig sand castles, swim, or sun, Dorothy camps in a sheltered cove, knits, mends, or reads' (ibid.: 68). Notably, this exposure to the beach front is pointedly described as 'health-giving' for the children; all three are pictured in long sleeves or sweaters, and Dorothy avers that these outdoor excursions occur 'while the day and the three little girls are cool, fresh' (ibid.). Certainly, the coolness suggested by the words and images abates the threat supposedly carried by infectious diseases in the scorching heat of the summer months when bared bodies in close proximity spelled physical danger; this woman's family – and her worthiness as a mother – are saved by the refreshing north-Atlantic breezes that keep the deadly summer heat at bay twelve months a year.

The anxiety on display in this subtext, surrounding Mom's ability to mother safely and effectively, is mirrored in the subtextual debate played out in the articles and columns devoted specifically to children's health. Certainly, for the treating of everyday ailments such as colds and bruised elbows, Mother's assignment to the post is not surprising. Yet in a time when grave physical illness threatened potentially every family, we might expect a shift in command from frantic Mother to distant, authoritative Dad. Such an ideological shift is displayed frequently enough in these publications; if Dad is not physically pictured taking over the reins of power, Mother's ability to care for her children's health – and even her own – is impugned by the magazines' hired medical authorities on multiple occasions.[12] In 'The Convalescent Child' (Kenyon 1952), inane questions like 'Is it easy for a mother to take care of a child during convalescence?' – of course the answer begins with 'No' – and 'Can a mother properly care for a convalescent child and also continue outside social activities?' insinuate that Mother is too weak-minded and/or self-absorbed to care for sick children without these heavy-handed prompts, so should perhaps not be given the job in the first place. Significantly, Dad is assigned the task of making sure that boy children are not 'babied' (i.e. sissified) by Mom during the convalescent process, especially in the case of long illnesses like polio.

The frightening international situation regarding communism and the atomic bomb mirrored more domestic, polio-related concerns faced by families during this period with respect to personal and environmental health and failed strategies of containment. If women's role on the world stage, following their return from wartime production lines, was minimal, their position on the front lines against polio surely provided them a vital and all-consuming redeployment. And yet this survey of post-war women's magazines indicates the conflicted message found therein: mothers were enjoined, alternately, to be optimistic about the problem or to ignore it entirely, and rare was the direct 'treatment' of the issue its readers certainly eagerly sought. Would that the Evelyn R. Zeek, the author of 'Mother Takes the Best Pictures' (1953), had been allowed to transfer the insights provided there to writings whose topics included home preservation, medical information gathering and child safety in this polio period;[13] in addition to her camera work on a sunny afternoon, then, Mother would have been credited with the presence of mind and body, skilful hand and careful eye that would have more than qualified her to guide the children through the doctor's visits and life-threatening illnesses and to deal calmly and effectively with the full disclosure of such subjects in her favourite women's publications.[14]

NOTES

1. Elaine Tyler May, *Homeward Bound: American Families in the Cold War Era* (New York: Basic Books, 1988), p. 58; Judith Sealander, 'Families, World War II, and the Baby Boom (1940–1955)', in Joseph M. Hawes and Elizabeth I. Nybakken (eds), *American Families: A Research Guide and Historical Handbook* (New York: Greenwood Press, 1991), p. 160. See also Arlene Skolnick, *Embattled Paradise: The American Family in an Age of Uncertainty*

(New York: Basic Books, 1991), especially pp. 66–7.

2. Skolnick, *Embattled Paradise*, especially, p. 71.

3. Ibid. p. 72.

4. While only one in a 1,000 actually succumbed to the polio virus in the USA's most epidemic moments – and in the UK the odds were perhaps one in 6,500 – still the prospect of infection struck fear into the hearts of every parent during this period. Ruth Martin (1954) writes to reassure her British audience that the odds of infection are quite low, yet the alarming increase in cases she reports – 655 in 1946, 7,646 in 1947 and 7,752 in 1950 – should have indicated to readers how serious this epidemic had become. Barry North (*Something to Lean On: The First Sixty Years of the British Polio Fellowship* (South Ruislip: BPF, 1999)), documenting the history of the British Polio Fellowship, agrees that 'the disease brought great fears, especially amongst parents, for their children' (p. 20). In America, 1952 was the peak year, with 58,000 cases; totals for 1946 and 1953 were 25,000 and 35,000, respectively (Jane S. Smith, *Patenting the Sun: Polio and the Salk Vaccine* (New York: Anchor Books, 1990), p. 43).

5. Between April and June 1954, Jonas Salk ran field trials on first- and second-graders in towns and cities throughout the USA, with some testing in Canada and overseas. The results from 1.8 million children were tabulated, and in April 1955 Salk and his team announced that the vaccine, based on trial results, was safe and effective. Salk's vaccine was a 'killed-virus' type; Albert Sabin's attenuated-virus vaccine, later judged to be more effective for several reasons, was licensed by the US Public Health Service in 1961. See Smith, *Patenting the Sun*.

6. A brief index search of American publications indicates that, from 1948 to 1955, *Life* magazine ran thirty-two articles related to polio, while *Time* and *Newsweek* presented seventy-two and seventy-eight pieces, respectively; by contrast, *Ladies Home Journal* ran only seven articles during that same period, while *Good Housekeeping*, *McCall's* and *Better Homes and Gardens* each presented four. In the UK *The Times* ran dozens of items every year between 1947 and 1955, and the *Observer* positioned a weekly notice of new cases on the front page during epidemic periods; meanwhile, a limited search of the women's magazines *Woman* and *Woman's Own* (about fifty issues between 1948 and 1955) uncovered only three relevant articles. Since *McCall's* was not listed in the *Reader's Guide* prior to 1953, this number is likely to be mildly undercounted.

7. Smith, *Patenting the Sun*, pp. 85, 87.

8. See, for example, Maxine Davis (1950), Richard Frey (1950), Magaret Clark (1953) and Ruth Martin (1954).

9. See, for example, Maxine Davis (1950), Maggie Miller (1952), Leo Smollar (1952), William F. McDermott (1953) and Joan Williams (1954, 1955).

10. *Woman's* 'Woman's Mirror' feature that concluded each issue throughout the mid-1950s not only housed the regular medical help column but often featured stories of individual and family catastrophe as its headlining item. 'Saying 'Hallo" to Sick Children' (Cooper, 1954) describes volunteers with 'crippled' children in a hospital; a family's home burns down in an instalment from 1955 (Sandilands). In America, the *Journal's* semi-regular feature 'How America Lives' was a dependable source of hard-luck stories of struggling young marrieds or families of eight, whose meagre home environments were depicted in minute detail and in the grim greys of black-and-white photography; the equally intrusive text examines the family's exhausting schedule, unmet debts and budget shortfalls to the minute and penny.

11. Emily Martin, *Flexible Bodies: Tracking Immunity in American Culture from the Days of Polio to the Age of AIDS* (Boston: Beacon Press, 1994).

12. In Smart's photo essay (1952) (and tonsillectomies during the summer months were considered as gateways to polio infection), both Mom and Dad don hospital gowns and enact the surgical moment at home, to prepare the youngster for his hospital stay. In 'Help your Child GET WELL' (Taylor 1952), both watch carefully as a doctor puts a son's leg

through a range of motion. Irma Simonton Black's monthly column for *Redbook* provides an example of the hortatory tone one discerns in 'advice' writings. Her exclamatory titles – 'Don't Fence Me In!' (1952b) (about 'playpen overuse') and 'Let the Kids Cook!' (1952a) – and texts that insist much more than suggest presume an audience of inept and negligent mothers.

13. In fact, a piece for *McCall's* concedes that 'Mother is the Best Cure for a Sick Child' (Welch and Moore 1951), emphasising her capacity for providing 'TLC' and even demonstrating the bed-changing skills necessary for patients who are so sick they cannot be moved (or cannot move) off the bed; the piece is striking, however, for its brevity and singularity across the many pages surveyed here.

14. I wish to thank the Office of Research and Technology Transfer at the University of North Texas for a Faculty Research Grant, which enabled the writing of this chapter, and the British Polio Fellowship, which provided helpful information.

REFERENCES

Black, Irma Simonton (1952a), 'Let the Kids Cook!', *Redbook* (October), p. 93.

Black, Irma Simonton (1952b), 'Don't Fence Me In!', *Redbook* (November), p. 73.

Clark, Margaret (1953), 'Polio is Being Defeated', *McCall's* (January), pp. 48 ff.

Cooper, Barbara (1954), 'Saying "Hallo" to Sick Children', *Woman*, 16 October, p. 61.

Davis, Maxine (1950), 'First Complete Handbook on Infantile Paralysis', *Good Housekeeping* (August), pp. 56 ff.

Fontaine, André (1950), 'The Town that Fought for its Kids', *Redbook* (July), pp. 46 ff.

Frey, Richard (1950), 'Your Child's Camp and POLIO', *Good Housekeeping* (May), pp. 54 ff.

Herbert, Elizabeth Sweeney (1952), 'This is How I Keep House', *McCall's* (July), pp. 68 ff.

Kaufman, Suzanne (1950), 'Summer Bachelor', *McCall's* (September), pp. 28 ff.

Kenyon, Josephine H. (1952), 'The Convalescent Child', *Good Housekeeping* (February), pp. 28 ff.

Ladies Home Journal (1952), 'If Polio Strikes my Home' (June), p. 86.

McCall's (1952), 'Mother, Beware' (October), p. 22.

McDermott, William F. 1953, 'The House that Kindness Built', *McCall's* (August), pp. 36 ff.

Martin, Ruth (1954), 'How Dangerous is Polio Today?', *Woman's Own*, 22 April, pp. 22 ff.

Miller Laura Owen (1952), 'Dangerous Summer', *McCall's* (May), pp. 39 ff.

Miller, Maggie (1952), 'The Fair-Weather Kind', *McCall's* (February), pp. 46 ff.

Redbook (1952), 'Polio Pledge', (September 1952), p. 86.

Reiten, Grace (1954a), 'Our Daughter had Polio', *Woman's Own*, 11 November, pp. 26 ff.

Reiten, Grace (1954b), 'Our Daughter had Polio', *Woman's Own*, 18 November, pp. 26 ff.

Smart, Mollie (1952), 'Smitty Gets his Tonsils out', *McCall's* (January), pp. 10–12.

Sandilands, Chiquita (1955), 'Death Came in Flames', *Woman*, 9 April, p. 61.

Smollar, Leo, MD (1952), 'It Won't Kill You!', *Redbook* (May), pp. 21 ff.

Taylor, Toni (1952), 'Help your Child GET WELL' *Redbook* (August), pp. 64 ff.

Temple, Helen (1954), 'Chilblain Cheaters', *Woman*, 27 November, p. 16.

Temple, Helen (1955), 'After that Cold', *Woman*, 29 January, p. 13.

Welch, Aiken and J. Leonard Moore, MD (1951), 'Mother is the Best Cure for a Sick Child', *McCall's* (September), pp. 104–7.

White, Lionel (1952), 'The Girl who Never Gave up', *Redbook* (June), pp. 47 ff.

Williams, Joan (1954), 'Talking about Health' ('tonic summer'), *Woman*, 5 June, p. 35.

Williams, Joan (1955), 'Talking about Health' ('rejoice in the sun'), *Woman*, 11 June, p. 49.

Zeek, Evelyn R. (1953), 'Mother Takes the Best Pictures', *McCall's* (February), pp. 20–2.

CHAPTER TWO

Gender and Sexuality

All about the Subversive Femme:
Cold War Homophobia in All about Eve

Robert J. Corber

By focusing on the representation of Eve, the duplicitous, manipulative lesbian in Joseph L. Mankiewicz's 1950 camp classic *All about Eve*, this chapter aims to initiate a more complex scholarly discussion of the Cold War construction of the lesbian, one that does not conflate it with the Cold War construction of the gay man but instead takes into account more fully the differences between the two. Although scholars have long recognised that the state persecution of gays and lesbians in the United States played a central role in the production of the Cold War citizen-subject, the scholarship on this aspect of Cold War culture has focused with few exceptions on gay men. Too often the analysis in this scholarship is assumed to apply equally to gays and to lesbians. But this approach has obscured an important historical process, one in which the Cold War construction of the lesbian played a crucial role, the transformation of the category of the femme. Because she was the one who could pass for straight, the femme overtook the butch in the discourses of national security as the lesbian whose deviant gender identity created the greatest homophobic anxiety. Virtually indistinguishable from that of the straight woman, the femme's femininity threatened to reveal that, rather than biologically man-dated, the normative alignment of sex, gender and sexuality was an ideological fiction that worked to maintain the dominance of heterosexuality. The chapter argues that this homophobic construction of the lesbian, which can be traced to Cold War anxieties about the fluidity of heterosexual identities, deeply informed Mankiewicz's representation of Eve, played by Ann Baxter.

Starting with Vito Russo in his classic study *The Celluloid Closet*, scholars of images of gays and lesbians in classical Hollywood cinema have argued that Eve belongs to a long line of predatory celluloid lesbians in the Production Code era of Hollywood films, beginning with Mrs Danvers, the creepy housekeeper played by Judith Anderson who terrorises the nameless heroine in Alfred

Hitchcock's 1940 film *Rebecca*, and ending with Jo, the jealous and possessive madam of a New Orleans brothel played by Barbara Stanwyck who sexually preys on her girls in Edward Dmytryk's 1962 film *Walk on the Wild Side*. Eve does bear some resemblance to these other lesbian villains. Ruthlessly ambitious, she manipulates her way in the rarefied world of the ageing Broadway star Margo Channing, played by Bette Davis, by passing herself off as one of the star's most devoted fans. She then proceeds to undermine Margo both personally and professionally, even going so far as trying to steal her man. But, as the chapter shows, this is only part of the story. Eve's villainy differs from that of other lesbians of the Code era in one crucial respect. She has an ability to impersonate normative femininity that they do not, and thus she resembles the lesbian of the discourses of national security. In foregrounding the differences between Eve and other celluloid lesbians of the studio era, the chapter seeks to deepen our understanding of the role of Hollywood cinema in the production of the Cold War citizen-subject. Not all representations of lesbians in Hollywood films of the 1950s and 1960s can be explained in terms of Cold War homophobia. Indeed, most of these representations can be attributed to the persistence of the homophobic stereotype of the 'manly lesbian' whose cross-gender identification was thought to be a sign of mental illness. Only those representations that attributed to the lesbian an ability to pass for straight can be understood as participating in the sexual paranoia on which Cold War nationalism depended so heavily. What makes such representations so significant is that they helped to pry apart gender and sexuality, which until the 1950s were thought to have a causal relation to each other. In so doing, such representations contributed to the displacement of gender as the organising principle of sexuality. For this reason, they need to be seen as having played a crucial role in the consolidation of the hetero-homosexual binary, which depended on a decline in the importance of gender for classifying sexual acts and actors.

In the final scene of Joseph L. Mankiewicz's 1950 Academy Award-winning film *All about Eve*, Eve Harrington, the film's manipulative and duplicitous villain, is startled to find a female intruder asleep in her apartment when she returns home from the Sarah Siddons Award ceremony where she has received the best actress award. Although she picks up the phone to call the police, she puts it down when the intruder introduces herself as Phoebe, the president of the Eve Harrington Fan Club at Erasmus Hall, an all-girls high school in Brooklyn. Phoebe explains that she sneaked in while the maid was turning Eve's bed down 'just to look around' and that she is preparing a report on the actress, 'how you live, what kind of clothes you wear, what kind of perfume and books, things like that'. Annoyed but no longer frightened, Eve sits down on the sofa and lights a cigarette, which, because it is the only time in the film she is shown smoking, seems intended to signal a shift in her character. At first she responds impatiently to Phoebe's eager questions about her plans for a career in Hollywood, but when the girl begins to pick up after her, Eve's manner changes markedly. In a soft, caressing voice that contrasts with the husky voice she first uses when talking to the girl, she asks Phoebe how she got to Manhattan from Brooklyn. As Phoebe replies that it took her only a little more than an hour on the subway, the film dissolves to a close-up of Eve, who, posed seductively on the sofa, says, with a hint of invitation in her voice: 'It's after one now. You won't get home till all hours.'

Starting with Vito Russo in his classic study, *The Celluloid Closet*, scholars of images of gays and lesbians in classical Hollywood cinema have used this scene to argue that Eve is coded as a lesbian.[1] Because the Production Code, which by the consensus of the studios regulated the content of Hollywood films from 1930 to 1968, stated that 'sex perversion or any reference to it is forbidden', Eve's lesbianism can never be overtly expressed but can only be hinted at in scenes like this.[2] For many scholars, Eve belongs to a long line of predatory celluloid lesbians in films of the Code era, beginning with Mrs Danvers, the twisted housekeeper played by Judith Anderson who terrorises the nameless heroine in Alfred Hitchcock's 1940 film *Rebecca*, and ending with Jo, the jealous and possessive madam of a New Orleans brothel played by Barbara Stanwyck who sexually preys on her girls in Edward Dmytryk's 1962 film *Walk on the Wild Side*.[3] Eve does bear some resemblance to these other lesbian villains. Ruthlessly ambitious, she manipulates her way into the rarefied world of the flamboyant Broadway star Margo Channing (Bette Davis), a character based loosely on Tallulah Bankhead, who was widely rumoured to be lesbian and who was involved in a notorious professional rivalry with Bette Davis, by passing herself off as one of the star's most devoted fans. She then proceeds to undermine Margo both personally and professionally, even going so far as trying to steal her man.

But this is only part of the story. Eve's villainy differs from that of other Code-era lesbian villains in one crucial respect: it has a political resonance theirs lacks. As we shall see, Eve's impersonation of normative femininity, which is first exposed in the scene in which she tries to blackmail Karen (Celeste Holm) into getting her the part of Cora in her husband Lloyd's new play and drops the submissive, unassuming manner that has marked her behaviour until then, suggests that her character was at least partly inspired by Cold War constructions of the lesbian. What makes her so threatening as a lesbian is precisely her ability to impersonate normative femininity. As I discuss in more detail below, one of the ways in which the discourses of national security contained opposition to post-war norms of masculinity and femininity was by exploiting the fear that there was no way to tell homosexuals apart from heterosexuals.[4] In emphasising their invisibility, these discourses linked gays and lesbians to the communists and fellow travellers who were supposedly conspiring to overthrow the nation, a link that encouraged the view that gender and sexual nonconformity were un-American.

My goal in highlighting the differences between Eve and other lesbian villains in Hollywood films of the 1940s and 1950s is to show that, despite its status as a camp classic, *All about Eve* needs to be understood as a Cold War movie. Since Michael Rogin first defined this category of Hollywood film in 1987, cultural studies scholars have expanded it to include movies that, unlike those examined by Rogin, do not deal directly with the Cold War but that nevertheless underwrite or legitimate Cold War ideologies, especially those regulating the construction of gender and sexuality.[5] As we shall see, Eve's queerness, which consists of a combination of femininity and lesbianism that unsettles homophobic stereotypes, indirectly ratified the form of heterosexual femininity that became normative in the Cold War era. Mankiewicz, who wrote as well as directed *All about Eve*, claimed that he conceived of Eve as a lesbian and that he coached Baxter in how to play her as one.[6]

But in suggesting that one of the effects of the film's representation of Eve was to ratify Cold War homophobia, I also aim to complicate our understanding of Cold War culture. Scholars have tended to approach the 1950s as a particularly homophobic period in American history, one in which homosexuals were actively persecuted by the state and functioned, along with communists and fellow travellers, as the Other in the discourses of national identity.[7] As a result, the decade has emerged as the 'Dark Ages' of the lesbian and gay past, a period in which lesbian and gay life is thought to have been pathologically secretive and repressed. Although this view of the 1950s is not unfounded, it glosses over the inconsistencies and contradictions in Cold War ideologies. Taking those inconsistencies and contradictions more fully into account promises to illuminate an overlooked aspect of Cold War culture, what we might call its queerness, by which I mean the way that the discourses of national security, in highlighting the ability of gays and lesbians to pass for straight, inadvertently called attention to the mobility of sex, gender and sexuality in relation to each other. If homosexuals could pass, then there was no necessary or causal relationship between masculinity and femininity, on the one hand, and heterosexuality, on the other. Nor were masculinity and femininity fixed or immutable essences but rather roles even gays and lesbians could master through imitation and repetition. In this way, the discourses of national security unintentionally foregrounded the performative aspects of gender, denaturalising masculinity and femininity in the process, and demonstrating the lack of congruity between sex and sexuality. As we shall see, underlying the film's representation of Eve is an attempt to resolve this contradiction in Cold War ideology, an attempt that ultimately fails because the film cannot restabilise the normative alignment of sex, gender and sexuality that its homophobic representation of the lesbian throws into crisis.

Finally, in situating *All about Eve* in relation to Cold War homophobia, I would like to initiate a more complex examination of the Cold War construction of the lesbian, one that does not conflate it with the Cold War construction of the gay man but instead takes into account more fully the specificity of its impact. Although scholars have long recognised that the state persecution of gays and lesbians played a central role in the production of the Cold War citizen-subject, the work on this aspect of Cold War culture has focused with few exceptions on gay men. Too often the analysis in this work is assumed to apply equally to gays and to lesbians.[8] But this approach has obscured an important historical process, one in which the Cold War construction of the lesbian was deeply implicated, the transformation of the category of the femme. Because she was the one who could pass, the femme overtook the butch in the discourses of national security as the lesbian whose deviant gender identity created the greatest homophobic anxiety. What is so striking about this development is that historically the femme was invisible; that is, her lesbianism became visible only in the presence of the butch. The tendency of Cold War discourse to isolate the ability of gays and lesbians to pass as perhaps the only characteristic that distinguished them from heterosexuals may explain this development. In this context, the femme's femininity posed an even greater threat to dominant gender ideologies than did the butch's masculinity. Virtually indistinguishable from that of the straight woman, the femme's femininity threatened to reveal that, rather than biologically mandated, the normative alignment of sex, gender, and sexuality was an ideological fiction that worked to maintain the dominance of heterosexuality. I will try to show that this homophobic construction of the lesbian, which can be traced to Cold War anxieties about the fluidity of heterosexual identities, deeply informed the film's representation of Eve.

DECOUPLING THE BUTCH AND THE FEMME

In 1950, at about the same time that Mankiewicz began working on the screenplay for *All about Eve*, the Senate Appropriations Committee held widely publicised hearings on the government employment of homosexuals and 'other sex perverts' in which the chief officer of the District of Columbia vice squad created a stir when he testified that thousands of federal employees had been arrested on morals charges, many of them across from the White House in Lafayette Square, a notorious cruising venue. Following the hearings, the Committee issued a virulently homophobic report in which it asserted that male and female homosexual government employees posed a serious threat to national security because they were supposedly vulnerable to blackmail by foreign espionage agents. But it emphasised that, unless such employees already had a police record, it would be virtually impossible to ferret out and purge them. Citing recent medical findings that challenged homophobic stereotypes of gay men and lesbians, the report stated that 'all homosexual males do not have feminine mannerisms, nor do all female homosexuals display masculine characteristics in their dress or actions'.[9] Indeed, it went on, 'many male homosexuals are very masculine in their physical appearance and general demeanor, and many female homosexuals have every appearance of femininity in their outward behavior'.[10] In making these claims, the report linked homosexuals to the communists and fellow travellers who were then also being investigated by Congress. If gays and lesbians could not be easily identified, then they too could infiltrate the government without being detected and subvert it from within by perverting 'normal' employees. Because they supposedly had no distinguishing characteristics, the report claimed, 'one homosexual can pollute a government office'.[11]

What made the Cold War shift in thinking about homosexuality so significant was that it transposed the positions that the butch and the femme traditionally occupied in homophobic discourse. To simplify a complex history, since the sexologists began to develop classifications for non-normative genders and sexualities in the late nineteenth century, the masculine lesbian has been subjected to more intense scrutiny than the feminine lesbian. Although it is important to avoid subsuming the history of the female sexual invert into that of the butch, there are continuities between the two that justify seeing the female sexual invert as an antecedent of the butch.[12] Because Victorian gender norms associated femaleness with sexual passivity, a woman literally had to become manlike before she could be seen as a sexual being.[13] Thus the sexologists claimed that the masculine lesbian was not a woman but a man trapped in a woman's body. In so doing, they heterosexualised her desire for other women, a conceptual move that helped to maintain the ideological fiction that the relationship between sex, gender and sexuality was causal rather than mobile. At the same time, the gender of the female sexual invert, which did not line up with her anatomical sex in the socially prescribed way, showed that men could not claim a monopoly on masculinity. Thus the masculine lesbian directly threatened patriarchal privilege, which depended on the alignment of masculinity with maleness and heterosexuality. In explaining her sexuality in terms of her gender, the sexologists neutralised this threat.

But, even as it helped to consolidate patriarchal social arrangements, this explanation of the female sexual invert's sexuality rendered the feminine lesbian, the object of her desire, a puzzle that sexology could not solve. Because the feminine lesbian's gender was in alignment with her anatomical sex, her desire for other women could not be adequately explained, except in terms of the dominant gender norms. In accordance with Victorian constructions of femininity, the feminine lesbian was seen as the passive recipient of the masculine lesbian's sexual advances, a view that deprived the feminine lesbian of sexual agency.[14] In his influential book *Studies in the Psychology of Sex*, published in 1900, Havelock Ellis, one of the founders of sexology, claimed that feminine lesbians 'were the pick of the women whom the average man would pass by'.[15] In other words, because feminine lesbians could not get even an average man, they were reduced to having affairs with female sexual inverts. Thus the sexologists did not consider these women, who would later be called femmes, to be true lesbians; on the contrary, the belief was that they would willingly forsake their deviant lifestyles to be with a heterosexual man. The feminine lesbian did not begin to attract the same kind of homophobic scrutiny as the masculine lesbian until sexual object choice began to displace gender as the organising principle of sexuality in the early twentieth century.[16] But this process occurred unevenly and over several decades, and Cold War constructions of the lesbian need to be understood as having played a crucial role in it.

As Elizabeth Lapovsky Kennedy and Madeline Davis have shown, stereotypical thinking about femmes was not limited to sexology and other forms of homophobic discourse, but even permeated butch–femme communities of the 1940s and 1950s.[17] Both butches and femmes tended to think that the butch was the true lesbian and that the femme's entry into the subculture was dictated more by circumstance than by a sense of fundamental difference from other women. Indeed, many butches did not think femmes were wholly reliable members of the subculture, because they supposedly could always revert to heterosexuality to avoid the social stigma of having a butch as a lover. This subcultural view of the femme did not begin to change until the late 1950s, when sexual attraction to women rather than masculinity became the basis of lesbian identity.[18] As we have seen, the Cold War discourse of homosexuality tended to reverse the homophobic view of the femme of earlier decades. The femme was now thought to pose an even greater threat to the existing social order than the butch. Her ability to use her femininity to disguise her lesbianism supposedly enabled her to infiltrate the institutions of heterosexuality and subvert them from within by converting the straight woman to her perverted sexual practices.

ALL ABOUT EVE AND MARGO

All about Eve's representation of its eponymous villain needs to be understood as simultaneously drawing on and contributing to Cold War constructions of the lesbian. In the opening shots of the flashback that makes up the bulk of the movie, when Eve emerges from the shadows of a darkened alley wearing a soiled men's overcoat and rain hat, she seems more butch than femme. Even her voice seems to mark her as butch. In marked contrast to the soft-spoken, almost girlish Eve of later scenes, she here calls out to Karen in a deep husky voice, one she does not use again until the final scene, where she seduces Phoebe. This butchness clashes with her later identity as the feminine lesbian who can pass for straight, but the only way in which the film can render her lesbianism visible is by using the visual codes developed by Hollywood to get around the prohibitions concerning the treatment of homosexuality, and those codes relied on a conceptual model that defined lesbianism as a form of sexual inversion.[19] Marking Eve as butch in this scene also helps to make clear that her femininity in later scenes is a performance, and thus it is crucial to the film's ideological project, even though it also seems to suggest that at her core the lesbian is masculine, even the lesbian who can pass for straight. The impression created by Eve's masculine appearance is quickly dispelled once she enters Margo's dressing room and adopts the stereotypical feminine demeanour that characterises her in most of the film's remaining scenes. Eve's demeanour in this scene borders on a parody of stereotypical femininity, which reinforces the impression that she is performing a role. She apologises for intruding on Margo, as though she is not worthy of being in Margo's presence, and when Karen encourages her to talk about herself, she hesitates, as if she were reluctant to make herself the centre of attention. But Karen's desire to hear her story provides her with an opportunity to show how good an actress she is and she cannot pass it up.

She concocts a clichéd story of tragic heterosexual romance that seems intended to disguise her lesbianism. As some sentimental theme music begins to play on the soundtrack, she tells them that she married a young soldier in the Air Force shortly before he was shipped off to the South Pacific and that she took a job in a brewery to support herself while he was gone. But one day when she was supposed to meet her husband in San Francisco while he was on leave, she got a telegram informing her that he had been killed in battle, and so her dreams of domestic bliss ended tragically. Eve seems to make up this story to mask her ruthless ambition to become an actress, so it does not masculinise her. She claims to have turned to acting as compensation for her drab life as a widow and a secretary. The way in which this scene is shot heightens the sense that Eve's femininity is not 'real' or authentic but a performance designed to deceive Margo and the others. Margo and the others sit on one side of the dressing room with Eve on the other, an arrangement that makes Margo and the others resemble an audience. Close-ups of Eve as she tells her hackneyed love story are cross-cut with close-ups of Margo and the others, who seem spellbound by Eve's powers of narration. Birdie (Thelma Ritter), Margo's personal assistant, is the only one in the 'audience' who is not taken in by Eve's performance, even though she too appreciates its power. When Margo wipes the tears from her eyes and blows her nose, Birdie comments dryly, 'What a story! Everything but the blood-hounds snapping at her rear end.' Eve's consummate skill in playing the part of the stereotypical woman in this scene enables her to gain entry into Margo's world. Margo is so moved by her story that she takes Eve home with her and hires her as an assistant.

Eve's resemblance to the lesbian of the discourses of national security is not limited to her ability to impersonate stereotypical femininity. She also resembles her in having the power to convert the heterosexual woman to her 'perverted' sexual practices. That this combination of qualities threatens to subvert the institutions of heterosexuality becomes clear in the scene in which Eve accompanies Margo to the airport to see off Bill (Gary Merrill), Margo's lover–director, who is leaving for Hollywood. In this scene, Margo emerges as the straight woman of the Cold War discourse of homosexuality whose supposedly fluid sexuality puts her at risk of being converted by the passing lesbian. This scene is as close as the film can come without violating the Production Code to suggesting that Eve's and Margo's relationship is based on sexual attraction. As Bill and Margo kiss goodbye, Eve stands behind them, with her eyes averted, as though the sight of them kissing made her jealous. When Bill turns away and begins walking toward the plane, the camera dissolves to a medium shot of Eve, who approaches Margo from behind with a caressing look on her face. She begins to place her hands on Margo's shoulders but stops when Bill turns and shouts from the runway, 'Hey, Junior, keep your eye on her, don't let her get lonely, she's a loose lamb in a jungle.' The camera then cuts to another medium shot of Eve, who, in response to Bill's words looks longingly at Margo. Because of this look, her reply, 'I will', sounds more ominous than reassuring. The final sequence of shots shows her and Margo walking down the airport corridor arm-in-arm looking like a butch–femme couple. The contrast between the two women could not be greater. Eve is still dressed in her soiled men's overcoat and rain hat, while Margo is wearing a sexy, tight-fitting cocktail dress and fur coat. Margo's voice-over as the scene fades out reinforces these visual codes, further indicating that, with Bill gone, the two women now form a couple: 'That same night we sent for Eve's things, her few pitiful possessions. She moved in to the little guest room on the top floor. The next three weeks were out of a fairy tale, and I was Cinderella in the last act . . . The honeymoon was on.'

In the film, the passing lesbian's power to convert the heterosexual woman emerges as a perverted form of reproduction grounded in the homoerotic relations of looking central to female spectatorship.[20] The potential of the heterosexual woman to be converted seems to have made Mankiewicz particularly anxious about this aspect of female spectatorship, which becomes one of the movie's major themes. Eve's desire to have Margo is inextricably bound up with her desire to be her. One of Margo's most devoted fans, Eve has travelled from city to city so as not to miss a single one of her idol's performances. As Margo's new assistant, she has an opportunity to study the star more closely. Before Birdie leaves, she warns Margo that Eve 'thinks only about you, like she's studying you, like you was a book, or a play, or a set of blueprints, how you walk, talk, eat, think, sleep'. The alternation in Eve's desire between wanting to have and wanting to be Margo seems to be what brings her and Margo's honeymoon to its premature end. The more Eve wants to be Margo, the more annoyed Margo becomes with her. The complex play of identification and desire underlying Eve's fascination with Margo is captured in the scene in which Margo discovers Eve on stage holding up Margo's costume and bowing to an empty theatre. The scene begins with Eve watching one of Margo's performances from the wings of the stage. Close-ups of her looking at Margo are cross-cut with long shots of Margo bowing to an audience that remains off-screen. The shot/reverse shot structure of this sequence positions Eve as a stand-in for the unseen audience, but, because she is playing the part of the adoring fan, the distinction between star and spectator collapses. As Margo exits backstage, she passes by Eve and teases her for crying at the performance, which she has seen repeatedly: 'Not again!' In the following scene, Margo's and Eve's positions in relation to each other are reversed. Star becomes spectator, and spectator, star. Margo emerges from her dressing room in search of Eve, who has volunteered to return her costume to wardrobe, and finds her on the empty stage with it. Standing in roughly the same place as Eve in the earlier scene, she watches as Eve pretends to be her and bows to an imaginary audience. Although she has already become disenchanted with Eve, she smiles indulgently, as if she were flattered by the impersonation.

With this reversal of Margo's and Eve's positions, it becomes unclear exactly who has the power to convert whom. Margo's stardom has implanted in Eve a desire both to have her and to be her, which suggests that Margo occupies the position of the passing lesbian as well as that of the converted heterosexual woman in relation to Eve. It is worth noting again here that Mankiewicz based Margo's character on Tallulah Bankhead, an actress widely rumoured to be lesbian, and that many reviewers assumed that Bette Davis's performance was an imitation of the flamboyant Bankhead.[21] The connection between Margo and Bankhead only added to Margo's coded identity as a lesbian who has converted Eve through her magnetic appeal as a star.

Margo's physical appearance in this scene is especially revealing, as it contrasts markedly with her appearance in the preceding one, where we see her onstage and in costume. Dressed in an old bath robe and smeared with cold cream – in short, stripped of all of the accoutrements of femininity that make her a glamorous star – she looks plain, dowdy and middle-aged, the very antithesis of Margo Channing the glamorous star. In this way, the film calls attention to the performative aspects of her glamorous femininity. Her femininity is like one of her roles, requiring wardrobe, make-up and a glamorous hair style, as well as an enormous amount of concealed labour, both her own and that of others. In this respect, her femininity is not all that different from Eve's. After all, she shares Eve's penchant for performing offstage as well as on, and, like Eve, she tends to perform her femininity to excess. This is not to overlook the enormous differences between the types of femininity the two embody. As we have seen, Eve's is the conventional femininity promoted by Cold War nationalism, whereas Margo's is the flamboyant femininity of the diva, which is by definition excessive and theatrical. My point is simply that neither Margo's nor Eve's femininity appears to be authentic or natural. Rather, we are encouraged to see them as an act or a role Margo and Eve perform like any other.

In collapsing the distinction between the lesbian and the heterosexual woman, the film registers the fear that the lesbian's powers of conversion will enable her to reproduce herself almost endlessly. In the movie's final shots, Phoebe, the intruder Eve discovers in her apartment when she returns home from the awards ceremony, takes Eve's award into the bedroom and puts on the sequined cloak Eve wore to the ceremony. Holding up the award, Phoebe stands in front of the bedroom mirror in long shot. As she begins to bow to her own reflection, the camera cuts to a medium shot, showing her image multiplied almost infinitely in the three-way mirror. The scene echoes the one I discussed above in which Margo occupies the position of the femme in relation to Eve, suggesting that the complex play of desire and identification that began with Margo and Eve continues with Eve and Phoebe. But the difference is that Phoebe emerges as a virtual clone of Eve. When Addison DeWitt (George Sanders) shows up with Eve's award, which she carelessly left in the taxi, we discover that Phoebe is just as manipulative and duplicitous as her idol. She coyly bats her eyelashes at Addison as she tells him that she knows who he is, and when Addison leaves and Eve asks who was at the door, she lies: 'It was just the taxi driver returning your award.' Moreover, the multiplication of her image in the mirror suggests that, like Eve, she is a lesbian whose ability to pass gives her the power to reproduce herself in others, the only difference being that her power seems infinite by comparison. With this image of Phoebe's power, the film indirectly ratifies the findings of the Senate Appropriations Committee, which, as we have seen, claimed that it took only one homosexual to 'pollute' a government office. Like the homosexual employee conjured by the committee's report, Phoebe threatens to become legion.

QUEERING COLD WAR CULTURE

As I suggested at the beginning, in emphasising the central role homophobia played in the production of American national identity in the 1950s, scholars have overlooked the queerness of Cold War culture, a queerness that was intimately related to its homophobia. The construction of the lesbian as a national security risk was riddled with contradictions that destabilised the category of woman by calling into question its foundation in heterosexuality. In locating the lesbian's threat to patriarchal social arrangements in her ability to pass as a straight woman, the discourses of national security inadvertently severed the connection between femininity and heterosexuality, even as they sought to preserve it. *All about Eve* tries to resolve this contradiction by restoring Margo to the institutions of normative heterosexuality. Margo's normalisation entails transforming her femininity so that, unlike Eve's, it appears to be the 'real thing'. Eve's powers of conversion prove temporary. As I have already noted, the more Eve treats her like a 'set of blueprints' to be followed, the more antagonistic Margo becomes. In the sequence of the party, Margo is particularly nasty to Eve. Mounting the stairs to her bedroom, she turns to Bill when he asks suggestively if she wants any help, and says, 'Put me to Bed? Take my clothes off, hold my head, tuck me in, turn out the lights, and tiptoe out? Eve would, wouldn't you, Eve?' When an embarrassed Eve replies, 'If you'd like', Margo snaps, 'I wouldn't like!' Margo's comments here could not be more coercively homophobic. She all but forces Eve to out herself. For Eve to maintain her compliant, stereotypically feminine demeanour, she must reveal that she is willing to engage in intimacies with Margo 'properly' reserved for a heterosexual lover. Adding to the homophobia, Margo's reply, 'I wouldn't like!' seems intended to make clear that she is different from Eve, that, unlike her, she is 'normal'. Now that Bill is back, she prefers to have him keep her from getting lonely, and he follows her upstairs to put her to bed.

In reclaiming Margo for heterosexual romance, the film tries to destabilise the category of woman that its own representation of the lesbian has put into crisis. In the scene where, stranded in the car with Karen, Margo apologises for having treated her and the others as her 'supporting cast', as Karen puts it in the scene at the party, Margo makes a distinction between Margo Channing the star, 'something spelled out in light bulbs', and Margo Channing the woman who loves Bill 'more than anything else in this world'. To teach Margo a lesson, Karen has emptied the car of petrol so that Margo will not make it back to New York in time for her performance and Eve, her understudy, will have to go on in her place, thus getting her big break. Much to Karen's chagrin, Margo deeply regrets the sacrifices she has made to become a star. 'Funny business a woman's career,' she begins ruefully; 'the things you drop on your way up the ladder so you can move faster. You forget you'll need them again when you get back to being a woman.' Margo asserts here that a woman cannot have a career and remain a woman. Indeed, what she did not realise while moving up the ladder of success was that womanhood itself is a career. For a woman, the only career that should matter is being a woman, and if she does not allow being a woman to take precedence over her other careers, then, like Eve, she is not really a woman. Margo goes on to say that womanhood is 'one career all females have in common, whether we like it or not – being a woman – and sooner or later we've got to work at it no matter how many other careers we've had or wanted'. And what do women need to work at most, what is being a woman all about? Getting a man, because, without a man, a woman is not really a woman. Margo concludes her rueful self-examination by stating that 'in the last analysis nothing's any good unless you can look up just before dinner or turn around in bed and there he is. Without that you're not a woman.' Here the film attempts to rearticulate being female with being feminine and heterosexual, the very normative alignment of anatomical sex, gender and sexuality it has disrupted through its representation of Eve as the lesbian of the discourses of national security who is all but indistinguishable from the heterosexual woman. If, as Margo claims, being a woman depends on having a man, then, despite her femininity, Eve is not one.

But restabilising the category of woman requires more than containing Margo's fluid sexuality through heterosexual romance. Perhaps the film's greatest obstacle to resolving the contradictions in Cold War gender and sexual ideologies was Bette Davis's campy performance. As I have already indicated, many reviewers assumed that Davis modelled her performance on Bankhead. Her hairdo, facial expressions, husky voice (the result of being hoarse, or so Davis claimed when pressed by reporters to explain why she sounded so different in *All about Eve* from her other movies), and exaggerated mannerisms all resembled Bankhead's, as did her wardrobe, which Edith Head designed after looking at film stills of Bankhead.[22] The reviews in *Time*, *Life* and *Newsweek* all noted the resemblance, which they took to be deliberate. Bankhead was known for her gender-bending as well as for her lesbianism. Her weekly radio show, 'The Big Show', which aired on NBC, beginning in 1950, always ended with her musical director Meredith Wilson wryly uttering the line, 'Thank you, Miss Bankhead, sir!'[23] The resemblance between Davis and Bankhead gave Davis's performance a camp inflection it might otherwise have lacked, especially for gay male spectators who were fans of both her and Bankhead, a camp icon. But, even without the resemblance, Davis's performance would have lent itself to camp appropriations. Davis was one of the actresses of Hollywood's 'golden age' most often impersonated by drag queens in the 1950s and 1960s for good reason. Famous for her exaggerated mannerisms and facial expressions, Davis was one of Hollywood's most flamboyant stars, and impersonating Bankhead only intensified her exaggerated acting style. Some critics have gone so far as to describe Margo as a drag queen impersonating Bette Davis to capture the camp quality of Davis's performance in *All about Eve*.[24] In promoting a camp mode of reception, this quality undercut the film's ideological project of realigning femininity with femaleness and heterosexuality. One of the effects of Davis's exaggerated performance was to denaturalise femininity by highlighting its performativity, or constructedness. Davis's glamorous femininity was literally a copy of a copy, Bankhead's. As I have already mentioned, Davis's model was a gender-bending lesbian whose femininity was thought to be 'fake' or an act designed to conceal a core masculine identity ('Thank you, Miss Bankhead, sir!'), and thus there was nothing authentic or natural about it. For this reason, Margo's definition of femininity in the scene in the car, a definition that essentialises it by grounding it in both femaleness and heterosexuality, may have seemed unbelievable to many spectators.

In foregrounding the film's campiness, which underlay its status as a gay male cult film in the 1950s and 1960s, I do not mean to simplify or gloss over its relation to the Cold War discourse of national identity. This aspect of the film existed in tension with its homophobia, competing with but never displacing it. In foregrounding the film's contradictory relation to Cold War gender ideologies, I have tried to show that it is precisely the uneasy relationship between the campy and the homophobic elements of Mankiewicz's film that defines the queerness of Cold War culture. As we have seen, the film's homophobic construction of the lesbian disrupts the alignment of sex, gender and sexuality on which the category of woman depended in the Cold War era by highlighting the mobility of femininity in relation to both femaleness and heterosexuality. But, as we have also seen, despite the fact that Eve can pass for straight, her core identity seems to be masculine, or at least her butchness in the opening shots of the flashback and then again in the final scene with Phoebe allows for this understanding of her identity. This contradiction in the film's representation of Eve can be traced to the persistence of the stereotype of the masculine lesbian, or the lesbian who was thought to be a man trapped in a woman's body. The Cold War discourse of homosexuality may have displaced this stereotype by accelerating the process whereby sexual desire for women overtook masculinity as the basis of lesbian identity, but it did not completely disappear and continued to shape how the lesbian was perceived so that the butch continued to be seen as somehow more lesbian than the femme. As a result, the lesbian's masculinity continued to be seen as real or authentic, whereas her femininity was assumed to be fake, a kind of disguise she put on to conceal her lesbianism. But even the film's essentialist construction of Eve's identity cannot recontain the mobility of femininity that her ability to pass for straight foregrounds. The examples of queer femininity in the film are too compelling, especially the one provided by the film's star, Bette Davis, whose campy performance undermined the film's project to underwrite the institutions of normative heterosexuality. As we have seen, these examples of queerness denaturalise femininity even as they seek to immobilise it by reanchoring it to the straight female body and in so doing open up the possibility of a camp appropriation of the film. Thanks to this possibility, *All about Eve* is not only one of the most homophobic but also one of the queerest films made during the Cold War era.

NOTES

1. Vito Russo, *The Celluloid Closet: Homosexuality in the Movies* (New York: Harper and Row, 1987), p. 94.
2. Quoted in Patricia White, *Uninvited: Classical Hollywood Cinema and Lesbian Representability* (Bloomington, IN: Indiana University Press, 1999), p. 1.
3. Exemplary discussions of Code-era celluloid lesbians include Russo, *The Celluloid Closet*, and Andrea Weiss, *Vampires and Violets: Lesbians in Film* (Harmondsworth: Penguin Books, 1993). See also Richard Barrios, *Screened Out: Playing Gay in Hollywood from Edison to Stonewall* (New York: Routledge, 2002).
4. I develop this argument more fully in Robert J. Corber, *Homosexuality in Cold War America: Resistance and the Crisis of Masculinity* (Durham, NC, and London: Duke University Press, 1997).

5. Michael Rogin, *Ronald Reagan, the Movie: And Other Episodes of Political Demonology* (Berkeley and Los Angeles: University of California Press, 1987), pp. 236–71.

6. Kenneth L. Geist, *Pictures Will Talk: The Life and Films of Joseph L. Mankiewicz* (New York: Scribner's, 1978).

7. John D'Emilio, *Sexual Politics, Sexual Communities: The Making of a Homosexual Minority in the United States, 1940–1970* (Chicago: University of Chicago Press, 1983), pp. 40–53.

8. I include my own work on Cold War homophobia here. See in particular Robert J. Corber, *In the Name of National Security: Hitchcock, Homophobia, and the Political Construction of Gender in Postwar America* (Durham, NC, and London: Duke University Press, 1993).

9. US Senate, 81st Cong., 2nd sess., Committee on Expenditures in Executive Departments, *The Employment of Homosexuals and Other Sex Perverts in Government* (Washington: Government Printing Office, 1950), p. 2.

10. Ibid. p. 2.

11. Ibid. p. 4.

12. The female sexual invert is also the antecedent of the female-to-male transsexual. For a genealogy of the female-to-male transsexual that traces him to the female sexual invert, see Judith Halberstam, *Female Masculinity* (Durham, NC: Duke University Press, 1998), pp. 75–110.

13. For a more detailed discussion of this, see George Chauncey, 'From Sexual Inversion to Homosexuality: The Changing Medical Conceptualization of Female "Deviance"' in Kathy Piess and Christina Simmons (eds), *Passion and Power: Sexuality in History* (Philadelphia: Temple University Press, 1989), pp. 87–117. See also Esther Newton, 'The Mythic Mannish Lesbian: Radclyffe Hall and the New Woman', *Signs*, 9/4 (Summer 1984), pp. 557–75.

14. On the feminine lesbian, see Chauncey, 'From Sexual Inversion to Homosexuality'; Halberstam, *Female Masculinity*, pp. 75–110; and Martha Vicinus, '"They Wonder to Which Sex I Belong": The Historical Roots of the Modern Lesbian Identity', in Martha Vicinus (ed.), *Lesbian Subjects: A Feminist Studies Reader* (Bloomington, IN: Indiana University Press, 1996), pp. 233–60.

15. Havelock Ellis, *Studies in the Psychology of Sex: Sexual Inversion* (Honolulu, HI: University Press of the Pacific, [1906] 2001), p. 133.

16. On the emergence of sexual object choice as the organising principle of sexuality, see Chauncey, 'From Sexual Inversion to Homosexuality'. Chauncey examines this emergence more fully in his *Gay New York: Gender, Urban Culture, and the Making of the Gay Male World, 1890–1940* (New York: Basic Books, 1994).

17. Elizabeth Lapovsky Kennedy and Madeline Davis, *Boots of Leather and Slippers of Gold: The History of a Lesbian Community* (New York: Penguin Books, 1994).

18. Ibid. pp. 323–71.

19. On the visual codes developed by Hollywood for representing lesbians in the era of the Production Code, see Barrios, *Screened Out*.

20. For particularly good analyses of the homoerotics of female spectatorship, see Jackie Stacey, 'Desperately Seeking Difference', *Screen*, 18/1 (Winter 1987), pp. 48–61; Jackie Stacey, 'Feminine Fascinations: Forms of Identification in Star–Audience Relations', in Christine Gledhill (ed.), *Stardom: Industry of Desire* (London: Routledge, 1991), pp. 141–63; Diana Fuss, 'Fashion and the Homospectatorial Look', *Critical Inquiry*, 18/2 (Summer 1992), pp. 713–37; and White, *Uninvited*.

21. On this aspect of the reception of *All about Eve*, see Sam Staggs, *All About 'All about Eve'* (New York: St Martin's Griffin, 2000), pp. 219–21.

22. On Bankhead and Davis's notorious rivalry, see ibid. pp. 218–22.

23. Ibid. pp. 217–31.

24. Ibid. p. 218.

CHAPTER THREE

Politics

Mapping Containment:
The Cultural Construction of the Cold War

David Ryan

Following the 'lessons' of the 1930s, the post-war US agenda necessitated a thorough engagement with Western Europe, not just to keep the Soviets out and the Germans and the European left down, but also to keep the Americans in. The Depression demonstrated that the US 'way of life' could not be sustained in an autarkic global system. Washington needed to promote an ideology that ensured the survival of US-style liberal democratic capitalism. Given the various forms of European resistance to the encroachment of US power, culture and ideology played an indispensable role in the construction of US policy. The cultural constructs of the early Cold War period created a consensus and narrowed the range of ideological options. Instead, a bipolar construct was presented as a natural outcome of the post-war period in which the Soviets attempted to overrun Europe and threaten the West more generally.

This orthodox consensus needs to be situated into the context of US expansionism: political, economic, ideological and cultural. Without the Soviet 'threat', US expansionism was deprived of a focal point around which to mobilise not just US culture but also that of Western Europe. The writings of George Kennan, the public rhetoric of the Truman administration and the internal Policy Planning Studies and NSC-68 advanced a Manichaean construct of the world that was buttressed by an extensive set of overt and covert operations designed to shape public consciousness of the situation.

This bipolar vision not only exaggerated the Soviet threat, and elided US motivations; it also obscured the West European political and cultural resistance to an enhanced US power and presence. Ideology, public diplomacy and culture helped to embed the idea of the Soviet threat and the need for a continued US presence in Europe. The frequent and strident characterisation of the Soviets and the creation of a new 'West' masked the transatlantic divisions and metaphorical discordance between Washington and the West

Europeans. Moreover, the construction of the Soviet threat, long before it actually became one, facilitated US integration with Western Europe. Within the context of an isolationist Republican and a more accommodating Democratic left who either argued that the United States should stay home or seek compromise with the Soviets, the division of Europe was in a sense essential to US post-war objectives. What other discourse, beyond national security, could mobilise and motivate the reluctant sectors of US society and the resistant sectors of Europe?

Such binary divisions that now pitted a liberal democratic capitalist West against the Soviets created a new Western identity that masked many tensions in that relationship. Though Washington stood for freedom and democracy, it had simultaneously to explain away its internal problems with civil rights and its thorough integration with European colonial powers. Though Washington had relations with both Nazi Germany before the war and the Soviets during the war, these had to be forgotten in order to preserve the new and ontologically benevolent identity of the West. The Cold War narratives, cultural constructs and cultural artefacts from magazines to movies reinforced the essential narrative. Moreover, the power of the Cold War Western narrative posited a new beginning to a new story. The story began with Soviet expansionism and situated the US response as a benign reaction to 'contain' the new menace. As with all narratives, the author chooses the point of departure.

Such beginnings facilitated the construction of a cohesive and coherent West in the face of the Soviet threat, even though there were significant differences between the West Europeans and the United States and some reticence to US power. The culture of the Cold War provided the atmosphere and the tools that enabled Washington to enhance its consensus, achieve its objectives and largely win the battle for the hearts and minds of West Europeans. But far from the idea of a passive transfer of culture, Washington initiated numerous programmes designed to bring about its desired ends. And, although US culture was renegotiated in Europe, in broad outline US policy was largely a success: a new West was created in which old inconsistencies were forgotten and new identities were advanced.

The power of a metaphor derives from the interplay between the discordant meanings it symbolically coerces into a unitary conceptual framework and from the degree to which that coercion is successful in overcoming the psychic resistance such semantic tension inevitably generates in anyone in a position to perceive it.[1]

(Clifford Geertz, *The Interpretation of Culture*, 1993)

IN SEARCH OF MONSTERS TO DESTROY

At the point that the Cold War collapsed as a viable narrative with the destruction of the Berlin Wall and the autonomous liberation of the peoples of Eastern Europe, an employee of the State Department, Francis Fukuyama, had the audacity to proclaim the end of 'History'. It ended because there were no further paths of ideological development; US-style liberal democracy constituted 'the end point of mankind's ideological evolution and the final form of human government'. To stretch a point, life, liberty and the pursuit of happiness (or property) had come full circle. Fukuyama opined: 'we might summarize the content of the universal homogenous state as liberal democracy in the political sphere combined with easy access to VCRs and stereos in the economic'.[2] With the end of the Cold War the USA had consumed the dialectic in History. The Soviet challenge was the last major ideological battle. While such arguments may seem reductive and absurd, there was a concerted effort to promote US ideology, culture and 'way of life' after the Second World War.[3]

Daniel Bell and Herbert Marcuse dealt with similar ideas from widely different perspectives. Marcuse argued in *One Dimensional Man* (1964) that the affluent period of the 1950s had turned history off 'by narcotizing its members – they were sexually gratified, well fed, well housed and fashionably clothed, and they were taught to think no thoughts that would derail the society'. The utopianism of the progressive ideologies had been pacified. For instance, Richard Hofstadter's post-war works, *The American Political Tradition* (1948) and *The Age of Reform* (1955), argued that capitalism was the true organic tradition of the American people and that 'populist democracy was their false consciousness'. So during the troubled times of the Cold War it was better for Americans to shun the mass participatory impulses of the people and let experts guide the nation. As such, Hofstadter 'served as midwife' to a reigning idea in post-war academic thought that national identity was rooted in consensus.[4] Consensus was the central message of Daniel Bell's infamous essay, 'The End of Ideology'. The prosperity of the post-war period had dampened radicalism and encouraged the Western working classes to settle for 'good enough, rather than Utopia; the horrors of communism had put up the price of Utopia, and the welfare state had lowered the costs of capitalism'.[5] Creating a clear consciousness of the benefits of the American way of life was imperative. These adhesive narratives found an audience in the USA, with some help from the Americans for Democratic Action (ADA), initiated by Arthur Schlesinger and others to promote a liberal domestic agenda with a strong anti-communist foreign policy.[6] It was another thing to project these beliefs into Europe.

US political, economic and cultural imperialisms have been resisted at various points throughout Europe, while they have also been assimilated, adapted and renegotiated. The US strategy towards becoming the Western hegemony was multifaceted and needs to be viewed as a whole. US political authority paved the way for the Marshall Plan, which guaranteed access to European markets for American goods. Following post-war European austerity, these cultural products were attractive and desirable but also considered crass and superficial. But the products rarely travelled across the Atlantic alone. They came with strong and seductive political messages. In various ways and through various adaptations, American goods, from cigarettes to jeans, promoted narratives of freedom, often explicitly in advertisements.[7]

France provided most resistance. Its culture had never let go of the idea of a French universalism that clashed frequently and ignominiously with that of the Americans, who were aware of the problem of cultural resistance to the American dream. In 1952 Reinhold Niebhur outlined a problem: 'The progress of American culture toward hegemony in the world community as well as toward the ultimate in standards of living has brought us everywhere to limits where our ideals and norms are brought under ironic indictment.' The US confidence in the compatibility of prosperity and virtue was challenged,

> particularly in our relations with Europe. For the European nations, France especially, find our culture 'vulgar', and pretend to be imperilled by the inroads of an American synthetic drink upon the popularity of their celebrated wines. The French protest against 'Cocacolonialism' expresses this ironic conflict in a nutshell.

The US confidence of happiness with a foundation of prosperity was challenged by the anxiety 'which our world-wide responsibilities bring upon us'.[8] Responsibilities? Such words and that characterisation of US foreign policy grew out of the concurrent desire to extend its sphere of influence, its power and its way of life, yet American leaders did not want to be characterised as imperialists. Instead, concepts of leadership, responsibility and manifest destiny echoed the paternalistic language of nineteenth-century imperialism, but avoided its explicit characterisation.[9] The construction of cultural narratives was fundamental to facilitate this extension of US power.

After decades of historians struggling over the interpretation of the early Cold War period, Leffler concludes that the US 'preponderance of power' was designed to bring about a certain structure and order to the world. The USA wanted to contain, not just the Soviet Union, but also various forces unleashed through the Second World War: nationalism, the popularity of the left in Western Europe and the disruption of global commerce. US national security strategies were devised to protect the American way of life. Despite all the hyperbole of US Cold War rhetoric, recent research indicates that Stalin had no plans to invade Western Europe, and wanted to avoid war with the United States. The Soviet posture was essentially defensive.[10] But, if Stalin's abilities, if not ambitions, were limited, how could Washington push the desired consensus throughout Western Europe? It was imperative to define the emerging Cold War struggle early to obtain conditions that would bring about not just certain outcomes, but attitudes and distributions of wealth. George Kennan, director of Policy Planning in the State Department, argued that

> we have about 50% of the world's wealth but only 6.3% of its population . . . In this situation, we cannot fail to be the object of envy and resentment. Our real task in the coming period is to devise a pattern of relationships which will permit us to maintain this position of disparity without positive detriment to our national security.[11]

But that 'pattern of relationships' relied on certain global configurations of power. The world had endured the autarkic depression of the 1930s, whose chief lesson to US policy-makers was that isolationism was not an option. Its economy, its prosperity and its way of life depended on integration and engagement. The dreams that were the stuff of proverbial and parochial narratives, that filled the pages of popular US publications such as *Time* and *Life*, rested on US economic access abroad. Washington had to spread the American dream,[12] especially in Europe.[13] The Marshall Plan was not just the benevolent act of a state that sought to assist war-torn Europe. It was not just an attempt to keep the Soviets out, or the European left down; it was not just aimed at the revival of capitalism; it was also an attempt to ensure that the USA was thoroughly integrated into the West European economic system.[14] It was even more ambitious than that. Through these European metropolitan capitals, Washington had the opportunity to gain access to the raw materials, labour and markets of their colonies.[15]

But there were considerable lingering doubts about these Americans. They were not just the liberators with nylons, Hershey candy bars, chewing gum and cigarettes, the stuff of countless movies that later formed the basis of much collective memory, aspirations and emulation. They also generated widespread scepticism and fear. Capitalism was not as strong in Europe as in the States; the Depression had seriously dented its appeal to leading European opinion-makers, who could undermine the American dream.

The still substantial European left(s) considered American-style capitalism beyond reform; it needed radical change. Moreover, despite the atrocities, because of their tremendous contribution to victory over Nazi Germany, the Soviets held great appeal in Western Europe. The argument over Western identity in Europe was divided between those who identified their West with the United States against those who rejected the commercialism and religious elements for a polity that sought progressive social transformation.[16] They thought American commercialism threatened European traditions and culture; capitalism threatened to displace the primacy of politics and the existing European elite; and further capitalism and the Americans threatened the European empires and their illusionary, but puissant, belief in their importance.

Washington had to overcome these divisions in Western Europe and try to promote consensus. This necessitated developing a political, commercial, military and cultural hegemony that would facilitate the continued US presence in Europe. Despite the internal contradictions in US policy, between democracy and capitalism, between liberty and democracy, and even between capitalism and liberty, references to a select narrative from the past and reference to an impending threat in the future ameliorated such discordance. The US collective memory of its diplomatic history relies considerably on rituals and almost deified traditions and documents that explain its purpose and position in the world. The cultural constructions that run through the foundational myths to the Declaration of Independence, the Monroe Doctrine, the Fourteen Points, the Four Freedoms, the Atlantic Charter and the Truman Doctrine played a tremendous part as morality tales that sought inspiration from the past, real or imagined. But these tales also inspired and mobilised; they provided a common purpose.[17] In the early post-war period it was essential to create a consensus that was not just American, but Western. Such a construction could not acknowledge the recent past: the US–Soviet relationship, the US–German relationship or the common ground between liberalism and totalitarianism.[18]

Instead, a new West was imagined – one that would rest on the benign meta-narrative of the essential Western identity that papered over the recent past. Reference to the sacred documents and traditions of US foreign policy buttressed the castles built of sand and simultaneously constrained potential dissent. By the early Cold War period US policy-makers drew on this tradition liberally; they argued that US freedom had not grown out of European imperialism, but against it. But now Washington was the saviour of even imperial Europe's freedom against the menace of a new construct: Red Fascism. This new threat was used to justify US leadership. Washington simultaneously 'denied imperialism and enacted it'. Following Hiroshima and Nagasaki and the potential of Soviet weapons, and despite the dreams of a global system moving to the End of History, the Cold War had undermined traditional understandings of victory. The struggles in Western Europe over the Western identity and in Europe between the East and the West, indeed the struggles for the world, were, as Appy writes, also a struggle for the word. Propaganda, cultural diplomacy and culture were essential elements of the early Cold War period that supplemented the traditional tools of power.[19] As the influential liberal Louis Hartz wrote in the 1950s:

> It is the absence of outright war, or the presence of what we call the 'Cold War', which makes these orientations plain; for military struggle . . . is the great simplifier, reducing complicated social issues to the simple lines of the battle chart. Because the current struggle against Communism is in significant part an ideological competition for human loyalties, it has brought into the plainest view America's psychological pattern. One of the issues it involves is the issue of a social 'message' to compete with the appeal of Communism.[20]

The propaganda, both official and other, demonised the Soviets and created an essential and enduring West based on a series of constructions that facilitated US policy and its integration into European affairs. Indeed, when George Kennan penned his article in the pages of *Foreign Affairs* in 1947, he concluded that 'there was never a fairer test of national quality' nor will there be cause for complaint. Instead:

> He will rather experience a certain gratitude to a Providence which, by providing the American people with this implacable challenge, has made their entire security as a nation dependent on their pulling themselves together and accepting the responsibilities of moral and political leadership that history plainly intended them to bear.[21]

THE IMPORTANCE OF BEING GEORGE

The pursuit of 'leadership' ran up against European agendas and their suspicion of an overbearing American influence. Moreover, there was resistance from the left in the US Democratic Party and the isolationist Republican right. The new Western identity was threatened by significant internal confusion. European powers still maintained colonial empires. How could that be construed as promoting liberty and self-determination? The Soviets were weak and withdrawn. The European left was still attractive. And, finally, Germany was still occupied. Such complexity hindered social mobilisation. How could the United States support European colonial monarchies? How could it overcome resistance to a greater US global agenda? How could Washington overcome the resistance of the European left? The Cold War narrative had to be raised above the particularities and inconsistencies in the transatlantic relationship. The concept of the West was indispensable to mobilise Congress with its fiscal prerogatives. The Western hemisphere, once that geographical and ideological territory west of the Atlantic, now transcended the ocean in the new West. The expanded West would encompass these colonial powers and maintain the narrative of freedom and self-determination. Such metaphorical discordance could be accommodated only through references to the Soviet threat. What other device could facilitate US integration into Europe?

The division of Europe had been informally worked out in the closing stages of the Second World War. The infamous 'percentages agreement' between Stalin and Churchill in 1944 largely reflected where real power rested after the war. The Red Army advanced over Eastern Europe as a result of the Western Allies' choice of the peripheral strategy through North Africa and Italy in 1942 and 1943, and the Russians stayed in the East to ensure their own security against a West that now possessed the atomic bomb. By February 1946 Stalin indicated that capitalism and communism were incompatible in a speech designed for domestic consumption.[22] Stalin cared little for the pursuit of worldwide class-based revolution; his primary motivation was state-centred: to secure the Soviet Union. The following month Churchill described the division of Europe by an 'Iron Curtain', and also called for an Anglo-American alliance. George Kennan, working in the US Embassy in Moscow, penned the famous long telegram, some 8,000 words that advanced the basic argument for the containment of expansive Russian tendencies. Kennan pointed out that these tendencies did not result from any 'objective analysis of the situation beyond Russia's borders', but were a result of 'basic inner Russian necessities'. Nevertheless, according to this telegram, Russian leaders were bent on US destruction: that 'the internal harmony of our society be disrupted, our traditional way of life destroyed, the international authority of our state be broken if Soviet power is to be secure'.[23]

The Truman administration closely monitored US public attitudes. Administration officials read editorials of over 100 papers, kept an eye on what columnists were writing and reviewed the public statements of political leaders. The Truman administration wanted to shape opinion and attitudes. In Kennan's telegram, Secretary of Defense James Forrestal found the perfect vehicle to engrave 'the Nazi totalitarian image onto Soviet foreign policy'.[24]

The telegram was distributed widely throughout Washington, and, like the Iron Curtain speech, it reduced a complex situation to a more palatable Manichaean formula.

The telegram was the most influential explanation of Russian intentions. Stalin made his position clear; Churchill set the agenda for the conservatives. In Washington, the Secretary of Commerce, Henry Wallace, pushed the liberal agenda and advocated cooperation with the Soviets. Kennan's telegram helped Truman oppose this proposal. The telegram provided the intellectual tools to conflate 'concerns about totalitarianism and communism in dealing with the Soviet Union'.[25] By the summer of 1947 'containment' became a more familiar term with the publication of Kennan's 'The Sources of Soviet Conduct' in *Foreign Affairs* under the pseudonym Mr X. He argued that US policy must involve a 'long-term, patient but firm and vigilant containment of Russian expansive tendencies'.[26] The Truman administration urged the publication of the article to send a signal that Washington was clear on its policies and in the hope that it would encourage congressional funding of the Truman Doctrine.[27]

By early 1947 the British indicated that they could no longer sustain their position in the Near East, especially in Greece and Turkey. Though the situation in Greece had very little to do with Moscow, policy-makers in Washington insisted that it did. US policy could not be couched in terms of supporting another corrupt and repressive European monarchy.[28] Instead, overlooking the situational particulars, the Truman Doctrine, announced on 12 March 1947, developed a construct of the West and the challenge that faced it.

Just two months earlier, leading US magazines talked positively about the prospects of US–Soviet cooperation. Moreover, new congressional representatives were elected with little concern for foreign affairs or the desire to increase taxes necessary to pay for US ambition. Such attitudes convinced the Truman administration that Americans had to be 'shocked' into action. In late February Undersecretary of State Dean Acheson presented the situation to congressional leaders in apocalyptic terms. Congress would surely support the president, Senator Vendenberg indicated, if such terms were repeated. The administration had to 'scare [the] hell' out of the American people.[29]

President Truman did not identify the Soviets specifically, but chose instead to rely on that catch-all term, totalitarianism. The speech kept clear of particularities. Speech-writers found it difficult to justify aid to Turkey, but it was kept in the bargain. The depiction of the Greek situation was somewhat inaccurate. Nevertheless, such broad terms and the general characteristics of the Other facilitated the conceptual image of a bipolar world.[30] A defining choice in world history between democractic freedom and communist totalitarianism had to be made. The characteristics of the two 'ways of life' were stark and diametrically opposed to each other.[31] Such binary divisions demonised the Soviets. The Truman Doctrine affirmed the messages in Kennan's long telegram that it was pointless to try to understand or to negotiate with Moscow under its present system. Accommodation or reconciliation was out of the question. The message echoed that of Stalin's speech. The division of Europe was essential to US policy and objectives. In time it was reflected throughout society, but it was especially evident in films throughout the 1950s. The epic biblical tales in *Quo Vadis* (1951), *The Ten Commandments* (1956) and *Ben-Hur* (1959) echoed the Manichaean framework, positioning narratives of 'benevolent superiority', anti-slavery, anti-colonialism and liberation in the context of the Cold War.[32]

The implications of such a binary construct meant that there was little political room for dissent. Not only had the Soviets been caricatured; the Truman Doctrine also constructed an essential US identity. This identity was quite consciously linked to the long succession of principled US texts that were frequently invoked in US public diplomacy to silence critics and reaffirm the benevolence and moderation of US policy. Between 1947 and 1949 the 'Freedom Train' crossed the United States visiting 322 cities in all forty-eight states. It attracted 3.5 million people, who saw 127 documents that contrasted the sacred texts of American history with those of Nazi Germany. Run by the Department of Justice, it was conceived as a means 'of aiding the country in its internal war against subversive elements and as an effort to improve citizenship by reawakening in our people their profound faith in the American historical heritage'. President Truman fully endorsed the touring train. Its essential objectives were echoed in US policy to take the American message to 'freedom loving people throughout the world'.[33] US national identity was bound within a limited framework that obfuscated its former relationship with Nazi Germany and its continued relationship with colonial Europe. Instead, these negative associations were increasingly projected onto Soviet behaviour. References to Red Fascism and to the Soviet *colonial* policies advanced apace. The tactic is captured well within the decade. On the eve of African decolonisation, in 1957 Eisenhower's NSC opined that, on the colonial question, care should be taken to 'avoid US identification with those policies of the metropolitan powers, which are stagnant or repressive, and, to the extent practicable, [to] seek effective means of influencing the metropolitan powers to abandon or modify such policies'; and to 'emphasize through all appropriate media the colonial policies of the Soviet Union and particularly the fact that the Soviet colonial empire has continued to expand throughout the period when Western colonialism has been contracting'.[34]

Through the 'strategy of Otherness', domestic dissent was precluded; identified with supporting the Soviets, it was considered disloyal.[35] McCarthyism ultimately represented the apotheosis of this process. The emerging Cold War culture narrowed the parameters of debate; an increasing homogeneity of outlook emerged and ultimately coalesced into what became known as the Cold War consensus. The bounds of expression, debate and therefore viable policy alternatives were constrained through these ideological limits.[36]

The division of Europe was essential to US objectives. US expansion into Europe was considered imperative, given the ghosts of the 1930s and their attendant deceptions. Truman had to push the US boat out into the world and become entangled in European affairs, against the cultural tide of Washington, Jefferson and Quincy Adams's admonitions to avoid entangling alliances. The Soviets were essential to this agenda. It is difficult to think how economic recovery in the United States could have been brought about without the Soviets. Why would the inward-looking, fiscally conservative Congress support a financial programme for Greece and Turkey – let alone the much more expensive Marshall Plan – had these not been cast in a binary construct predicated on a national security discourse? If the Marshall Plan had to deal with Eastern Europe, devastated even more by the war, the plan would have been drained by the scope of the project. 'Without an "enemy" to focus on, how could the bedevilling European rivalries of the interwar years have been overcome?'[37]

THE ENDS OF US FOREIGN POLICY

There are multiple interpretations of US foreign policy at the origins of the Cold War, which have produced historiography that is both rich and acrimonious. Despite the plurality of interpretation within academia, culturally, the traditional interpretation is dominant. It informed the production of films and television, and generally laid the basis for American collective memory.[38] These media and early historical writings echoed Kennan and amplified the gist of the Truman Doctrine: the need to 'contain' the Soviet expansive tendencies. The Manichaean formula provided an attractive basis for cultural interaction. Most Americans had convinced themselves that their culture and outlook were not ideological. Objectivity was considered the basis of free thought in a pragmatic and progressive society.[39] By 1958 Edward Shils situated the bipolar outlook in a long line of ideological antecedents that had informed politics throughout the nineteenth and twentieth centuries, epitomised best in the USA through the politics of McCarthyism and the Truman Doctrine. The ideology was, for Clifford Geertz,

> dualistic, opposing the pure 'we' to the evil 'they', proclaiming that he who is not with me is against me. It is alienative in that it distrusts, attacks, and works to undermine established political institutions. It is doctrinaire in that it claims complete and exclusive possession of political truth and abhors compromise. It is totalistic in that it aims to order the whole of social and cultural life in the image of its ideals, futuristic in that it works toward a utopian culmination of history in which such an ordering will be realized.[40]

There was no point in trying to understand the Soviets' position or their legitimate interests: they were simply the enemy that needed to be contained. There were no options or prospects for accommodation, because the Soviets had no legitimate interests. Diplomacy and compromise under such circumstances were futile.[41]

The narrative power of the Truman Doctrine and the X article cannot be underestimated. Not only did they set out the ideas, language and metaphors used in the texts; they also drew on the nation's sense of mission and manifest destiny, its sense of superiority and its cultural exceptionalism. The Truman administration created an evangelistic mood for a Cold War against an evil other.[42] The consensus and benign interpretations of US policy were enhanced by the characteristics of a good narrative. Narratives obviously have a beginning selected by the author. The impact of 'containment' as a policy and a word immediately suggested that the Soviets took the initiative and that the Americans responded as part of a defensive posture concerned with national security. Within this framework, the United States was identified as the guarantor of Western security, the regenerator of its economy, and the instigator of a period of freedom and prosperity. Precluded from this framing were alternative narratives that explained the hostilities as a function of US economic, political, ideological and cultural expansion across the Atlantic. This narrative identified the artificial origins of the period and let Washington recast the drama. Moreover, rather than recalling the immediate past of cooperation with the Soviets and economic engagement with the Nazis or other awkward colonial relationships, the initial and most powerful Cold War narratives called on the sacred documents of US diplomacy, providing continuity, benevolence, comprehension and closure to the unfolding story.[43] Narratives are not only vital for both individual and social identity; they provide cultures with stories that make action possible.

They provide a meaning that facilitates social and cultural mobilisation.[44] Containing the Soviets was one part of the proposition. Integrating Europe and more importantly integrating the United States with Europe was another.

In 1948 the Policy Planning Staff were primarily concerned with Europe, Britain and the United States. Kennan argued that, for the free nations of Europe to survive against a united East, some form of political, military and economic union was necessary. A European union would not be strong enough unless it included Britain. Yet this would not be enough for Britain; Europe could not provide the food and raw materials it needed. So Britain might be better off with close association with the USA and Canada. But, given the loss of Eastern Europe, traditionally an area that supplied the West, the only way that the prospective European union could become economically healthy was through closer relationships with either the western hemisphere or Africa. The former option was anathema, because the association would have to be 'so intimate' and require a currency and customs union, and free migration between Europe and the United States. The second option was more attractive, involving a more loosely constituted transatlantic relationship, coupled with 'a union of Western European nations [that] would undertake jointly the economic development and exploitation of the colonial and dependent areas of the African continent'.[45]

Transatlantic integration was essential. Kammen describes an array of cultural responses in the early Cold War period that were still 'cohesive and patterned like a carefully designed fabric' that echoed official narratives. The Hiss, Rosenberg and Oppenheimer security cases brought attention to the internal Other and the sense of anxiety that was echoed in plays like Arthur Miller's *The Crucible* (1953). Even the Junior Metropolitan Museum of Art's supervisor developed a project that ran for three years on the integration of the United States between 1783 and 1800, *E Pluribus Unum*. The press release noted the connections between the Cold War and the founding of the United States. Just as the States had struggled to unite, now the states of the free world were struggling to unite. Popular fiction to academia echoed the themes raised by the Truman administration. Perry Miller advanced the notion that American literature could be used as a weapon against communism. Such writings could communicate with 'free men everywhere. Because this is a literature of criticism in the name of the fundamental man, it is a literature of freedom.'[46]

The stakes were continually raised through the late 1940s. The Czech coup and Berlin blockade of 1948 were followed by the 'loss' of China to communism and the Soviet explosion of an atomic bomb in 1949. Early in 1950 Truman ordered a review of US security. The resulting report, NSC-

68, reinforced the Manichaean outlook, stressed the urgency of the situation and called for a significant military build-up. The document was an alarmist account rehearsing the prevailing narratives. Further, it outlined the fundamental characteristics of both the Soviets and the Americans in diametrically opposite terms. The urgency of the language, the appeal to US tradition and history and the articulation of the dichotomous nature of the conflict established 'a single point of view from which the new post-war world is "mapped" and national security choices are understood'.[47]

The binary construction pushed forward a militant nationalism and created a consensus by focusing on the evil Other. Such discourse fitted easily with the traditions of US diplomacy. Such binary constructions removed shades of grey and options to pursue a middle ground. Europeans had to choose where they stood. If they were often doubtful, Washington ran covert operations to convince them otherwise.[48] Though the state had long been involved in 'spreading the American dream', there was some resistance to its involvement in creative enterprises.[49] Such reticence disappeared after the war, when diplomats began to see culture as an invaluable weapon to sell the American way of life. 'The politicians, writers, and journalists who regarded their developing cultural programs abroad as worthy weapons to eliminate totalitarianism in the world' led the transfer of American culture. The efforts were overt and covert – ranging from the impact of the United States Information Agency to the Fulbright academic exchange programmes and the 'Campaign for Truth'.[50] The CIA and other agencies of the US government spent vast resources on spreading US propaganda throughout Europe through the production and distribution of a 'vast arsenal of cultural weapons: journals, books, conferences, seminars, art exhibitions, concerts, awards'.[51] There was the elite propagation of the cultural Cold War. The Congress for Cultural Freedom tried to get academics, writers and journalists to enter the fray. To abandon their detachment and contemplative manner 'in favour of a strong stand against totalitarianism'.[52] More broadly, Lucas has demonstrated the extensive ties between state and private networks, such as the American Federation of Labor, the Museum of Modern Art, CBS television, the US Davis Cup tennis team, who assisted government programmes defeat the USSR.[53]

Though NSC-68 was not declassified until the 1970s, the message was widely distributed through official testimony, speech and other campaigns. Concurrently, Edward Barratt, Assistant Secretary of State for Public Affairs, advanced NSC 59/1 and Washington's intended propaganda strategies. The Voice of America was strengthened and by 1950 a 'Campaign for Truth' was launched, described as a 'Marshall Plan in the field of ideas'. The strategic content of NSC-68 was buttressed by the Campaign for Truth. The campaign gained funds from the programme and in turn it disseminated the central message of NSC-68 widely.[54] In addition, the Committee on the Present Danger, a group of 'worthy citizens', was given access to the document and widely promoted its message for three years.[55]

THE NEW WEST AND 'OTHERS'

The metaphor of the West, the new west, encompassing colonial Europe while simultaneously projecting that colonial identity onto the Soviets, re-created and perpetuated the identity and notion of US benevolence. The dominant histories and, more importantly, US collective memory advanced a benign meta-narrative of US diplomatic history. The American 'empire' was removed from US history and consciousness, or dismissed as an aberration. The United States is still missing from the realm of postcolonial studies, though its real cultural power flourished during this period. This absence has reproduced 'American exceptionalism from without'. The United States is absorbed into a collective notion of the West, understood as a monolithic west. The histories of US westward expansion and that of European colonialism are treated as separate phenomena, thus preserving the narrative of American exceptionalism.[56]

The politics of identity and projection became paramount because of the widespread scepticism of the United States within Europe. That the scepticism rested more at the elite levels in European society made the role and propagation of US culture even more important. But the political, economic and cultural projection of the United States into Europe cannot be separated. The influence of the concept of the West, defined by Truman and echoed culturally, represented the lowest common denominator between the USA and Europe. The imperial extension of US culture and politics was denied, while simultaneously Soviet imperial policies were highlighted. As Amy Kaplan argues, 'if the vehemence and persistence with which something is denied mark its importance and even formative power, the characterization of a nation's ideological opponents reveals as much about that nation's self-conception as it does about its enemies'.[57] The dichotomies created in the long telegram, the Truman Doctrine, and the X article and through the cultural dissemination of the content of NSC-68, represent the reduction of the identities of the Soviet Union and the West. Perhaps obviously, the complexities could not be admitted because ultimately there was a fundamental contradiction in the Cold War West. Europeans and Americans disagreed on what liberty and democracy meant. Many in Europe still favoured the progress of collectivism and equality, whereas the Americans, generally, preferred to advance conceptions of liberty and democracy synonymous with enterprise and 'ordered liberty'. As David Gress argues, 'to enroll such contradictory ideas in a common front required that the distinctions be ignored or elided'. In the early Cold War period most European intellectuals found it difficult simply to convert to this militant strain of anti-communism, to the extent that mainstream American intellectuals had. Though much of what the United States professed derived from ideas shared with some Europeans, François Furet thought that Europeans suspected American democracy to be 'too capitalist . . . not to suspect that it concealed the domination of money under the slogans of freedom'.[58]

The conception of the West had to be advanced at several levels for long-term ideological acceptance. Politically, the narratives were well advanced by the early 1950s. The metaphors generated were of utmost importance and derived their powers through the all-encompassing concept of the West. Economically, the West was largely substantiated in the consolidation of the economies this side of the Iron Curtain through the Marshall Plan. Only now the United States was wedded to a West that also had access to a multitude of colonial areas. And, culturally, there was much work to be done to overcome the lingering doubts about US power.

There was urgency to the political message. Any doubts about containment were dispelled by analogies with Munich and appeasement. Munich and the word 'containment', the Iron Curtain and the metaphor of the West, all conjured up mental images of a geographical threat and an ideological unity. The geographical content of US diplomatic and cultural language buttressed the ideological messages. The frontier, as it were, had been shifted eastward. Images of a divided Europe mapped out the essential differences; the neat geographical demarcations reinforced the binary vision and ideological construction of the West. Politically, economically and culturally, the Americans were the principal cartographers. Theirs was a teleological route towards the *affluent society* and to the end of History; given the lessons of the 1930s, such a journey was difficult outside an Atlantic framework. They implicitly constructed the '*paths*, or channels along which a person regularly travels' and the '*landmarks* or signs to which he refers for self-location',[59] and the orientation of others.[60]

Notes

1. Clifford Geertz, *The Interpretation of Cultures* (London: Fontana, 1993), p. 211.
2. Francis Fukuyama, *The End of History and the Last Man* (London: Penguin, 1992), p. xi.
3. Scott Lucas, *Freedom's War: The US Crusade against the Soviet Union, 1945–56* (New York: New York University Press, 1999).
4. David W. Noble, 'The Reconstruction of Progress: Charles Beard, Richard Hofstadter and Postwar Historical Thought', in Lary May (ed.), *Recasting America: Culture and Politics in*

the Age of Cold War (Chicago: University of Chicago Press, 1989), p. 74. See also Daniel Bell, *The End of Ideology: On the Exhaustion of Political Ideas in the Fifties* (New York: Free Press, 1962); Herbert Marcuse, *One-Dimensional Man: Studies in the Ideology of Advanced Industrial Society* (London: Routledge, [1964] 1991).

5. Alan Ryan, 'Introduction', in Ryan (ed.), *After The End of History* (London: Collins and Brown, 1992), pp. 2–3.

6. Christopher Shannon, *A World Made Safe for Differences: Cold War Intellectuals and the Politics of Identity* (Lanham, MD: Rowman and Littlefield, 2001), p. 13.

7. Rob Kroes, 'American Empire and Cultural Imperialism: A View from the Receiving End', *Diplomatic History*, 23/3 (Summer 1999), p. 465.

8. Reinhold Niebuhr, *The Irony of American History* (New York: Charles Scribner's Sons, 1952), pp. 57–8.

9. Edward Said, *Culture and Imperialism* (London: Chatto and Windus, 1993), p. 345.

10. Melvyn P. Leffler, *A Preponderance of Power: National Security, the Truman Administration, and the Cold War* (Stanford, CA: Stanford University Press, 1992), pp. 515–17; Melvyn P. Leffler, 'Inside Enemy Archives: The Cold War Reopened', *Foreign Affairs*, 75/4 (July–August 1996), pp. 120–134.

11. Report by the Policy Planning Staff, PPS/23, Review of Current Trends in US Foreign Policy, 24 February 1948, *Foreign Relations of the United States*, vol. 1, (1948), pp. 510–29.

12. Emily Rosenberg, *Spreading the American Dream: American Economic and Cultural Expansion, 1890–1945* (New York: Hill and Wang, 1982).

13. Lucas, *Freedom's War*; Frances Stonor Saunders, *Who Paid the Piper? The CIA and the Cultural Cold War* (London: Granta, 1999); Stephen J. Whitfield, *The Culture of the Cold War* (1991), 2nd edn (Baltimore: Johns Hopkins University Press, 1996); Alan Nadel, *Containment Culture: American Narratives, Postmodernism, and the Atomic Age* (Durham, NC, and London: Duke University Press, 1995); Christian G. Appy (ed.), *Cold War Constructions: The Political Culture of the United States Imperialism, 1945–1966* (Amherst, MA: University of Massachusetts Press, 2000); Walter L. Hixson, *Parting the Curtain: Propaganda, Culture and the Cold War, 1945–1961* (London: Macmillan, 1997).

14. Joyce and Gabriel Kolko, *The Limits of Power: The World and United States Foreign Policy, 1945–1954* (New York: Harper and Row, 1972).

15. Robert E. Wood, 'From the Marshall Plan to the Third World', in Melvyn P. Leffler and David S. Painter (eds), *The Origins of the Cold War: An International History* (London: Routledge, 1994), pp. 202–5; David Ryan, *US Foreign Policy in World History* (London: Routledge, 2000), pp. 110–15.

16. David Gress, *From Plato to NATO: The Idea of the West and its Opponents* (New York: The Free Press, 1998), pp. 410, 415.

17. Ryan, *US Foreign Policy*, p. 9; Filipe Fernandez-Armesto, *Millennium* (London: Bantam, 1995), p. 7; Peter Novik, *That Noble Dream: The 'Objectivity Question' and the American Historical Profession* (Cambridge: Cambridge University Press, 1988), p. 4.

18. Gress, *From Plato to NATO*, p. 415.

19. William H. McNeill, 'The Changing Shape of World History', *History and Theory*, 34/2 (1995), p. 16; Christian G. Appy, 'Struggling for the World', in Appy (ed.), *Cold War Constructions: The Political Culture of United States Imperialism, 1945–1966* (Amherst, MA: The University of Massachusetts Press, 2000), pp. 2–6.

20. Louis Hartz, *The Liberal Tradition in America* (New York: Harcourt, Brace and Company, 1955), p. 305.

21. Mr X/George Kennan, 'The Sources of Soviet Conduct', *Foreign Affairs*, 25/4 (July 1947), pp. 566–82; reprinted in George F. Kennan, *American Diplomacy, 1900–1950* (Chicago: University of Chicago Press, 1951), pp. 89–106.

22. Speech delivered by J. V. Stalin, at a meeting of voters of the Stalin electoral district, Moscow, 9 February 1946, http://ptb.lashout.net/marx2mao/Stalin/SS46.html

23. George Kennan, telegram to Secretary of State, Washington (The Long Telegram), 22 February 1946, http://www.gwu.edu/~nsarchiv/coldwar/documents/episode-1/kennan.htm

24. Leffler, *Preponderance of Power*, pp. 107–9; Abbott Gleason, *Totalitarianism: The Inner History of the Cold War* (New York: Oxford University Press, 1995), pp. 74–5.

25. Ryan, *US Foreign Policy*, p. 122; H. W. Brands, *What America Owes the World: The Struggle for the Soul of Foreign Policy* (Cambridge: Cambridge University Press, 1998), p. 151; John Lewis Gaddis, *The United States and the Origins of the Cold War, 1941–1947* (New York: Columbia University Press, 1972), pp. 355–6.

26. Mr X/George Kennan, 'The Sources of Soviet Conduct', reprinted in Kennan, *American Diplomacy, 1900–1950*, p. 99.

27. Brands, *What America Owes the World*, p. 152.

28. Gabriel Kolko, *Century of War: Politics, Conflict, and Society since 1914* (New York: New Press, 1994), p. 385.

29. Leffler, *Preponderance of Power*, p. 145; Walter LaFeber, *America, Russia and the Cold War, 1945–1990* (New York: McGraw-Hill, 1991), p. 53.

30. Lucas, *Freedom's War*, pp. 6–9.

31. President Truman, address to a Joint Session of Congress, 12 March 1947, in Raymond Dennett and Robert K. Turner (eds), *Documents on American Foreign Relations*, vol. 9 (Princeton: Princeton University Press, 1949), p. 7.

32. Melani McAlister, *Epic Encounters: Culture, Media, and US Interests in the Middle East, 1945–2000* (Berkeley and Los Angeles: University of California Press, 2001), pp. 43–55.

33. Michael Kammen, *Mystic Chords of Memory: The Transformation of Tradition in American Culture* (New York: Vintage Books, 1993), p. 574.

34. National Security Council, US Policy toward Africa South of the Sahara Prior to Calendar Year 1960, NSC 5719, 31 July 1957, Record Group 273, pp. 9–10.

35. Michael J. Hogan, *A Cross of Iron: Harry S. Truman and the Origins of the National Security State, 1945–1954* (Cambridge: Cambridge University Press, 1998), pp. 17–18.

36. Ryan, *US Foreign Policy*, p. 119; Robert R. Tomes, *Apocalypse Then: American Intellectuals and the Vietnam War, 1954–1975* (New York: New York University Press, 1998), pp. 9–20.

37. Lloyd C. Gardner, *Spheres of Influence: The Partition of Europe from Munich to Yalta* (London: John Murray, 1993), p. 263.

38. Whitfield, *The Culture of the Cold War*, pp. 127–151.

39. Novik, *That Noble Dream*, p. 299.

40. Geertz, *Interpretation of Cultures*, p. 198.

41. Leffler, *Preponderance of Power*, p. 108; Ryan, *US Foreign Policy*, pp. 121–2.

42. Robert L. Ivie, 'Fire, Flood, and Red Fever: Motivating Metaphors of Global Emergency in the Truman Doctrine Speech', *Presidential Studies Quarterly*, 29/3 (September 1999), pp. 570–1.

43. Alun Munslow, *Deconstucting History* (London: Routledge, 1997), p. 13.

44. Joyce Appleby, Lynn Hunt and Margaret Jacobs, *Telling the Truth about History* (New York: W. W. Norton, 1994), pp. 235–6.

45. Report by the Policy Planning Staff, PPS/23, Review of Current Trends in US Foreign Policy, 24 February 1948, *Foreign Relations of the United States*, vol. 1, (1948), pp. 510–11.

46. Kammen, *Mystic Chords of Memory*, pp. 572–3.

47. Emily S. Rosenberg, 'Rosenberg's Commentary', in Ernest R. May (ed.), *American Cold War Strategy: Interpreting NSC-68* (Boston: Bedford Books, 1993), p. 161.

48. Wendy L. Wall, 'Italian Americans and the 1948 Letters to Italy Campaign', in Appy (ed.), *Cold War Constructions*, pp. 89–109.

49. Rosenberg, *Spreading the American Dream*.

50. Jessica C. E. Gienow-Hecht, 'Shame on US? Academics, Cultural Transfer, and the Cold War – A Critical Review', *Diplomatic History*, 24/3 (Summer 2000), pp. 467–9.

51. Stonor Saunders, *Who Paid the Piper?*, pp. 1–2.

52. Quoted in ibid. p. 84.

53. Scott Lucas, 'Mobilising Culture: The CIA and the State–Private Networks and the CIA in the Early Cold War', in Dale Carter and Robin Clifton (eds), *War and Cold War in American Foreign Policy 1942–62* (London: Palgrave, 2002), p. 99.
54. Rosenberg, 'Rosenberg's Commentary', p. 163.
55. McAlister, *Epic Encounters*, p. 53.
56. Amy Kaplan, '"Left Alone with America": The Absence of Empire in the Study of American Culture', in Amy Kaplan and Donald E. Pease (eds), *Cultures of United States Imperialism* (Durham, NC: Duke University Press, 1993), p. 17.
57. Ibid. p. 13.
58. Gress, *From Plato to NATO*, pp. 418, 431.
59. Alan K. Henrikson, 'Mental Maps', in Michael J. Hogan and Thomas G. Paterson (eds), *Explaining the History of American Foreign Relations* (Cambridge: Cambridge University Press, 1992), pp. 177–8, 189.
60. I would like to thank Scott Lucas for helpful comments.

CHAPTER FOUR

Mobility

Movable Containers: Cold War Trailers and Trailer Parks

Dina Smith

Continually represented as America's most dazzling decade, the 1950s, according to historian James Patterson, are regarded as those 'buoyant years' – when new phrases such as 'gung ho, ponytail, panty raid, sock hop, cookout, windfall profit, togetherness, hip, Formica and Barbie Dolls' pronounced the triumph of a decade far removed from the Depression and war years.[1] However, the 1950s economy, in its seeming abundance, was one of immense contradiction, for, after all, its rabid consumerism promised Americans the realisation of a single, unified domestic culture, one that culminated in the usually ill-defined nirvana of classless prosperity. This 'golden era' of consumerism emerges as a nostalgic historical model, in which mobility is seamlessly connected to the visible purchase of commodities. As visual signifiers of physical and social mobility, the trailer and trailer park, as this chapter traces, are integral components of this larger, contradictory discourse on post-war mobility.

During the post-war years the United States witnessed the most dramatic internal demographic shifts in its history, leading to a new era of physical, social and economic mobility. The house trailer offered a generation of American home-owners technologically advanced, mobile housing, the material expression of Cold War mobility and, paradoxically, containment. It was during the 1950s that the United States experienced incredible cultural and political shifts: the explosion of the first H-bomb, Vietnam falling to communists, the proposal of a new massive interstate highway system, the US GNP reaching $365 billion or $1 billion per day while the unemployment rate reached a new low, *Brown* v. *Board of Education of Topeka, Kansas*, the Army– McCarthy hearings, Salk's discovery of the polio vaccine and, as this chapter explores, the introduction of the 'mobile home' as an alternative form of low-income, starter housing.

This chapter then examines how the early trailer stood (or moved) as a shining testimony to the wonders of factory-made, affordable housing, re-defining the domestic and the experience of the domestic (as both home and nation). In its originality, the American house trailer mimicked the aesthetic energies of modernism itself and was used in a series of new and often exciting ways. From Le Corbusier's 'machine aesthetic' to Frank Lloyd Wright's Usonian house, this chapter then reads and situates the trailer and trailer park as part of a growing modern design trend that attempted to reimagine urban and community space as mobile, fragmented, free and open to a limited number of (re)fabrications.

As we will see, challenging the abundance model of 1950s consumerism, the post-war trailer presented a new form of taylorised consumption. Post-war Fordism's daily logic pivoted on certain recurring motifs: stability, mass production, standardisation and centralised corporate control. The trailer industry combined a rationalised Fordism with a flexi-time mode of produc-tion associated with late capitalism. The trailer's adaptability, its ability to serve a number of purposes and populations, made it the perfect structure for a rapidly changing economy/culture(s). Trailers and makeshift trailer camps facilitated wartime conversion, allowing key defence industries to mobilise a Second World War workforce. They also mediated and aided post-war reconversion, providing housing for a generation of returning veterans and their 'booming' families. Mediating these shifting economic and cultural registers, the trailer represents a completely unique, proto-postmodern architectural form.

The trailer's form, like the American suburb, suggests an impermeable exterior, not so unlike 1950s Tupperware, a container that enclosed its inhabitants. As the trailer enclosed, it also concealed, forming a crucial component of McCarthyism, imagining a mobile network of surveillance and counter-surveillance that came to be associated with Cold War culture. This chapter then reads the trailer and trailer park within and against the frame of Cold War containment culture, connecting its emergence to the growth of the American suburb, itself a means of social and physical contain-ment. As many newly-weds purchased their sparkling new Levitt homes, many more purchased house trailers, becoming part of a booming, mobile, 'trailerite' culture, largely forgotten by American cultural historians. As Levittown became a symbol of upward mobility, the mobile home and trailer parks inevitably became associated with immobility, a site for obsolete populations, America's 'trash'. Trailers and trailer parks are now perceived as cultural failures, even though they form such a crucial part of the cultural landscape. This chapter then reads (or maps) the various levels of Cold War trailer discourse, literal and imaginary, in order to locate a submerged cultural history of the United States. In the American trailer and trailer park, we find a history of a desire for mobility and also the contradictions attached to such a distinctively American cultural narrative.

In 2002 the Los Angeles Cultural Heritage Commission requested that the city council designate the Monterey Trailer Park a historic 'monument'. Dating back to the 1920s, the Monterey Trailer Park will now join the 'Hollywood' sign as a unique Los Angeles historic/cultural site.[2] Ironically, the modern trailer and trailer park's critique of modernist, monumental architecture, and seeming ubiquity, parodied the post-war American suburb and rendered it somewhat invisible to cultural historians. And yet, in the early twenty-first century one in ten American dwellings is a trailer/mobile home. Although crucial components of the American geography and imaginary, the trailer and trailer park are perceived as cultural failures, modernism's trashy remainder. They are seemingly depositories of dead-end populations.

Significantly, however, trailers, as imaginary objects, appear at pivotal historical junctures: namely, symbolising 1930s New Deal legislations, or 1950s containment culture, as well as the period's mobile (atomic) technologies (for example, Oak Ridge, Tennessee, an atomic development site, was constructed entirely out of Schult Co. trailers). Today they are signifiers of 'trash', or 'trailer trash', presenting a challenge to American notions of upward mobility as well as a reminder of late capital's culture of obsolescence. Trailers have become, to borrow Fredric Jameson's term, a 'vanishing mediator' – a hybrid object/discourse – that negotiates, or militates against the trauma of, certain crucial historical, cultural and economic shifts.

THE TRAILER'S HISTORY

The trailer began by offering travel luxury to the newly initiated car-owner. Charles Lindbergh owned a 'Gypsy Wagon' trailer; Ford, Edison and Harding had at one time camped together in a 'Covered Wagon' trailer.[3] These awkward, early trailers offered 'superior technology', mobility and pioneer nostalgia to those who craved – and could afford – travel on the early, open roads. The trailer was simultaneously coded in terms of its efficiency and travel luxury. While more affluent populations used trailers for travel, as a means of escaping the 'degraded', modern city, with its bustling immigrant labour force, migrant workers and other itinerant labour (in the circus, carnival, and so on) increasingly purchased or built their own trailers, using them for mobile or temporary housing while they searched for work.

During the 1920s and 1930s, then, trailers were seen either as luxury camping or as mobile, non-taxed, squatter housing.

During the early period in the trailer's history (1930s–50s), the unconventional 'trailerites', as trailer-owners were called, became a visible part of the American landscape; and a lively trailerite culture emerged, complete with trailer magazines and newsletters that circulated across the country. By the early 1930s, there were roughly 2,000 trailer camps, of all sorts, to accommodate American travellers. Their increasing visibility led some to speculate that trailers, along with the rail, car and air industries, would become the key technologies to remobilise the US economy of the Depression era. Some went so far as to link the trailer's popularity to the beginnings of a future mobile society. Economist Roger Babson predicted that by 1956 'more than half of the population of the United States will be living in mobile trailers'.[4]

Trailers played a significant role during the Second World War and post-war reconversion. Commissioned by the military, trailer manufacturers converted their trailer assembly lines to accommodate the war effort, using the travel trailer's frame to provide a variety of transport vehicles, such as ambulances and buses. Such mobilisation of the means of production, employing primarily women and elderly men, ensured the industry's viability during the wartime economy. The industry also continued to manufacture trailers as temporary housing for war-workers. 'In 1940 various government agencies began buying trailers for temporary "stopgap" housing until conventional housing could be built in areas impacted by heavy influxes of war workers.'[5] The industry sold approximately 35,000 trailers to be used for civilian housing during the war; such wartime housing ironically aided the industry, since it introduced to the American public trailers as alternative models for middle-class housing.[6]

Crucial to the construction of what was to become the 'military–industrial complex', trailers and trailer parks tended to become permanent fixtures adjoining defence plants. While some camps were dismantled after the war, many became semi-permanent communities, leading to a surge in trailer-park development. Thus, one could find trailer parks not only alongside new highways, a complement to the expanding automobile tourist culture, but also near cities, such as San Francisco, that had become military/defence sites. The industry provided not only start-up housing for returning veterans but also married-student housing for a generation of university students, opening up the once elite colleges and universities to lower-income, ethnically diverse populations.[7] The trailer then offered young couples the latest technological innovations and mobility for a minimum down payment. As a trailer dealer wrote in the 1954 issue of *Mobile Life Magazine*, with the purchase of a trailer you are getting MOBILITY – that magic word of our industry that means freedom to so many now in the mobile population. It is a new kind of freedom – a freedom unknown twenty years ago. It is the freedom to go where you want to go – when you want to go.[8]

Prior to easy finance and the proliferation of credit cards, new trailers were a difficult initial investment, as were new cars, yet they remained cheaper, more available and more adaptable than the suburban home. Indeed, they condensed the rhetoric of post-war mobility, as well as domestic security, into a nicely packaged interior – 'a package that contains a new home with everything you have ever wanted'.[9] While not yet half of the population, as Babson had predicted, two million Americans were living in trailers in 1954, and by 1962 this number had doubled.[10]

Yet, what exactly were trailer-park communities during the 1950s like, and who lived in them? According to a 1959 poll of 1,629 trailer-park dwellers, most parks had paved streets, underground power lines and laundry facilities. They tended to be located in small towns, rural areas or on the periphery of America's most rapidly growing cities. With a median rent of $28 per month, trailer parks were affordable communities with a median size of fifty-eight spaces. Most trailer-park inhabitants were married, between 24 and 65 years old, and were skilled or semi-skilled workers (38 per cent), military personnel, retirees or professionals/semi-professionals (25 per cent). The study contends that most lower-income families tended to stay within cities, closer to city transportation networks, shelters and established community support.[11] Moreover, according to a 1962 study, most couples who lived in mobile homes did so because they could build equity.[12] As property, mobile homes were better than apartment living, so they began to meet the permanent housing needs of many post-war Americans.

THE TRAILER'S HYBRIDITY

Significantly, the trailer opens up a series of inversions that complicate any teleological reading of history/culture. Trailers express a desire for individualism/autonomy and yet, unlike traditional suburbs, trailer parks helped form a sense of community/communalism, since so much of everyday life spilled out of the narrow confines of the trailer's space and into community courtyards. Trailers are used for leisure/recreation and for the necessity of working-class housing; they are associated with speed/motion, but also with control/containment; finally, they present a sense of freedom from fixity and surveillance – and yet, in the 1950s, they were the ideal site for surveillance, a location in and from which the Cold War deviant was found. These kinds of dualisms are worth exploring, since, as Alan Nadel has argued of such contradictions in twentieth-century cultural narratives, they dialectically signal some of the contradictions linking the modern to the postmodern.[13]

Although housing so-called mobile homes, the Cold War trailer park eventually comes to be associated with a mobility that goes nowhere. However, like capital itself, the trailer is an adaptable system – a system that constantly changes and is changed by its users. It is a flexible amalgam that nevertheless has come to represent immobility. In his important survey of the American trailer, historian Allan Wallis describes the mobile home's functional aesthetic as that of an 'aesthetics of process' – an object whose survival depends upon continual adaptation toward new uses.[14] This process aesthetic can be broken down into the following features:

- light/portable design
- collage of vehicular and house-like design
- its 'appliqué' form which consists of loose meanings and rapidly introduced and recycled innovations
- its constant circulation: mobility, transformability and disposability
- its pluralism as well as individual inventiveness
- its adaptability categorically: it changes function, even name, according to need.

Indeed, this either/or status of trailers extends to their form. The trailer, after all, is a modern architectural hybrid, linking Le Corbusier's 'machine aesthetic', which imagined the home as a 'machine for living in', with Frank Lloyd Wright's Usonian (proto-ranch) home, a streamlined version of his Prairie House. Le Corbusier's 1920s image of the home invoked the factory/ city. Enhancing the worker's private 'situation', Le Corbusier attempted to ameliorate the divide between work and home, for, after all, 'the primordial instinct in every human being is to assure himself of a shelter'.[15] On the other hand, Wright's vision embraced the American landscape, linking the frontier to new architectural technologies. Inspired by the naturalistic philosophies of Thoreau and Emerson, Wright's organicism grew out of a desire to meld the external world with the world of luxury services; his homes, for instance, showcased floor heating, corner windows, skylights, built-in seating and recessed lighting. This organicism was then tied to commodities and eventually inspired the ubiquitous ranch home: a boxy, open-plan home that is close to the ground and presumably a part of its natural surroundings. These twin, if competing, visions of modern architecture tend to collapse into the mobile home's structure: a boxy, factory-produced machine that allowed its users to integrate and reintegrate into various natural settings. Reconciling the machine and organic split of modernist design discourses, trailers were literal 'machines in the garden', structurally yoking the factory to the country.

And yet, the trailer industry utilised a somewhat different factory model, by combining the centralised assembly line with a flexi-time, made-to-order, mode of production. 'The industry's manufacturers, dealers, park operators, material suppliers, and transporters functioned as a loosely organised but efficient system, capable of responding to changing market demands and the vicissitudes of seasonal and economic cycles.'[16] The trailer's production and distribution were mobile, ad-hoc systems. In the early 1950s one could open up a trailer dealership for only $5,000 or a plant for $10,000–$15,000.[17] Prospective dealers simply bought a stretch of land next to an expanding highway, bulldozed and levelled the ground for trailer set-up, opened up a store to accommodate the various needs of trailer-owners, thereby constructing a second source of revenue, and sold trailers to prospective buyers. Since the demand for parking space exceeded the number of existing trailer parks during the 1950s, dealers could tie the rental of a park space to the purchase of a trailer, thus ensuring a steady stream of trailer buyers. Extending this loose yet efficient system of production and distribution, trailer manufacturers tended to build to order, since many suppliers extended them credit and allowed for the easy delay of payments until after the units were sold. The trailer industry then responded to local and specific needs and was a relatively easy, low-risk venture, requiring less planning and capital than suburban development.

Accordingly, the incredible growth of the trailer industry and trailer parks illustrates some of the dramatic shifts in the Cold War economy. The 1950s has been acknowledged for its perceived affluence, or what we now term Post-war Fordism, a period of mass production, through the deployment of large corporate power, leading to a standardised product and consumption patterns, a moment where production and consumption came together almost seamlessly. The rise in real GNP rose some 50 per cent between 1949 and 1960, stimulated by the Korean War's military expansion.[18] In addition to the defence budget, large manufacturing sectors relied on the production of consumer durables, of which houses and home appliances were prime examples, built and maintained by a regimented factory system designed on continuity and regularity. Not only was Post-war Fordism a system of mass production, it also constituted, according to David Harvey, 'a total way of life'.[19]

By the mid-1970s, this system had collapsed, ushering in a new era of flexible accumulation, to which the trailer, as a product and design, was easily adapted. The trailer helped mobilise a portable population, or a semi-permanent, flexible workforce, easily hired and laid off, the hallmark of late capitalism. This shift towards flexibility in production and labour has been accompanied by rapid obsolescence: 'The half-life of a typical Fordist product was', as Harvey notes, 'from five to seven years, but flexible accumulation has more than cut that in half in certain sectors'.[20] What distinguishes the trailer from most other traditional housing forms is its built-in obsolescence, for its design assumes a limited duration of occupancy (ten years was supposed to be the maximum duration for occupancy). And yet trailers are rarely disposed of; indeed they tend to retain their use value, continually recycled for new users, rarely, if ever, 'trashed'. The trailer's efficiency, then, runs in two direction: a reminder of Cold War capital expansion but also of a generation of working-class Americans moving, ever steadily, towards a space littered with immobile shanty/trailer parks.

These shifting economic registers find expression in the discourse of adaptability that has suffused twentieth-century architectural design and theory, especially during the post-war era. As early as 1926, Frederick Kiesler, in his manifesto for a 'Space City' architecture, demanded 'elasticity' in buildings, which would set 'us free from the ground' with 'no walls, no foundations'.[21] Kiesler challenged the traditional, nineteenth-century site-built home, a bourgeois structure anchored to a fixed place. This home became a motif of economic determinism and exclusion. As a reminder of the many economic and social barriers to home ownership, the site-built, Victorian home confined its inhabitants, and also barred entry to those who built its foundations. Extending this discourse, Guy Debord, in the 1960 'Situationist Manifesto', proclaimed that 'architecture must advance by taking as its subject exciting situations rather than exciting forms'.[22] In the writings of the Situationists, architecture appears as a dialectical process, never confined to one form. Architecture is thus not a 'site', but rather a series of situations, a shifting, inherently unmappable social space. By the early 1970s, eliding the rhetoric of class struggle, a group of theorists stretched the notion of adaptable architecture to imagine a 'kinetic' or 'flexible' architecture. Kinetic architecture focused on designing movement within the building's 'body'. Drawing on the long history of prefabrication, 'kinetic' architecture, consisting of detachable and movable walls, sliding and collapsible ceilings and mobile homes, paralleled the new regime of flexible accumulation following the 1973 recession. Kinetic architecture – 'inherently displaceable, deformable, expandable, disposable, and in some other manner capable of kinetic movement'[23] – conceptually alludes then to a whole series of social and economic displacements associated with late capital: such as the dissolution of social welfare, the slow repeal of affirmative action laws, late capital's tendency to reposition its labour centres in non-unionised areas, as well as factory workers' growing redundancy. Kinetic architecture, with its focus on expanding, or mobilising, a specific place, rather than redefining the very nature of lived space, lacks the rhetoric of class struggle of early modernists and Situationists, illustrating how architecture intimately connects to the economy and culture producing it.

SUBURBIA, TRAILER PARKS AND COLD WAR DOMESTICITY

The trailer's invention and popularity coincided with the rise of the twentieth-century modern suburb, itself a mobilisation of housing away from American cities. The creator of 'America's ideal suburb', Fredrick Law Olmstead, during the nineteenth century conceived of the suburb as a site outside the city's borders, where builders, planners and home-buyers could, through a consensus, construct a place with 'pleasant openings and outlooks', a 'community in the park'.[24] By designing an efficient and complete community, separated from the inner city and its labour, Olmstead wished to avert the 'desolation' or devaluing of real estate that had previously occurred when immigrant squatters 'overran' new, unplanned villa communities. As Robert Fishman has argued, 'Olmstead's picturesque aesthetic and his attempt to envision a truly civilized community cannot be disentangled from his equally pressing aim of creating a tightly knit, exclusive society that would enjoy forever the unique benefits of its affluence'.[25] Part of the logic behind American suburban design, then, was to prevent the slow accretion of squatters near new bourgeois development along the city's periphery. The suburb would offer 'some assurance to those who wish to build villas that these districts [would] not be invaded' before the 'progress of the town' was complete – namely suburbs would provide long-term, permanent exclusion.[26] Above all, the suburb's design and various restrictions preserved racial, class and spatial order, all of which protected the family's real-estate investment.[27]

Since the early 1980s, such spatial markers of class have facilitated what Mike Davis terms 'low-intensity warfare' against the urban poor and the homeless, late capital's version of Olmstead's squatters. As a result of contemporary urban regentrification projects, homeless populations, as Davis describes in Los Angeles, have increasingly been contained to certain urban sections, which are devoid of public toilets, showers and accessible dustbins, thereby turning these areas into 'outdoor poorhouses'.[28] Invoking the rhetoric of Cold War 'containment', a reminder that such discourses are not so easily contained, the social 'deviant' is placed under surveillance and denied movement, contained in a boxlike community that is the city, but not the city, that is a community, but not a community.

Cold War social and urban planning focused on containment, either in the slow creation of virtual fences surrounding lower-income urban areas or in the construction of securely planned, gated and isolated suburbs. By 1950 thirty-seven million people had relocated to the suburbs; by 1970 the number had doubled. Notably, this suburban population was 95 per cent white and self-identified as socially mobile.[29] Suburban development was just one element of the incredible expansion of the American infrastructure – an attempt spatially to stabilise the USA as a geopolitical centre. And yet much of this infrastructure centred on 'mobility'. The era saw the growth of massive highway systems (the Federal Highway Administration was created in 1956) and a motel culture (Holiday Inn opened its doors in 1952), forcing states and communities to open up to a new traveller/tourist culture that included 'booming' suburban families. The post-war years witnessed the most dramatic internal demographic shift in US history – from the 1940s to the 1970s roughly 70 per cent of Americans changed residences every year.[30] To accommodate these shifts and the concomitant population boom, a record fifteen million housing units were constructed between 1945 and 1955.[31] The GI Bill (1944–56) financed this generation of home-owners, providing aid for home purchases, loans to start businesses and monthly stipends.

And it was by the mid-1950s that the American suburb had, like the trailer, become a recognised commodity. Suburban homes full of heavy consumer durables, as Nixon reminded Kruschev in the much publicised 'kitchen debate', were distinctly American and thus must be celebrated as the 'essence of Western culture'.[32] And yet this image of the 1950s appliance-filled kitchen militates against the notion of a constantly expanding frontier, illustrating how the frontier rhetoric was cordoned off by the image of the white picket fence or the house weighted down with heavy consumer durables. The frontier then moves inside, to the American home's interior, to the accumulation of new technologies such as televisions and washing machines. As Reyner Banham comically notes, 'right from the start, from the Franklin stove and the kerosene lamp, the American interior has had to be better serviced if it was to support a civilized culture'.[33] In contrast to this vision of the fully equipped suburban home, trailers – already furnished – possessed a limited space for the storage of objects.

In other words, trailers were mobile commodities that strangely defied the logic of consumption. Unlike the suburban home full of heavy things that signified its owner's social mobility, trailers redefined the domestic through mobile commodities that came to represent economic stagnation, since they also signalled a new form of taylorised consumption. As a scene from the popular period film The Long, Long Trailer (1954) illustrates, the domestic space of the trailer allows for only one casserole dish or the economical and functional designs of the latest Tupperware. The trailer husband and wife, as the film comments, would have to 'strip to the bone' in order to fit inside their trailer. Trailers implicitly challenged the logics of Cold War consumption to which Nixon paid homage. Suburbia, on the other hand, promised a seemingly infinite site for consumption.

Drawing on the imagery of the community-in-a-park model of suburbia, trailer parks increasingly became, by the mid-1950s, an alternative, uncanny version (a *Doppelgänger*) of the post-war suburb. After all, according to Freud, the uncanny (*das Unheimlich*) is the process of becoming Other to ourselves; it marks or announces the return of the unrecognised, the 'unhomely'. Italian theorist Franco Rella defines it as the 'atopic', that 'without a place'.[34] Thus, within this discourse, the uncanny trailer park always leads us back to suburbia in as much as it is an expression of how the suburb, a squatter settlement itself, is always permeable to the Other: to migrant workers, homosexuals, unmarried women, and so on. And yet the trailer park abducts the very logics of suburban design, thereby imploding Cold War regulatory, zoning practices. They were municipally 'unplanned' parked communities, permanently or temporarily situated nearby the American suburb, punctuating and challenging the spatial/temporal permanence of suburbs. Moreover, the trailer park's tight, efficient, rectangular lots paralleled and therefore called into question the rectangular lots of the American suburb, whose front lawns attempted to mask how these homes had been seemingly 'parked' on a box of bought land. The trailer and trailer park unmasked the very exclusionary, artificial logics of the community-in-a-park model of the post-war American suburb. The trailer park merges the parking lot with a suburb, reminding us of how suburbs often appear as a series of garages hitched to living rooms.

However, during the late 1940s and 1950s, the heyday of trailerite culture, mobile homes and trailer parks were increasingly denounced, either explicitly or implicitly, as a challenge to permanent communities and the proper acquisition of property. Unregulated and defying zoning laws, trailer parks, especially year-round facilities, were deemed a social 'menace' by some sociologists. One such critic, in a 1951 article in *The Survey*, warns of a

> new kind of slum, the permanent trailer camp, [which] offers all the bad features of the urban 'blighted area', [with] none of the vacation adventure for which trailers were made . . . Their very condensation, their capsule-like concentration, makes the evil dosage that much more potent and brings the festering irritation to the head.[35]

An 'evil dosage', the trailer park becomes a dangerous additive, a suburban narcotic. 'Dose' was also slang for 'venereal disease', or gonorrhoea. Within such a sociological frame, trailers and trailer parks 'contain' and 'secrete' the noxious excess of the 1950s social body, and, like all such communicative diseases, their mobility, or potential mobility, may spread the contagion to other areas.

Such critiques tended to linger on the open-door policy of many trailer parks. Though predominantly white, a trailer park's inhabitants might include the middle-class retired couple, the semi-skilled factory-worker or a single woman writer. As such they were socially varied communities, offering amazing diversity in an era that valued homogeneity, denying any easy, sociological quantification. Even J. Edgar Hoover chimed in during the 1940s, stating that 'there is today a new home of crime in America, a new home of disease, bribery, corruption, crookedness, rape, white slavery, thievery' – and that home, of course, was the mobile home. Hoover reminds his readers that these kinds of activities 'flourished in the worst days of segregated districts' and 'have now appeared again in suburban retreats'.[36] The trailer park becomes the displaced image of the suburb itself, of its own aporia, and, as in *Doppelgänger* mythology, it returns as the 'evil twin' of suburbia. By the mid-1950s trailer magazines advocated the use of trailer parks for Cold War surveillance. In the 1954 article 'How You can Help the FBI', the writer discusses how the many trailerites can, 'by keeping their eyes and ears open, perhaps contribute a great deal as loyal Americans in helping our FBI in its arduous task of preventing subversive acts against our Republic'. Trailerites' mobility allows them to 'talk with thousands of people in their travels', since they 'see many things, and hear a great deal'.[37] Trailerites then had the potential to become patriotic informers, reminding us that 'it took the Cold War to include informing among the inventory of "American traditions"'.[38]

In an attempt to avoid the label of Cold War deviant, trailerites and industry representatives wrote a series of articles concerning the typicality of trailer life. Throughout the early 1950s, these magazines were devoted to constructing a distinctly patriotic image of trailer parks and living. In a 1953 article in *Mobile Life Magazine*, the trailer-owner is defined as quintessentially American, 'perhaps better clothed, housed, and fed than the average, with an income slightly higher, but an American for all that, and there is no such thing as a "typical American"'. But if there were such a thing as a typical American, 'he would certainly be a trailerist; comfortable, congenial, friendly, but not pushing, self-contained, able to go anywhere, good company in leisure moments, a willing help in time of stress'.[39] Ambivalent in its tone, this article suggests the trailerites' own uncertainty regarding where to place themselves. Though not 'typical', the trailerite nevertheless conforms to the image of a well-adjusted, conformity-driven American. Many of these periodicals act as the rearguard to the trailer industry, advocating/selling the life of trailer living not only for those who live in trailers but also for those who are contemplating such a shift. They project an image of a safe, tightly knit community possessing a Cold War inflected, pioneer spirit.

Both trailer parks and suburbs became sexually coded communities. As Elaine Tyler May has argued, the 1950s suburb was a sexually charged, domestic retreat from a variety of Cold War anxieties, but one that people knew was inadequate: hence, the need for trailer parks as an image of poverty and compromised security/morality. If the suburban home was a 'sexually charged retreat' from Cold War fears, then the image of the mobile home as a 'sex-crime suburban retreat' condensed and magnified this image, forming a libidinal container, a displacement, for desires not so easily contained. By the late 1950s and early 1960s, sleaze novels capitalised on this image, with titles such as *Trailer Park Tramp*. Increasingly the mobile home came to be coded in terms of and conflated with women's sexuality, offering a longer version of the back seat of a car. And, given the repetition of the discourse of sexuality alongside the 'unsanitary' conditions of trailer parks, with their inadequate sewage facilities, trailer parks were rhetorically situated as a dirty/unclean, or 'trampy', version of the suburb.

In response to such fears, and to the pressure from local municipal authorities, the industry attempted to self-regulate. By the late 1940s and early 1950s, the Trailer Coach Manufacturer's Association published *Trailer Park Progress*, a newsletter advertising America's cleanest and most advanced trailer parks. The association also began distributing 'officially approved trailer park' signs to association members, constructing a standard for trailer parks across the country. This attempt to regulate, or domesticate, trailer parks paralleled the steady increase in housewife-related stories in trade journals, such as *Trailer Topics*, *Mobile Life* and *Trailer Travel*. The 'Homemaker's Section' of these magazines attempted to address women's questions regarding the 'proper' way to live in a mobile home. The preface to a question-and-answer section asked its women readers: 'You want to know if you will be accepted not only by park people, but by the community at large? You're wondering if you'll have the peace of mind that comes with such things as ample protection for your home; the ease of body that comes with few chores to be done at day's end.'[40]

In response to a question regarding the kind of people permitted to lease a space in a mobile-home park, the author replies: 'You'll find that many of the fine parks cater only to adults; some to adults with children; and others to retired old people . . . Some parks, also, accept only the better quality mobile homes.'[41] Placating the homemaker's fears, park-owners could choose the type of residents they desired, suggesting the possibility for covert restrictive leases, preventing certain racial, ethnic groups. The 'mobile homemaker' was central to the creation and selling of trailer-park community life. Indeed, following The Second World War, with the high numbers of veterans purchasing mobile homes, *Mobile Life* magazine produced a 'Mrs Mobile Homemaker'. This contest celebrated the protean achievements of resourceful mobile-home homemakers, many of whom were married to veterans. The Mrs Mobile Homemaker of 1959, Mrs William R. Charette, or 'Louise', is representative of such contest winners, as the magazine admits:

> Louise is a natural for the title. She is young (24) and attractive. She has two cute daughters. She keeps house in a 50–foot long, 10–foot wide mobile home, the third one owned by the Charettes. Husband Bill fits the picture exceptionally well. He is a quiet, stocky sailor assigned to a submarine in the Navy's growing underwater fleet. He is a national hero, having won the Congressional Medal of Honor for conspicuous gallantry and intrepidity on a Korean battlefield.[42]

With pictures illustrating Louise's adept ironing skills in the trailer's confined space, the article conflates her homemaker achievements with husband Bill's wartime achievements. Describing how she was chosen for Mrs Mobile Homemaker, Louise confesses that it had much to do with Bill's military honours:

> In May last year, Bill was chosen to select the Unknown Soldier of World War II in a special ceremony at sea. There was a lot of publicity about it and I guess the industry people remembered us. At any rate, I'm very surprised and very happy to be selected 'Mrs Mobile Homemaker' and I'll do my best during the year to tell other homemakers about the many high points of mobile living.[43]

As the Mrs Mobile Homemaker contest illustrates, these articles featured women who creatively constructed comfortable, intimate mobile homes, safe havens from the outside world, akin to their husband's protection of the nation. These domesticity-oriented articles, often authored by women journalists, betray a fascination with newly-wed honeymooners cocooned in their cosy trailer interiors. These trailers grounded newly-weds in the prevalent heteronormative ideology of the period, drawing on the discourse of suburban domestic containment. The erotic marriage made the container, the home, or in this case the mobile home, all the more attractive. Indeed, 'marriage', according to May, 'was considered the only appropriate container for the wieldy American libido'.[44] In other words, precisely, and ironically, at the moment when Roger Babson had predicted that the USA would be an entirely mobile-home-oriented society, American domestic ideology locked, or contained, the suburban home to a high moral, albeit fecund, ground.

Interestingly, May begins her ground-breaking book *Homeward Bound* by describing a couple entering into a bomb shelter as their honeymoon retreat: two weeks in a bomb shelter with canned peas and spam was the stuff of romance in 1950s America. Such seemingly contradictory discourses – the bomb shelter as simultaneously a retreat *for* love and a retreat *from* nuclear disaster – form the centre of May's text, which illustrates how sex, domesticity and Cold War containment were inextricably linked. Within this context, the trailer as mobile container, a condensed version of the suburban home, filled with food and supplies, mimes the spatial rhetoric of the bomb shelter. The submerged shelter locks its inhabitants into a hermetically sealed, vertical grave, allowing families to 'duck and cover' from an atomic blast. The mobile home, on the other hand, allows for containment through the spatiality of mobility; the mobile home can horizontally escape the atomic blast, expanding the radius of safety. As one critic noted, mobile homes 'could well be dispersed as a precaution against concentrated bomb attacks'.[45] And one need only remember the famous scene in the film *Independence Day* (1996), in which a band of recreational vehicles and mobile homes act as a post-apocalyptic cavalry of survivors. With the modern-day trailerites as the only Americans apparently alive after the alien attack, the film pays homage to Cold War containment, where, once again, the 'alien' threat is contained through technology, coded as a natural by-product of capitalism and might. The film conflates the mobile home with the bomb shelter, for the mobile homers and the American military, who remain safely tucked away underground in a military bomb shelter, eventually band together to save the world. The popular show *X-Files*, a homage to 1950s Cold War paranoia, also linked trailers to mobile containment/threat. In episode after episode, im/mobile trailers either housed freaks – from vampires to technology geeks – or transported alien technologies. These texts inevitably link mobility to nuclear/ideological containment.

In a bizarre connection, after the recent September 11th attacks, orders for mobile homes/recreational vehicles surged in the United States. With the understandable fear that there may be more attacks on 'monumental' buildings, Americans looked to trailers, as undetectable, disposable dwellings, as movable shelter. Yet, mobile homes may also work as a movable offensive network. It has been speculated that Saddam Hussein's 'weapons of mass destruction' are undetectable precisely because they are in constant circulation, never in one place, because they have been concealed inside mobile truck or travel trailers. Recent American television newscasts have desperately constructed 'artist renderings' of these alleged Iraqi mobile trailers housing sophisticated weapons laboratories. For inspiration, there is the late Cold War film *Stripes* (1981), which showcased idiot-savant American soldiers driving the 'EM-50, Urban Assault Vehicle' across Europe saving Americans while fighting communism. The EM-50 might also be credited with prefiguring today's ubiquitous SUV, another version of urban assault.

This rhetoric of mobile concealment may also underpin the fascination with the spatial logics of trailer parks, which, like suburbs, seem ordered and planned. Indeed, 1950s–60s photographs of suburbs and trailer parks merge iconically, with both communities frequently photographed or imagined in wide-panoramic, aerial shots. Though different – the one mobile, the other fixed – they look remarkably the same from above. These photographs refer to the limits of visibility, for, as with all deep-focus, long shots, the eye cannot easily focus on any one point. Exposed and underexposed, expansive and toylike, the suburb and trailer park, as imagined in these photos, are like the fake towns constructed in Utah to simulate the effects of atomic blasts on actual populations. Such towns used mannequins and transplanted trees, in order to construct a lifesize diorama of a town from which, at a safe distance, science could measure or 'map' the effects of atomic fallout.[46] Trailer parks then, within this context, become another model of suburban disaster, from which, at a safe distance, the questions surrounding suburbia are posed long before they can be consciously formulated. The imag(in)ing and photographing of these communities, with airforce technology remobilised after Korea, remind us not only of how very similar they were to each other but of how important it was to conceptualise this new kind of social space. Such photographs then lead us to wonder whether or not, as these new organised communities enclosed, they also concealed, lending themselves to a mobile network of surveillance and counter-surveillance that came to be associated with McCarthyism.

The cosy and hidden interior of the trailer with efficient storage space parallels the physical map of the suburb, a series of concentric circles, or interiors (suburb, subdivision, sunken living room, garage), which eventually contain the individual through a process of division. Reminiscent of 'Space City' architecture, the space of a trailer park has no clear borders, no distinct foundations, since the homes, and people, are always displaceable. Current local zoning laws often relocate and devastate trailer park communities, pushing them, and their inhabitants, to town peripheries. They have literally become zoned into obsolescence, as is the case with the Gulfstream Trailer Park in Marathon, Florida. A 2003 *New York Times* article discovered:

To live in a trailer park like Gulfstream, one of more than 2,600 in Florida, is to occupy a precarious niche in the housing system. Residents at Gulfstream own their homes, which cost $10,000 to $40,000, but rent the land. Most homes are mobile in name only, too old or anchored to survive a move. As the value of real estate skyrocketed through the 1990s, park owners found they could make more redeveloping the land for houses or condominiums or selling to redevelopers.[47]

Through such displacement, these owners, and their equity, are disposable. And yet, the utopic desires embodied in the trailer persist. In a 1954 *Mobile Life* story, the mobile home satisfied the needs of many Americans, and it still does so today:

> mobile homes offer you that grand opportunity to look to your locations before they become permanent. To do as your fathers and grandfathers did – to move from job to job and community to community until you find the place you wish to make your permanent home. Enjoy the traditional American freedom. That thought of freedom on the part of the young married group is the thought which was responsible for the discovery of the west – for the founding of the cities on the great plains.[48]

CONCLUSION

Trailers and trailer parks in the 1950s, the latter a condensed and displaced version of the American suburb, were (indeed still are) simultaneously too mobile and too immobile, challenging the very logics of Cold War surveillance and the stability of traditional suburban design. Moreover, their potential mobility and condensed, communal design also punctuated the insularity of the post-war suburb, challenging its rigid class and spatial boundaries. And yet, as self-contained communities whose residents increasingly did not move, trailer parks and their owners in effect became a version of the nineteenth-century squatters who plagued Olmstead's projects, a version, however, clearly coded as white and working class – providing a visual and class commentary on their suburban counterparts. Thus, whereas Levittown represented the starter home, a step towards upward mobility, the trailer and trailer park came only to signify a form of locatedness, and, in the process, turned adjoining areas into lower-class neighbourhoods – sites of obsolete, working-class populations. However, the trailer possessed and still possesses a utopic dimension, an iconic register, to use Tom Moylan's phrase, in that it inflects the world as we know it, filled with displacement, shifting borders, the constant reproduction of labour/capital, while imagining something and somewhere else, a site of community, invention, where there are no exclusionary borders.[49] Their containment and recontainment thus became necessary, even if the fluid discourses surrounding trailers and trailer parks defy such containment.

Notes

1. James Patterson, *Grand Expectations: The United States, 1945–1974* (New York: Oxford University Press, 1996).
2. Story Tools, 'Trailer Park Makes LA Historic Monument List', *Associated Press*, 8 November 2002, p. 1.
3. Carl M. Edwards, *Homes for Travel and Living: The History and Development of the Recreational Vehicle and Mobile Home Industries* (East Lansing, MI: C. Edwards, 1977), p. 8.
4. Roger W. Babson, 'We'll Soon Be Living on Wheels', *Trailer Travel* (January–February 1936), p. 10.
5. John Fraser Hart, John T. Morgan and Michelle J. Rhodes, *The Unknown World of the Mobile Home* (Baltimore: Johns Hopkins University Press, 2002), p. 12.
6. Ibid.
7. Alan Wallis, *Wheel Estate: The Rise and Decline of Mobile Homes* (New York: Oxford University Press, 1991), pp. 113–14.
8. Anon., 'Trailerite as Typical American', *Mobile Life Magazine* (yearbook) (1954), p. 13.
9. Ibid.
10. Eleanor Kent, 'Now comes the age of the . . . Dream House on Wheels', *Mobile Life Magazine* (yearbook) (1963), p. 35.
11. Margaret J. Drury, *Mobile Homes: The Unrecognized Revolution in American Housing* (New York: Praeger Publishers, 1972), p. 18.
12. Ibid. 42.
13. Alan Nadel, *Containment Culture: American Narratives, Postmodernism, and the Atomic Age* (Durham, NC, and London: Duke University Press, 1995), pp. 13–67.
14. Wallis, *Wheel Estate*, pp. 157–60.
15. Le Corbusier, *Towards a New Architecture*, trans. Frederick Etchells (London: Architectural Press, 1946), p. 14. For work on Frank Lloyd Wright, see Thomas Doremus (ed.), *Frank Lloyd Wright and Le Corbusier: The Great Dialogue* (New York: Van Nostrand, 1985) and Roland Reisley and John Timpane, *Usonia, New York: Building a Community with Frank Lloyd Wright*, foreword by Martin Filler (New York: Princeton Architectural Press, 2001).
16. Wallis, *Wheel Estate*, p. 123.
17. Ibid. p. 117.
18. William Leuchtenberg, *A Troubled Feast: American Society since 1945* (Boston: Little, Brown and Company, 1973), p. 38.
19. David Harvey, *The Condition of Postmodernity* (Cambridge, MA: Blackwell, 1989), p. 135.
20. Ibid. p. 156.
21. Frederick Kiesler, 'Space City Architecture', in Ulrich Conrads (ed.), *Programs and Manifestoes on Twentieth-Century Architecture* (Cambridge, MA: MIT Press, 2002), p. 98.
22. Guy Debord, ' "Situationists": International Manifesto', in Ulrich Conrads (ed.), *Programs and Manifestoes on Twentieth-Century Architecture*, p. 172.
23. William Zuk and Roger H. Clark, *Kinetic Architecture* (New York: Van Nostrand Reinhold Company, 1970), p. 11.

24. Robert Fishman, *Bourgeois Utopias* (New York: Basic Books, 1987), p. 130.
25. Ibid. p. 132.
26. Ibid. pp. 120, 133.
27. John Stilgoe, *Borderland: Origins of the American Suburb, 1820–1939* (New Haven: Yale University Press, 1990), p. 224.
28. Mike Davis, 'Fortress Los Angeles: The Militarization of Urban Space', in Michael Sorkin (ed.), *Variations on a Theme Park: The New American City and the End of Public Space* (New York: Hill and Wang, 1992), p. 161.
29. Leuchtenberg, *Troubled Feast*, pp. 75–6.
30. Ibid. p. 74.
31. James Patterson, *Grand Expectations: The United States, 1945–1974* (New York: Oxford University Press, 1996), p. 71.
32. Harvey, *Condition of Postmodernity*, p. 37.
33. Reyner Banham, 'A Home is Not a House', in Penny Sparke (ed.), *Design by Choice* (New York: Rizzoli, 1981), p. 57.
34. Franco Rella, *The Myth of the Other: Lacan, Foucault, Deleuze, Bataille*, trans. Nelson Moe (Washington: Maisonneuve Press, 1994), pp. 27–56.
35. Alexander C. Wellington, 'Trailer Camp Slums', *The Survey* (October 1951), p. 418.
36. J. Edgar Hoover with Courtney Ryley Cooper, 'Camps of Crime', in Todd B. Kimmell and Kristin P. Kimmel (eds), *Lost Highways* (Philadelphia: Lost Highways, the Classic Trailer and Mobile Home Club, 1940), p. 25.
37. Chauncey T. Hinman, 'How You Can Help the FBI', *Travel Trailer Magazine* (March 1953), p. 24.
38. Stephen J. Whitfield, *The Culture of the Cold War* (1991), 2nd edn (Baltimore: Johns Hopkins University Press, 1996), p. 102.
39. Charlene Segal, 'Young Marrieds Salute Mobile Life', *Mobile Life Magazine* (yearbook) (1953), p. 9.
40. Jack Foster, 'Mrs Mobile Homemaker of 1959', *Mobile Life Magazine* (yearbook) (1959), pp. 11–13.
41. Kent, 'Dream House on Wheels', p. 41.
42. Foster, 'Homemaker', p. 11.
43. Ibid. p. 13.
44. Elaine Tyler May, *Homeward Bound: American Families in the Cold War Era* (New York: Basic Books, 1988), p. 101.
45. Zuk and Clark, *Kinetic Architecture*, p. 32.
46. Daniel Tiffany, *Toy Medium: Materialism and Modern Lyric* (Berkeley and Los Angeles: University of California Press, 2000), pp. 199–244.
47. John Leland, 'Trying to Stay Put in Florida Mobile Homes', *New York Times*, 22 June 2003, p. 1.
48. Edward L. Wilson, 'Housing Dollar: Lowest Cost', *Mobile Life Magazine* (yearbook) (1954), p. 4.
49. Tom Moylan, *Demand the Impossible: Science Fiction and the Utopian Imagination* (New York: Methuen, 1986), p. 37.

CHAPTER FIVE

Race

Passing as a Cold War Novel:
Anxiety and Assimilation in James Baldwin's Giovanni's Room

Douglas Field

In his seminal book on Cold War culture, *Containment Culture*, Alan Nadel observes 'that American culture during the cold war – as is sometimes suggested by a 1950s revival mentality – was, for all *significant* purposes, white'.[1] Although recent scholarship has challenged this narrative, race (and racial politics) are often subsumed into familiar narratives of containment, a space where African-American culture is relegated to a footnote or treated as a separate phenomenon. Despite the occlusion of African-American culture in numerous key works on Cold War culture, a number of scholars have drawn attention to the importance of civil rights in relation to US diplomacy and foreign relations.[2] As the USA emerged as a world leader in the wake of the Second World War, the 'Negro problem' became damaging and detrimental to the narratives of democracy and equality that America sought to project. US racism, as a reporter from the *Ceylon Observer* wrote, was 'the greatest propaganda gift any country could give to the Kremlin in its persistent bid for the affections of the colored races of the world'.[3]

Not only was US racism fuel for communist propaganda (despite the efforts of the US Information Agency), but racial progress was inextricably linked with communist activity. Many in the government believed that African-American political organisations, such as the National Association for the Advancement of Colored People, were supported and funded by communist organisations. With racial advances such as the desegregation of the armed forces and the education system, there were concerns both that they were communist-inspired plots, and also that black culture would merge with and miscegenate white American culture.

During the early 1950s, a further threat to US security emerged: homosexuality. After revelations that numerous homosexuals were government employees, the House Un-American Activities Committee (HUAC) investigated thousands of suspected sexual deviants, concluding that homosexuals and lesbians were 'susceptible to blackmail by Soviet agents because they were emotionally unstable'.[4] Of particular concern was evidence that homosexuals could pass as straight, just as communists could operate undetected in the US government. In 1948 Alfred Kinsey's best-selling *Sexual Behavior in the Human Male* repudiated the assumptions both that few men had had same-sex encounters, and also that homosexuals could be identified by feminine attributes, revelations that contributed towards a national homosexual panic.

This chapter focuses on the reception of James Baldwin's second novel, *Giovanni's Room* (1956), in order to explore how this short novel feeds into and explores key Cold War anxieties about race and homosexuality. Despite the fact that his writing career began shortly after the Second World War (his first published review appeared in *The Nation* (1947)), little attention is paid to Baldwin as a Cold War writer. As a politically active and homosexual African-American, Baldwin was in fact under intense surveillance from the FBI, a fact of which he was both aware and deeply critical, particularly in his long essay, *The Devil Finds Work* (1976).

While *Giovanni's Room*, set in Paris with an all-white cast, is frequently held up as an exemplary post-war novel about homosexuality, a re-examination of the novel in relation to the Cold War reveals the ways that it probes, examines and critiques rigid post-war identity categories. As a novel by an African-American with no ostensibly black characters, *Giovanni's Room* fits uneasily into the American and African-American canons, disturbing the 'containment' of black American literature that critics such as Robert Bone sought to maintain. For Bone in particular, the rise in 'raceless' novels such as *Giovanni's Room* was a symptom of assimilation, a bastardised genre that sought to blur the boundaries between American and African-American literature and culture. Published two years after the desegregation of the education system, *Giovanni's Room* reflects pervasive anxieties that African-American culture would miscegenate and pollute white America culture. As a work of homosexual fiction, *Giovanni's Room* also taps into concerns that homosexuality could go undetected through Baldwin's employment of a masculine, ex-football player who is contrasted with the effeminate gay underworld.

I always wonder
what they think the niggers are doing
while they, the pink and alabaster pragmatists,
are containing
Russia

(James Baldwin, 'Staggerlee Wonders', 1983)[5]

On 14 July 1964 the *New York Herald Tribune* announced the forthcoming publication of a new work of non-fiction by the celebrated African-American novelist James Baldwin. According to Baldwin in an interview with *Playbill*, *Blood Counters* would be serialised in the *New Yorker*, exposing the FBI's treatment of African-Americans.[6] Despite rumours at Dial Press, the book never materialised. Discussion of the book, however, quickly found its way into Baldwin's bulging FBI file, a dossier that ran to some 1,700 pages. Baldwin, the reports erroneously claimed, was a communist. Following reports on his involvement in civil rights, Baldwin was placed on the Security Index ('the list of "dangerous individuals" who posed "a threat to national security"'). Alongside one FBI file, J. Edgar Hoover scrawled, 'Isn't James Baldwin a well-known pervert?'[7]

The FBI's surveillance of Baldwin is indicative of the ways in which government organisations during the Cold War scrutinised American citizens (both home and abroad) for evidence of subversive political activity in order to maintain rigid distinctions between an identifiable Self and Other. Films of the early 1950s, such as *I Was a Communist for the FBI* (1951) and *My Son John* (1952), urge the importance of hyper-vigilance at a time when it was increasingly difficult to identify the enemy. Whilst communists remained the primary object of detection, the Cold War consensus, as Baldwin's FBI files testify, was also motivated and maintained by the twin domestic fears of racial integration and sexual deviance, which in turn were quickly linked to communist activity.

This chapter re-examines the impact of Baldwin's second novel, *Giovanni's Room* (1956), in order to show the ways in which it picks up on and illuminates Cold War concerns over racial integration and sexual deviance. Baldwin's well-known second novel is notable for several reasons: not only because it is set in Paris but also because there are ostensibly no black characters. Although *Giovanni's Room* has become a seminal work of gay literature, a reassessment of the novel's impact through the lens of Cold War politics and culture reveals the ways that Baldwin's work – and in particular *Giovanni's Room* – troubles and critiques narrow post-war racial and sexual boundaries. Published two years after the desegregation of the education system and in a period that saw an increasing anxiety about homosexuals who could pass as straight, *Giovanni's Room* feeds into acute anxieties about the policing of racial and sexual boundaries.

I

Baldwin's references to what he called his 'obsession with the McCarthy phenomenon' were due to more than paranoia.[8] The first known FBI file on Baldwin appeared in 1951.[9] In *The Devil Finds Work* Baldwin recollects being accosted by two agents in 1945. Noting that his colour had already made him 'conspicuous', Baldwin concludes that the FBI 'frightened me, and they humiliated me – it was like being spat on, or pissed on, or gang-raped'.[10] Baldwin's recollection of the bureau's violation painfully emphasises the ways in which he was scrutinised for both his sexual 'perversion' and his racial identity by, as he recalled, 'J. Edgar Hoover, history's most highly paid (and most utterly useless) *voyeur*'.[11] Baldwin's move to Paris in 1948 offered him greater sexual and racial tolerance but it did not remove him from the impact of the Cold War. By the early 1950s, there was a proliferation of newspaper headlines in Paris, such as 'McCarthyism, Forerunner of Fascism in the USA' and *Le Monde*'s 'The Mania of the Witch Hunt: Every Day McCarthy Weighs More Heavily on the Lives of Americans', a message, as James Campbell notes, that also included Americans in Paris.[12] There were rumours that magazines such as *Paris Review* were being funded by the CIA, illustrated by Baldwin's wry remark that he covered the first International Conference of Black Writers and Artists in Paris, in 1956, 'for *Encounter* (or for the CIA)'.[13] In Paris, as the poet Jan Logue recalls, 'everybody thought everybody was informing on someone or other for somebody', paralleling Baldwin's recollection that, on his return to America, 'friends were throwing their friends to the wolves, and justifying their treachery by learned discourses . . . on the treachery of the Comintern'.[14]

Baldwin's surveillance by the FBI in America and France points to a wider connection between the bureau's monitoring of racial progress and the ways in which early civil-rights achievements were connected to subversive political activity. As early as 1942, Edgar J. Hoover had set up a thorough investigation of racial conditions (RACON), insisting that African-Americans were 'seeking to exploit "the disloyal and malcontent"' in the United States by disrupting the war effort.[15] Crucially, the connection between racial equality and political subversion was reinforced, not relaxed, in the immediate post-war years. At first glance the 1940s and 1950s read as a rapid dismantling of racial boundaries across disparate arenas in culture and politics: African-Americans broke the colour line in the National Football

League and major league baseball in 1946 and 1947 respectively. In film, The National Association for the Advancement of Colored People (NAACP) continued to lobby Hollywood, demanding an end to the portrayal of African-Americans as two-dimensional stereotypes, while an executive order prevented discrimination in application to federal government posts.[16] Most significantly of all, the army was finally desegregated in 1948, followed six years later by the desegregation of public schools in the case of *Brown* v. *Board of Education of Topeka, Kansas.*

During the rapid dismantling of racial boundaries in post-war America, two crucial and interconnected points emerge. The first is that underneath Truman's progressive racial policies lurked a private ambivalence towards desegregation. Racial advancement was viewed as a secondary priority to combating communism (unless of course the two coincided). After the Supreme Court had ruled that segregated public schools were a violation of the Fourteenth Amendment, Eisenhower privately held the ruling as 'morally repugnant', giving his assurances to Southern Congressmen that he would not uphold the court's decision to desegregate schools 'with all deliberate speed'.[17] The second – and more crucial – point is that the advances of racial progress were seen by many as tantamount to the collapse of the racial order. In this way, the post-war years simultaneously saw a relaxing, but also a sharp delineation, of racial boundaries.

Nowhere is this reinscription of racial boundaries made more acute than in the *Brown* v. *Board* ruling of 1954, which gave rise to fears that racial parameters were increasingly permeable. While Cold War critics have usually attributed the pervasive fear of what Andrew Ross terms 'germophobia' to the threat of communism and homosexuality (which I examine below), there were increasing concerns, as James F. Davis has noted, 'perhaps paranoid is not too strong a term – about the specter of "invisible blackness"'.[18] Davis has noted the ways in which 'much of the rhetoric advanced in the 1950s and 1960s against desegregating the public schools and other public facilities featured the assertion that racial integration would destroy the purity of the races'.[19] Robert Patterson, a founder of the first White Citizens' Council, opposed what he saw as the 'dark cloud of integration', objecting to what he described as 'the Communist theme of all races and mongrelization', pledging that 'we will defeat this communistic disease that is being thrust upon us'.[20]

In March 1956, the year that *Giovanni's Room* was published, ninety-six Southern Congressmen (every congressman from the Old Confederacy's eleven states and every Southern senator except three) pledged to overturn the recently desegregated education system, protesting in an open letter to the *New York Times.*[21] Thomas Brady, a well-known Southern judge, warned that the desegregation of schools would lead to 'the tragedy of miscegenation'.[22] Like William Faulkner, who famously predicted that 'the Negro race will vanish by intermarriage', adding that, 'if it came to fighting, I'd fight for Mississippi against the United States even if it meant going out into the streets and shooting Negroes', Brady pledged to die for the principles of racial purity.[23] Although Brady's and Faulkner's views on integration were clearly extreme, it is important to realise that they were by no means isolated. As Leerom Medovoi has posited, even liberal whites could accept integration in schools only 'through the piecemeal admission and assimilation of non-whites who could then be brought to cross-identify racially with the primarily white and white-staffed schools'.[24] Integration, as Medovoi notes, was perceived as 'the collapse of the racial order', fuelling concerns that whiteness would be indistinguishable from blackness, rendering permeable racial boundaries that hitherto had been sharply delineated.[25]

The mid-1950s in America witnessed a sharp redrawing of racial boundaries, illustrated most acutely by a resurgence of the Ku Klux Klan after the *Brown* v. *Board* decision.[26] Crucially, domestic racial concerns over miscegenation were increasingly linked to wider anxieties about the spread of communism, acutely illustrated by Albert Canwell, chair of the Washington State Legislative Fact-Finding Committee on Un-American Activities. 'If someone insists that there is discrimination against Negroes in this country,' Canwell declared, 'there is every reason to believe that person is a Communist'.[27] By linking racial progress to the geo-political threat of communism, integration moved from being a Southern to a national concern. As Benjamin Muse noted in his study of integration after 1954: 'Fear stimulated opposition to desegregation most stubbornly on two counts: fear of Communism, with which the crusade for Negro rights was believed to be somehow related; and a horror of racial amalgamation.'[28] The links between communist and African-American organisations such as the NAACP were widespread; not only was there a wide belief that the *Brown* v. *Board* decision was a 'communist plot', but, as a 1956 FBI report 'revealed', there was a '"tremendous" Communist presence among the State's Negro leadership'.[29]

The 'horror of racial amalgamation' was illustrated most violently in the South through a resurgence of lynchings (most famously in the murder of the 14-year-old Emmett Till in 1955 and the lynching of Matt Parker in 1959). In 1957 Ku Klux Klansmen from Birmingham castrated African-American war veteran Edward Aaron, calling out the name of the Supreme Court chief justice as they tortured him: 'Look here, nigger! You ever heard of a nigger-loving Communist named Earl Warren?'[30] While interracial sex remained the primary cause of anxiety, the fear of integration moved beyond concerns that whites and blacks would mingle, to a more general concern that black American culture would miscegenate or pollute (white) America. Although the influence of African-American culture was most evident in the growing popularity of black-influenced rock and roll, debates about assimilation and integration dominated numerous cultural practices, not least, as I examine below, in the boundaries of 'American' and 'African-American' literature.

II

Some day, Dr Lancaster was saying, perhaps a Negro writer will write a novel about white people.

(Carl Van Vechten, Nigger Heaven, 1926)[31]

'Integration', wrote Arthur Davis in 1956 (the year that *Giovanni's Room* was published), is 'the most vital issue in America today', with the African-American at 'the center of this violent controversy'.[32] The violent controversy to which Davis alludes was fought out in cultural as well as political arenas, not only between whites and blacks, but also amongst African-Americans, where the question of integration and assimilation was fiercely contested. As early as 1941, Arthur Davis, Sterling Brown and Ulysses Lee had forcefully urged African-American authors to reject a specifically black aesthetic. In the introduction to their co-edited anthology *The Negro Caravan*, Davis, Brown and Lee made explicit their rejection of the term 'Negro literature', a term, the editors argued, that placed black literature 'in an alcove apart'. Central to the editors' introduction is the imperative that African-American writers must dilute and even write out any traces of black culture and language, what they term the 'structural peculiarity' of black American writing.[33]

Although Davis and Co. sowed the early seeds of what would later be termed 'Integrationist Poetics', their ideas would not become mainstream until the mid-1950s.[34] In an essay titled 'The Literature of the Negro in the United States', Richard Wright predicted that, as 'the Negro merges into the mainstream of American life, there might result actually a disappearance of Negro literature as such'.[35] As America achieved more social equality, Wright believed that African-American literature would become less 'racial', resulting in 'a merging of Negro expression with American expression'.[36]

Wright's views are echoed in an important essay by Arthur Davis titled 'Integration and Race Literature', in which Davis maintained that the course of African-American literature had been governed by political and social changes, such as the Abolition Movement, Reconstruction and the First World War.[37] With the desegregation of schools in 1954, Davis predicted that 'the Negro will move permanently into full participation in American life – social, economic, political and literary'.[38]

Baldwin's decision to write a 'white' novel cannot be reduced to pressing arguments regarding integration and assimilation. To do so would be to ignore the complex entanglement of race and sexuality that Baldwin would have faced with the inclusion of black homosexual characters, something he later acknowledged that 'would have been quite beyond . . . [his] powers' in 1956.[39] And yet Baldwin's post-war writing – and in particular *Giovanni's Room* – feeds directly into debates about the policy of assimilation and anxiety over 'raceless' novels. According to Arnold Rampersad, Langston Hughes 'linked what he saw as Baldwin's excesses to the trend of integration sapping the strength of black youth'. In a letter to Arna Bontemps, Hughes warned that 'Integration is going to RUIN Negro business – as it apparently threatened to ruin the finest young writer of fiction [Baldwin] in the race'.[40] Like Hughes, Addison Gayle in a discussion of Baldwin's essay 'Stranger in the Village', complained of the 'tone of assimilation, the obsession with fusing the black and white cultures', accusing Baldwin of 'obliterating racial characteristics altogether'.[41]

Gayle's criticism of Baldwin's fusion of white and black culture can be traced to his essays of the 1950s. In *Notes of a Native Son* Baldwin frequently switches register, so that it is difficult to place the authorial voice. For example, in 'Many Thousands Gone', Baldwin's racial identity becomes textually ambiguous as he aligns himself with the (white) authorial voice:

> Up to today *we* are set at a division, so that *he* may not marry *our* daughters or *our* sisters, nor may *he* – for the most part – eat at *our* tables or live in *our* houses. Moreover, those who do, do so at the grave expense of a double alienation: from *their* own people, whose fabled attributes *they* must . . . deny.[42]

The passage begins with a 'we' that is at first ambiguous: it is not clear whether Baldwin refers to 'we' African-Americans, 'we' white Americans, or a collective 'we'. It soon becomes clear that the 'he' is the African-American male subject, objectified from a dominant (white) position. In the next sentence Baldwin collapses these divisions, where '*their* own people' becomes a shared possessive adjective.

Baldwin's use of racially interchanging pronouns infuriated and bemused a number of black and white critics alike.[43] Langston Hughes, for example, bemoaned that 'Baldwin's viewpoints are half American, half-Afro-American, incompletely fused'.[44] Hughes's suggestion that Baldwin's writing is somehow bastardised – neither authentically white nor black – is most acutely illustrated in the writing of the white critic, Robert Bone, in his survey of African-American literature, *The Negro Novel in America* (*NNA*), first published in 1958. In his chapter on Baldwin, Bone articulates profound anxieties about the ways in which *Giovanni's Room* and other 'raceless' novels merge dangerously with the body of 'white' American literature.

Whereas Bone lauds Baldwin's first novel, *Go Tell it on the Mountain*, for capturing 'the essence of Negro experience in America', he lambastes *Giovanni's Room*, criticising the novel's sketchiness, describing it as though it were a dismembered and deteriorating body: 'The characters', writes Bone, 'are vague and disembodied, the themes half-digested, the colors rather bleached than vivified. We recognize in this sterile landscape the unprocessed raw material of art.'[45] Although Bone's language – such as the word 'sterile' – suggests a not fully articulated homophobic response, his comment that the characters are bleached rather than vivified holds the key to Bone's unease. It is rather that, for Bone, the characters are really African-American, made white for the purpose of Baldwin's novel, compounded by his view that Baldwin 'simply transposes the moral topography of Harlem to the streets of Paris' (*NNA*: 226).

Bone's mistrust of *Giovanni's Room* is illuminated by his broader examination of African-American literature in relation to the wider debates over assimilation and integration. For Bone, literature is the expression of experience, something that is governed by cultural and racial backgrounds:

> In choosing an appropriate vehicle for his theme, the author's first consideration must be familiarity with surface detail . . . Every artist apprehends reality through a specific culture. Why should the Negro novelist imagine that he alone is exempt from the limitations of time and place? (*NNA* 249–50)

Bone's role as literary immigration officer is deeply problematic, not least because there is no discussion of white portrayals of black American culture. For Bone, an authentic African-American literature – and the term authentic is one that Bone employs – is one that reflects what he calls 'a Negro quality in his experience', what he elsewhere refers to as the 'fidelity to his deepest experience' (*NNA*: 3, 250). In contrast to 'authentic' black American literature, Bone claims that 'raceless' or 'assimilationist' novels are not only largely 'extra-literary', but they are 'truncated, rootless and artificial' (*NNA*: 168, 248).

Importantly, Bone explicitly acknowledges the relationship between 'race-less' literature and the growing move towards assimilation, a fact that he fiercely contests (*NNA*: 248). Rather than reflecting the African-American's acceptance into mainstream American culture, Bone argues that assimilation is 'a means of escape . . . a denial of one's racial identity'. For Bone, the 'assimilationist novel' illustrates 'the loss of contact with the realities of Negro life'. This, Bone concludes, 'amounts . . . to a kind of literary "passing"', what he also refers to as 'a kind of psychological "passing" at the fantasy level' (*NNA*: 248, 4).

Bone's pejorative use of the words 'fantasy' and 'passing' raises several important points that are central to a discussion of *Giovanni's Room* and Baldwin's earlier essays. By equating fantasy with (unwanted) assimilation, Bone acknowledges the ways in which fantasy can disturb the 'racial order' of a racially divided literature. In other words, 'raceless' novels, such as *Giovanni's Room*, threaten the stability of racial parameters, what Bone refers to explicitly as 'a wall' (*NNA*: 247).[46] By equating 'raceless' novels with 'passing', Bone also points to the ways in which *Giovanni's Room* upsets the boundaries that he is so adamant to defend. As Elaine Ginsberg has cogently argued:

> when 'race' is no longer visible, it is no longer intelligible: if 'white' can be 'black', what is white? Race passing thus not only creates, to use [Marjorie] Garber's term, a *category crisis* but also destabilizes the grounds of privilege founded on racial identity.[47]

Ginsberg points to the ways in which *Giovanni's Room* problematises the very categories of black and white literature, something that numerous critics have explored by decoding a racialised – and in particular African-American – character in Baldwin's second novel. The references to Joey, David's first lover, as 'quick and dark', 'brown' with 'dark eyes' and 'curly hair', have prompted some critics to argue that Joey's darkness represents the position of a black gay lover.[48] I want to argue rather that Baldwin deliberately teases the reader, disturbing the purity (and authenticity) of his 'white' text through suggestion. But, as I argue in the following section, by portraying a character whose homosexuality is not visible – a character who is able to pass in both the straight and the gay worlds – Baldwin also questioned the prevailing notion that sexuality could be readily identified by those attempting to scrutinise and categorise sexual differences.

III

Although I have focused on Bone at some length, most criticism of the 1950s was too appalled by the homosexual subject matter to address the novel's absence of black characters. While a handful of reviewers commended

Baldwin's sensitive treatment of homosexuality, the praise was largely
drowned out by criticism that praised the novel's style, while dismissing
its content.[49] Charles Rolo, typical of many reviewers, begins by lauding
Baldwin as a writer 'endowed with exceptional narrative skill, poetic intensity
of feeling, and a sensitive command of language'. But, Rolo quickly adds – in
a curiously sexual rhetoric: 'This endorsement is made despite the fact that
Mr Baldwin's subject is one of which I have had my fill.'[50] The refusal of
critics to engage seriously with the theme of homosexuality is indicative of
the prevailing attitudes to dissident sexualities, particularly in the ways that
left-wing politics during the 1950s undermined (or 'contained') the political
relevance of same-sex desire. As Robert Corber has noted in his analysis of
homosexuality during the Cold War, 'even supposedly progressive critics'
such as Leslie Fiedler deflected the political significance of gay male writing,
challenging its claim for a gay male identity.[51] In his review of *Giovanni's
Room*, for example (which I return to), Fiedler deflects the significance of the
homosexual plot, stating that 'it is a basic American plot – a staple of popular
fiction'. Baldwin's decision to cast Giovanni as homosexual, Fiedler contends, is little more than a 'gimmick', a substitution of 'the poor but worthy
girl [for] a poor but worthy fairy'.[52]

Although Fiedler is well known for espousing the centrality of homoeroticism in American literature (most notably in his 1948 essay 'Come Back to
the Raft Ag'in, Huck Honey!'), critics such as Robyn Wiegman have noted
how his figuration of homosexuality (which, by 1960, he changed to
'homoeroticism') in fact cast 'homosexuality as the immaturity of arrested
psychosexual development'.[53] In 'Come Back to the Raft', as Corber points
out, Fiedler's reading of *The City and the Pillar*, like his reading of *Giovanni's
Room*, refused to distinguish Vidal's novel from the mainstream of American
fiction; rather, as Corber notes, Fiedler saw 'its focus on gay male experience
business as usual because it supposedly conformed to the repressed and
sentimentalizing homoerotic character of American literature'.[54]

The connection between *Giovanni's Room* and *The City and the Pillar* was
made explicit by Baldwin's publishers. Readers at Knopf referred to the
homosexual scenes in *Giovanni's Room* as 'repugnant', while William Cole, in
a wonderful double entendre, concluded that 'it was judged not the time for
an out-and-out homosexual novel. There had only been Gore Vidal's.'[55]
Knopf's comparison with *The City and the Pillar* indicates both the boldness of
Giovanni's Room and also similarities between the two novels that go far
beyond the theme of homosexuality. Prefacing a revised edition of *The City
and the Pillar*, Vidal talks explicitly of how he wanted to shatter the stereotype
of homosexuals as 'shrieking queens or lonely bookish boys'. Instead, Vidal
recalls how his 'two lovers were athletes and so . . . entirely masculine

that . . . the feminine was simply irrelevant to their passion'.[56] Like Vidal's protagonist, Baldwin's David is blond and athletic (there are references to his footballing past), and, like Jim Willard, David is contrasted with the negative depiction of an effeminate homosexual underworld.

The indistinguishable homosexuality of both David and Jim Willard suggests ways in which both Vidal and Baldwin were pointing towards the 'naturalness' of a homosexual identity, one not defined in opposition to a dominant definition of masculinity, a point that Baldwin had made earlier in his 1949 article 'Preservation of Innocence'.[57] The decision of Baldwin and Vidal to cast their heroes as strong, athletic and masculine challenged the assumptions not only that homosexuality was easily recognisable but also that masculinity was incompatible with homosexuality. But, crucially, the ability of both protagonists to pass as straight fed into increasing anxieties over the policing of sexual boundaries.

As various cultural critics, such as John D'Emilio and Estelle Freedman, have noted, the post-war period in America saw simultaneously a relaxing and a tightening of sexual boundaries.[58] Nowhere was this confusing blend of sexual permissiveness and restraint more acute than in the treatment of homosexuality. The publication of Alfred Kinsey's reports on male and female sexual behaviour in 1948 and 1953 respectively shattered pervasive conceptions of sexual practice.[59] *Sexual Behavior in the Human Male* catapulted the private sexual experiences of American men into the public arena. Top of the best-seller lists in the *New York Times* for over six months, Kinsey revealed that 'a considerable portion of the population, perhaps the major portion of the male population, has at least some homosexual sexual experience between adolescence and old age'.[60]

The impact of Kinsey's report was far-reaching enough to precipitate over 200 hundred studies on sexuality between 1948 and 1949.[61] Although Kinsey had set out to show that punishment for homosexuality was irrational and illogical, his report in fact contributed to a national homosexual panic. Crucially, Kinsey dismissed early reports that had attempted to register the degree of male and female characteristics in homosexual men and women. Repudiating the myths that gay people could be identified by their 'fine skins, high-pitched voices, [and] obvious hand movements', Kinsey insisted that homosexuals could pass as straight, indistinguishable in appearance from heterosexual men.[62]

The increasing arrests for homosexuality in the 1950s point to the ways in which deviant sexuality became associated with threats to the nation's security.[63] During the hearings of the House Un-American Activities Committee (HUAC) in the 1940s and 1950s, the investigations were extended, not only to fears of communist infiltration, but, as Corber has noted, to 'homosexuals and lesbians who "passed" as heterosexual'.[64] Following claims that several homosexuals had been dismissed in 1950 from the State Department, Senator Joseph McCarthy ordered a Senate inquiry into same-sex behaviour, which concluded that there were 'no outward characteristics or physical traits' to positively identify homosexuals and lesbians. Effeminate men and masculine women, the medical report concluded, were not necessarily homosexual.[65]

As is well documented, the report's findings were interpreted to argue that homosexuals did indeed constitute a security risk. In attempting to show that homosexuals and lesbians 'be considered as proper cases for medical and psychiatric treatment', the official conclusion was that, since homosexuals were emotionally unstable, they were vulnerable to 'the blandishments of the foreign espionage agent'.[66] The perceived threat of homosexuality to national security resulted in the dismissal of thousands of suspected 'sexual deviants'. In fact, more men and women were fired from government offices under the suspicion of homosexual practice than for alleged communist connections.[67]

The complicated connections between communism, homosexuality and miscegenation are further grouped by a prevailing rhetoric of contamination. The Senate report's finding of 1950, for example (*Employment of Homosexuals and Other Sex Perverts in Government*), warned that one homosexual 'can pollute a Government office', echoing fears that the 'red disease' could infect the American body politic, or that integration would lead to the miscegenation of American life. Accompanying pervasive pollution metaphors was the concern that homosexuals, like communists, might not be identified, resulting, as Elaine Tyler May has shown, in the scrutiny of employees' sexual behaviour, whether in private industry, the army or government.[68]

The correlation between homosexual passing and communism was made explicit by Arthur Schlesinger, who, in his attempts to show the secrecy and conspiracy of the American Communist Party, compared the dissenters to participants of gay male subculture. According to Schlesinger, Communists communicated to one another by recognising certain signals in an analogy that explicitly drew on gay cruising, which, as George Chauncey has shown, was communicated in an articulate form of 'codes of dress, speech and style'.[69] Communists, Schlesinger insisted, could 'identify each other (and be identified by their enemies) on casual meeting by the use of certain phrases, the names of certain friends . . . and certain silences', paralleling Vidal's description of cruising as 'a quick glance . . . a form of freemasonry'.[70] Similarly, in *Giovanni's Room*, concerned that people are taking bets on his sexuality, David is aware of being watched by *le milieu*, 'in order to discover, by means of signs I made but which only they could read, whether or not I had a true vocation'.[71]

Schlesinger's correlation between communism and homosexuality – and in particular the inability to identify subversive activity – points to a larger Cold War concern with the policing of racial, sexual and political boundaries that Baldwin's second novel feeds into. At the root of these anxieties is the fear that boundaries are porous, that communists, homosexuals or African-Americans can pass, assimilating without detection into American culture, a point made explicit by Leslie Fiedler's review of *Giovanni's Room*:

> there are not even any Negroes – and this, I must confess, makes me a little uneasy . . . It is rather the fact that he [David] encounters no black faces in his movements through Paris and the south of France, that not even the supernumeraries are colored; so that one begins to suspect at last that there must *really* be Negroes present, censored, camouflaged or encoded.[72]

Fiedler's rhetoric of suspicion – 'censored, camouflaged or encoded' – calls to attention the policing and surveillance of Cold War America: a fear of spying, infiltration and contamination that I have outlined. For Fiedler, *Giovanni's Room* only appears to have an all-white cast, but he continues to probe the text, using a language that becomes increasingly illogical and confused. How can black characters be both present and censored? Censored by whom? Does he mean that Baldwin's protagonists are really black, camouflaged by their white personas?

Fiedler's review implicitly suggests that Baldwin – as an African-American – must leave a trace of his ethnicity in the white world that he describes.[73] And, like the eponymous sleuth in Twain's *Pudd'n head Wilson*, the detective-critic can scrutinise literary fingerprints to reveal an author's racial identity. But Fiedler's anxiety also stems from his inability to locate firm racial boundaries. By insisting that there must be 'camouflaged' black characters that he cannot locate, Fiedler suggests that Baldwin's scopically white (but racially 'black') characters have passed. Like Fanon, who writes of how the Jew 'can sometimes go unnoticed', or Freud's observation that people of mixed race 'resemble white people, but who betray their coloured descent by some striking feature or other', Fiedler struggles to locate a gesture or feature that will betray the characters' 'real' blackness.[74]

Fiedler's anxieties about the lack of visible black characters in *Giovanni's Room* articulate the ways in which the novel has been viewed as a hybridised or bastardised narrative. Neither wholly white nor wholly black, *Giovanni's Room* appears miscegenated, impure, disturbing the boundaries of American and African-American literature. As a novel that remains on the peripheries of the African-American canon, *Giovanni's Room* is a sharp reminder of the ways in which Baldwin resisted dominant Cold War categories of black and white, gay and straight, loyalty and disloyalty. As Baldwin wrote in 1962, 'one's aware, in an eerie way, that there are barriers which must not be crossed, and that by these invisible barriers everyone is mesmerized'.[75]

NOTES

1. Alan Nadel, *Containment Culture: American Narratives, Postmodernism and the Atomic Age* (Durham, NC, and London: Duke University Press, 1995), p. 7.
2. From the late 1990s there has been a renewed interest in domestic race politics and foreign affairs. See Carol Anderson, *Eyes off the Prize: The United Nations and the African American Struggle for Human Rights, 1944–1955* (Cambridge: Cambridge University Press, 2003); Thomas Borstelmann, *The Cold War and the Color Line: American Race Relations in the Global Arena* (Cambridge, MA: Harvard University Press, 2001); Mary L. Dudziak, *Cold War Civil Rights: Race and the Image of American Democracy* (Princeton and Oxford: Oxford University Press, 2000); Gary Gerstle, *American Crucible: Race and Nation in the Twentieth Century* (Princeton: Princeton University Press, 2001).
3. Quoted by Dudziak, *Cold War Civil Rights*, p. 18.
4. Robert J. Corber, *In the Name of National Security: Hitchcock, Homophobia and the Political Construction of Gender in Postwar America* (Durham, NC, and London: Duke University Press, 1993), p. 8.
5. James Baldwin, 'Staggerlee wonders', in Baldwin, *Jimmy's Blues: Selected Poems* (London: Michael Joseph, 1983), p. 7.
6. James Campbell, 'I Heard it through the Grapevine', *Granta*, 73 (Spring 2001), p. 167.
7. Ibid. pp. 155, 170.
8. James Baldwin, 'No Name on the Street', in Baldwin, *The Price of the Ticket: Collected Nonfiction, 1948–1985* (New York: St Martin's/ Marek, 1985), p. 466.
9. See Maurice Wallace, ' "I'm Not Entirely What I Look Like": Richard Wright, James Baldwin, and the Hegemony of Vision; or, Jimmy's FBEye Blues', in Dwight A. McBride (ed.), *James Baldwin Now* (New York and London: New York University Press, 1999), pp. 289–306.
10. James Baldwin, 'The Devil Finds Work', in Baldwin, *The Price of the Ticket*, p. 615.
11. Ibid. p. 612. See Baldwin's final novel, *Just above my Head* (London: Penguin, [1979] 1994): 'No one called the late J. Edgar Hoover a terrorist, though that is precisely what he was' (p. 350).
12. James Campbell, *Exiled in Paris: Richard Wright, James Baldwin, Samuel Beckett, and Others on the Left Bank* (New York and London: Scribner's, 1995), p. 92.
13. Baldwin, 'No Name on the Street', p. 475; for an excellent account of the CIA's involvement with left-wing journals, see Frances Stonor Saunders, *Who Paid the Piper? The CIA and the Cultural Cold War* (London: Granta 1999), especially pp. 184–9 on *Encounter*.
14. Campbell, *Exiled in Paris*, p. 91; Baldwin, 'No Name on the Street', p. 464.
15. John A. Noakes, 'Racializing Subversion: The FBI and the Depiction of Race in Early Cold War Movies', *Ethnic and Racial Studies*, 26/4 (July 2003), p. 731.
16. See ibid., expecially pp. 728–9.
17. Kenneth O'Reilly, 'Racial Integration: The Battle General Eisenhower Chose Not to Fight', *Journal of Blacks in Higher Education*, 0/18 (Winter 1997–8), p. 112. See also Borstelmann, *The Cold War and the Color Line*, especially, pp. 86–110.
18. Andrew Ross, *No Respect: Intellectuals and Popular Culture* (New York and London: Routledge, 1989), p. 45; James F. Davis, *Who is Black? One Nation's Definition* (Pennsylvania: Pennsylvania State University Press, 1991), p. 56.

19. Davis, *Who is Black?*, p. 17.
20. Dudziak, *Cold War Civil Rights*, p. 111. The White Citizens Council was formed in 1954. See A. Robert Lee, *Multicultural American Literature: Comparative Black, Latino/a and Asian American Fictions* (Edinburgh: Edinburgh University Press, 2003), who notes that 'to many [the White Citizens Council were] simply the Klan and its sympathisers under another name, and given to camouflaging its ideology under the mantle of state rights' (p. 252).
21. 'Southern Declaration on Integration', *New York Times*, 12 March 1956, reprinted in Anthony Cooper (ed.), *The Black Experience, 1865–1978* (Dartford: Greenwich University Press, 1995), pp. 239–40.
22. Davis, *Who is Black?*, p. 17.
23. Campbell, *Exiled in Paris*, p. 208.
24. Leerom Medovoi, 'Reading the Blackboard: Youth, Masculinity, and Racial Cross-Identification', in Harry Stecopoulos and Michael Uebel (eds), *Race and the Subject of Masculinities* (Durham, NC, and London: Duke University Press, 1997), p. 145.
25. Ibid. p. 145.
26. Benjamin Muse, *Ten Years of Prelude: The Story of Integration since the Supreme Court's 1954 Decision* (Beaconsfield: Darwen Finlayson, 1964), p. 45. Muse also mentions the revival of *Birth of a Nation* after 1954, which had not circulated widely since the 1930s, p. 41.
27. Quoted by Stephen J. Whitfield, *The Culture of the Cold War* (1991), 2nd edn (London and Baltimore: Johns Hopkins University Press, 1996), p. 21.
28. Muse, *Ten Years of Prelude*, p. 39. See also Numan V. Bartley, *The Rise of Massive Resistance: Race and Politics in the South during the 1950s* (Baton Rouge, LA: Louisiana State University Press, 1969), especially pp. 185–7.
29. O'Reilly, 'Racial Integration', p. 114. For a brief but useful account of Paul Robeson and communism, see Tom Engelhardt, *The End of Victory Culture: Cold War America and the Disillusioning of a Generation*, 2nd edn, (Amherst MA: University of Massachusetts Press, 1995), p. 127. See Whitfield, *The Culture of the Cold War*, who points out that *I Was A Communist for the FBI* 'shows the [Communist] Party taking credit for race riots in Harlem and Detroit in 1943' (p. 21).
30. Quoted by Borstelmann, *The Cold War and the Color Line*, p. 89.
31. Carl Van Vechten, *Nigger Heaven*, introduced by Kathleen Pfeiffer (Urbana and Chicago: University of Illinois Press, [1926] 2000), p. 104.
32. Arthur P. Davis, 'Integration and Race Literature' (1956), in Angelyn Mitchell (ed.), *Within the Circle: An Anthology of African American Literary Criticism from the Harlem Renaissance to the Present* (Durham, NC, and London: Duke University Press, 1994), p. 156.
33. Sterling A. Brown, Arthur P. Davis and Ulysses Lee (eds), *The Negro Caravan: Writings by American Negroes*, introduced by Julius Lester (New York: Arno Press and the *New York Times*, [1941] 1970), p. 7.
34. For a useful overview of this movement, see Houston A. Baker, Jr, 'Discovering America: Generational Shifts, Afro-American Literary Criticism, and the Study of Expressive Culture', in Baker, *Blues, Ideology, and Afro-American Literature: A Vernacular Theory* (Chicago and London: University of Chicago Press, 1984), pp. 64–112.
35. Richard Wright, 'The Literature of the Negro in the United States', in Wright, *White Man, Listen!* (Westport, CT: Greenwood Press, 1957), p. 148.
36. Ibid. p. 149.
37. For a useful historical account of desegregation, see John Hope Franklin, 'A Brief History', in Mabel M. Smythe (ed.), *The Black American Reference Book* (Englewood Cliffs: Prentice-Hall, 1976), pp. 1–90, especially pp. 69–71.
38. Davis, 'Integration and Race Literature', p. 160.
39. John Elgrably and George Plimpton, 'The Art of Fiction 1984: James Baldwin' (1984), in Fred L. Standley and Louis H. Pratt (eds), *Conversations with Baldwin* (Jackson and

London: University of Mississippi Press, 1989), p. 239.

40. Arnold Rampersad, *The Life of Langston Hughes, vol. 2: 1941–1967 I Dream a World* (New York and Oxford: Oxford University Press, 1988), p. 335.

41. Addison Gayle, Jr, 'The Function of Black Literature at the Present Time', in Gayle (ed.), *The Black Aesthetic* (New York: Doubleday and Company, 1971), pp. 389, 390.

42. James Baldwin, 'Many Thousands Gone', in Baldwin, *Notes of a Native Son* (London: Penguin, [1955] 1995), p. 31. Emphasis added.

43. See Morris Dickstein, *Gates of Eden: American Culture in the Sixties* (New York: Basic Books, 1977), where he notes that 'Baldwin's "we" sometimes wobbles in the early essays, acting out his predicament by assuming now a white, now a black face' (p. 173).

44. Quoted by David Leeming, *James Baldwin: A Biography* (New York: Alfred A. Knopf, 1994), p. 101.

45. Robert A. Bone, *The Negro Novel in America* (1958), rev. edn (New Haven: Yale University Press, 1965), pp. 218, 226; hereafter abbreviated as *NNA*.

46. See Rosemary Jackson, *Fantasy: The Literature of Subversion* (London and New York: Routledge, 1995), who notes that 'fantasy' is etymologically rooted in the Greek word *phantasikos* meaning 'to make visible' (p. 13).

47. Elaine K. Ginsberg, 'Introduction', in Elaine K. Ginsberg (ed.), *Passing and the Fictions of Identity* (Durham, NC, and London: Duke University Press, 1996), p. 8.

48. James Baldwin, *Giovanni's Room* (London: Penguin, [1956] 1990), pp. 12, 13, 14. For critics who have interpreted 'encoded' black characters, see Donald H. Mengay, 'The Failed Copy: *Giovanni's Room* and the (Re) Contextualisation of Difference', *Genders*, 17 (Fall 1993), p. 60. See also Horace Porter, *Stealing the Fire: The Art and Protest of James Baldwin* (Middletown, CT: Wesleyan University Press, 1989), especially pp. 141–2.

49. For some positive comments on Baldwin's treatment of homosexuality, see Granville Hicks, 'Tormented Triangle', *New York Times Book Review*, 14 October 1956, p. 5, and Nelson Algren, 'Lost Man', *Nation*, 1 December 1956, p. 484.

50. Charles Rolo, 'Other Voices, Other Rooms', *Atlantic Monthly*, 198/6 (December 1956), p. 98.

51. Robert J. Corber, *Homosexuality in Cold War America: Resistance and the Crisis of Masculinity* (Durham, NC, and London: Duke University Press, 1997), p. 1. Although Fiedler and other left-wing critics denied the legitimacy of a homosexual identity, see Donald Webster Corey, *The Homosexual in America: A Subjective Approach* (New York: Greenberg, 1951). Corey argued that homosexuality was a form of disempowerment comparable to ethnic minorities.

52. Leslie Fiedler, 'A Homosexual Dilemma', *New Leader*, 39/10 (1956), p. 17.

53. Leslie Fiedler, 'Come Back to the Raft Ag'in, Huck Honey!' (1948), in *The Collected Essays of Leslie Fiedler*, vol. 1 (New York: Stein and Day, 1971), pp. 142–51; Robyn Wiegman, 'Fiedler and Sons', in Stecopoulos and Uebel (eds), *Race and the Subject of Masculinities*, p. 50.

54. Corber, *Homosexuality in Cold War America*, p. 137.

55. W. J. Weatherby, *James Baldwin: Artist on Fire* (London: Michael Joseph, 1990), p. 119.

56. Gore Vidal, Preface to *The City and the Pillar* (1949); reprinted, with a new preface by Gore Vidal (London: Abacus, 1994), p. 3.

57. See James Baldwin, 'Preservation of Innocence', *Zero*, 1 (Summer 1949), pp. 14–15, where Baldwin challenges the naturalness of gender and sexual identities.

58. John D'Emilio and Estelle B. Freedman, *Intimate Matters: A History of Sexuality in America* (New York and Cambridge: Harper and Row, 1988), p. 260.

59. Alfred Kinsey, *Sexual Behavior in the Human Male* (Philadelphia and London: W. B. Saunders Company, 1948).

60. Ibid. p. 610.

61. John D'Emilio, *Sexual Politics, Sexual Communities: The Making of a Homosexual Minority in the United States, 1940–1970* (Chicago and London: University of Chicago Press, 1983), p. 35.

62. Kinsey, *Sexual Behavior*, p. 637.
63. See, for example, D'Emilio, *Sexual Politics*, especially pp. 49–50.
64. Robert J. Corber, *In the Name of National Security: Hitchcock, Homophobia and the Political Construction of Gender in Postwar America* (Durham, NC, and London: Duke University Press, 1993), p. 8.
65. Ibid. p. 61; see also Harry M. Benshoff, *Monsters in the Closet: Homosexuality and the Horror Film* (Manchester and New York: Manchester University Press, 1997), who cites an article from the gentleman's magazine, *Sir!* (March 1958). The author warns that 'Not All Homos Are Easy to Spot', and informs the reader that, although an estimated 15–20% of men are thought to be homosexual, less than 4% are 'are so effeminate they are recognizable' (pp. 131–2).
66. Corber, *In the Name of National Security*, pp. 62–3.
67. Ibid. p. 8.
68. Elaine Tyler May, *Homeward Bound: American Families in the Cold War Era* (New York: Basic Books, 1988), p. 95; see also David Savran, *Communists, Cowboys and Queers: The Politics of Masculinity in the Work of Arthur Miller and Tennessee Williams* (London and Minneapolis: University of Minneapolis Press, 1992), who notes the 'intense level of surveillance posted over the circulation of sexuality in and around the nuclear family facilitated an unprecedented level of social control' (p. 9).
69. George Chauncey, *Gay New York: Gender, Urban Culture, and the Making of the Gay Underworld, 1890–1940* (London: Flamingo, 1995), p. 4.
70. Quoted by Corber, *In the Name of National Security*, pp. 19–20; Vidal, *The City and the Pillar*, pp. 148, 149.
71. Baldwin, *Giovanni's Room*, p. 31. There are a number of instances in the novel where David is conscious that his actions will betray his sexuality. See, for example, his cruising of a sailor: 'We came abreast and, as though he had seen some all-revealing panic in my eyes, he gave me a look contemptuously lewd and knowing . . . And in another second . . . I was certain that there would erupt into speech . . . some brutal variation of *Look, baby. I know you*' (p. 88).
72. Fiedler, 'A Homosexual Dilemma', p. 16.
73. See also Leslie Fiedler, *The Return of the Vanishing American* (London: Jonathan Cape, 1968), where he writes: 'one suspects Baldwin's Giovanni of being a Negro disguised as a European, and the book consequently of being a disguised Southern' (p. 20).
74. Sigmund Freud, ('The Unconscious', in *On Metapsychology* (1915), trans. James Strachey, Penguin Fread Library, vol. 11 (London: Penguin, 1984), p. 195; Frantz Fanon, *Black Skins, White Masks*, trans. Charles Lam Markmann (London: Pluto Press, [1952] 1986), p. 115.
75. James Baldwin, 'Color', in Baldwin, *The Price of the Ticket*, p. 320.

PART TWO

Cultural Forms

CHAPTER SIX

Film

Disney's Song of the South *and the Birth of the White Negro*

Catherine Gunther Kodat

Released in 1946 to instant controversy, *Song of the South*, the Walt Disney adaptation of Joel Chandler Harris's 'Uncle Remus' tales, has never appeared in the US home video market and received only limited video distribution in Europe and Asia before being removed from circulation in 2001. The film, which mixed live action and animation in its portrayal of Remus and his Brer Rabbit tales, received two Academy Awards, despite being attacked by film critics and civil-rights activists as a 'sublimely unreconstructed fantasy of the Old South' presenting a 'dangerously glorified picture of slavery'.[1] Such criticism only increased over the course of an era that saw the rise of the civil-rights movement; and, though DVDs and VHS videotapes of the film still enjoy some underground circulation in the USA and internationally, it is highly doubtful that the Disney company will ever sanction public release of *Song of the South*.

But, as the recognition signalled by the awards suggests, the film enjoyed considerable popularity despite its repellent racial politics; thus, as shrewd as the criticisms of the film remain, they fail to explain the mass popularity of *Song of the South*, despite its highly fraught and deeply compromised artistic and political status, a popularity testified to by the frequent appearance of the animated sections of the film through the 1960s in Disney's Sunday evening television series; by the film's continuing life in theatrical rerelease (in 1956, 1972, 1980 and 1986) before its final suppression; and by the construction of the Splash Mountain flume rides in the two Disney theme parks, rides that keep the Brer Rabbit characters alive despite the disappearance of the film featuring them.

In one sense, *Song of the South* can be seen simply as another example of Hollywood's embrace of the minstrel tradition casting blacks as singing, dancing, happy-go-lucky folk. The relationship of Remus and little Johnny has recognisable antecedents in the Shirley Temple–Bill Robinson friendship in 1938's *Just around the Corner* and *Rebecca of Sunnybrook Farm*; the 1943 films *Cabin in the Sky* and *Stormy Weather*, though intended for adults, likewise portray black experience as one infused with song and laughter. And, while it is tempting (and easy) to attribute *Song of the South*'s popularity to its success in catering to racial fantasies of benevolent dominance and grateful submission among the white Americans who undoubtedly made up the majority of the film's audience, an explanation relying on these two factors would account for only some of the film's success, and then only super-ficially.

It is not enough, then, for the cultural critic faced with *Song of the South* simply to register the protest that greeted the film and to enumerate its many, and hoary, objectionable aspects; and though Marxist accounts of uneven cultural development account for the film's appeal to its most unreconstructed audience members, recent approaches in cultural studies open the possibility of *Song of the South* having unexpected effects. Thus the cultural critic must ask whether the film's backward glance to a supposedly 'simpler' time in US racial history, motivated though it almost undoubtedly was by a defensive and reactionary politics, may have contributed to the affective cultural work necessary to furthering the arrival of the mid-Cold War civil-rights movement that is generally seen as hitting its stride with the 1954 *Brown* v. *Board of Education of Topeka, Kansas* Supreme Court decision and climaxing (though hardly concluding) with the passage of the 1965 Voting Rights Act.

This chapter examines the work accomplished by *Song of the South* in the light of later cultural phenomena that incorporated its fondly nostalgic views of black–white race relations even as they sought to point up their racist paternalism. Bernard Wolfe's famous 1949 essay for *Commentary*, 'Uncle Remus and the Malevolent Rabbit', written in response not only to the renewed popularity of Remus but also to his own experience as co-author of Mezz Mezzrow's 1946 memoir *Really the Blues*, the white-to-black racial conversion narrative that played a decisive role in forming the 'hipster ethic' of the ostensibly anti-racist Beat generation, hints at a dialectic of 'Negro-philia' and 'Negrophobia' that casts the relationship between these presumed polar opposites as 'two sides of one coin'. Norman Mailer's 1957 essay 'The White Negro' furthers the possibility that white love of black cultural style, whether animal fables or jazz music, remains enmeshed in white racial fantasies of identification and denial even when it is deployed toward social justice.

'Mother, Uncle Remus is gone. Where did he go, mother?'
'I don't know, son.'
'But why did he go, why?'
'I'm afraid mother's to blame.'

(*Song of the South*, 1946)

For almost a generation now, Walt Disney's 1946 film *Song of the South* has been something of an animated shadow, a film few Americans under the age of thirty have seen but one that lives on in the 'Brer' animatronics populating the Splash Mountain flume rides at the Disney theme parks. The first post-war offering of Disney Studios, *Song of the South* mixed animation and live action in an adaptation of Joel Chandler Harris's well-known 'Uncle Remus' tales, stories first published in a series of best-selling collections from 1880 to 1918 and themselves literary adaptations of the African-American Brer Rabbit oral narratives. The film won a 'Best Song' Academy Award (for 'Zip-a-Dee-Doo-Dah'), and James Baskett, who played the live-action Uncle Remus and provided the voice for the animated Brer Rabbit, received a special Oscar for his performance. Far from registering an unquestioned esteem for *Song of the South*, however, the awards were bestowed in the face of strong criticism both of the film's formal awkwardness (most reviewers found its blend of live action and animation technically impressive but unsatisfying) and of its patronising and stereotyped portrayal of plantation life in the nineteenth-century South (criticism that has only grown stronger over the years, and that accounts for Disney's 2001 decision to withdraw the film from the home-video market). Walter White, the executive secretary of the National Association for the Advancement of Colored People, condemned the film for perpetuating 'a dangerously glorified picture of slavery', while Bosley Crowther, the film critic for the *New York Times*, described it as 'the most meretricious sort of slush . . . a sublimely unreconstructed fantasy of the Old South . . . one might almost imagine that [Disney believed] Abe Lincoln made a mistake'.[2] That both Crowther and White saw the film's racial landscape in terms of the master–slave relationship tells us something about the regressiveness of Disney's adaptation: Harris's stories, published during the turn-of-the-century emergence of the New South, employ a frame narrative set during Reconstruction – so, though faithful to his former masters, Remus is nominally free – but *Song of the South*'s depictions of blacks heading off to work in the fields recalls the antebellum world of *Gone with the Wind*.

Film critics were not the only ones troubled by the film's racial politics: the National Negro Congress picketed *Song of the South* during its Manhattan run, and the movie drew a telegram of protest from New York Representative Adam Clayton Powell, Jr.[3] Matthew Bernstein's editorial for *Ebony* magazine reminded readers that *Song of the South* flew in the face of recent, war-driven improvement in the lives of black Americans, improvement manifested in Hollywood by 'Negroes getting several really good roles, like the Negro soldiers in *Bataan* and *Sahara*' (both released in 1943). Screened against this backdrop, *Song of the South* emerges as the purest reaction, and Bernstein predicted dire consequences for civil rights: '*Song of the South* cannot but retard America's biggest minority in its battle to get a square deal.'[4]

Yet, as acute as these criticisms of the film's racial politics were (and remain), they fail to explain the mass popularity of *Song of the South* despite its highly fraught and deeply compromised artistic and political status, a popularity registered by the two Academy Awards and further testified to by the film's continuing life in theatrical rerelease (in 1956, 1972, 1980 and 1986) and the construction of those Splash Mountain rides. It is tempting to attribute this popularity to the film's success in catering to racial fantasies of benevolent dominance and grateful submission among the white Americans who made up the majority of *Song of the South*'s audience, but such an analysis only partially accounts for the film's success. For, though the immediate post-war and early Cold War years saw the continuation of *de jure* segregation in US race relations, they also saw the beginning of the end of that segregation. Gunnar Myrdal's two-volume study of US racial discrimination, *An American Dilemma*, had been published two years before the release of *Song of the South*; one month after the film appeared, President Truman appointed a biracial committee on civil rights. In October 1947 (just months after Jackie Robinson had joined the major league), Truman's committee produced the now-famous report, 'To Secure These Rights', which called for the abolition of racial segregation. In 1948 a second presidential committee called for the end of segregation in the military, and Truman responded with Executive Order 9981, which demanded 'equality of treatment and opportunity for all persons in the armed services without regard to race, color, religion, or national origin'.[5] That same year the Supreme Court decision *Shelley* v. *Kraemer* held that state courts could not uphold restrictive racial covenants in housing. Thus it is hard to make a convincing case for Bernstein's assertion that the film deeply damaged the civil-rights cause, given that the reform was already partly under way and that the USA's post-war emergence as a world power rapidly transformed the nation's habits of racial discrimination from a domestic embarrassment into an international scandal.[6]

It is not sufficient, then, for the cultural critic faced with *Song of the South* simply to register the protest that greeted the film and to enumerate its objectionable aspects; and though Marxist accounts of uneven cultural development can account for the film's appeal to its most unreconstructed audience members despite (or thanks to) its appearance during the early years of the civil-rights movement, more recent approaches in cultural studies open the possibility that *Song of the South* had other effects on viewers. Thus the cultural critic must ask whether the film's backward glance to a supposedly 'simpler' time in US racial history may have contributed to the affective cultural work that furthered the arrival of the mid-Cold War civil-rights movement generally seen as hitting its stride with the 1954 *Brown* v. *Board of Education* of *Topeka, Kansas* Supreme Court decision and climaxing (though hardly concluding) with the passage of the 1965 Voting Rights Act.

Of all the negative reviews given to *Song of the South* in the year of its release, only Manny Farber's for the *New Republic* begins to address this question. Like his contemporaries, Farber finds much to dislike in the film: 'the honey-sweet Dixie presented in . . . *Song of the South* shows plantation life as a paradise for lucky slaves', he writes, a 'paradise' where 'cotton-pickers, straggling home after a carefree twenty-three hours in the fields, sing and chuckle as the sunset drips gold all over them'. Still, Farber notes, *Song of the South* is 'the first movie in years in which colored and white mingle throughout, and where both are handled with equal care and attention'.[7] Thus as regressive and repellent as its vision of race relations clearly was, *Song of the South* did white viewers the rare favour of offering – in a manner not unlike Harris's stories, and for a similarly volatile time – a vision of racial reconciliation and reciprocity that many found deeply satisfying.

My reading of *Song of the South*, then, can be said to pick up where Farber so suggestively leaves off in positing the film as a vague and flickering precursor of a shift in the racial attitudes of white Americans over the course of the Cold War years, a shift that led large numbers of white Americans to make common cause with African-Americans in the fight to end racial injustice. That *Song of the South*'s anticipatory articulation of this change nevertheless remains invested in racist modes of cultural expression raises complicated questions about the degree to which white sympathies for civil rights remained psychologically, if not politically, linked to racist dramas of identification and denial, and one task of this chapter is to illustrate the usefulness of film as a medium for analysing the complicated motivations underlying that investment.

I begin my discussion of the cultural work done by *Song of the South* with an overview of that undertaken more than a generation earlier by Harris's fiction, thereby demonstrating how narratives of US race relations repeatedly employ a set of tropes and gestures that both enable and compromise progressive reform. An understanding of these tropes reveals unexpected but striking homologies between the racist paternalism suffusing Harris's

Uncle Remus books and *Song of the South* and the racial romanticism informing works such as Mezz Mezzrow's *Really the Blues* (1946) and Norman Mailer's 1957 essay 'The White Negro'. In proclaiming their identification with, and sympathy for, the black man forced to live by his wits in a racially hostile country, Mezzrow and Mailer imagined themselves as latter-day Brer Rabbits, but careful reading of their work shows they have more in common with Harris. *Song of the South*, in drawing on and refashioning the framing material of one of Harris's lesser-known Remus collections (*Told by Uncle Remus*, published in 1905), additionally makes its dream of racial harmony contingent on a misogyny casting excessively independent-minded women as the chief obstacle barring the way to an American democratic utopia, a view given vehement expression just four years before the release of *Song of the South* in Philip Wylie's best-selling *Generation of Vipers* (1942).

The sum effect of this analysis of *Song of the South* may be to leave us with a troubling sense of the degree to which Cold War racial discourse among whites in the US remained enmeshed in preconscious racist and misogynist scenarios, fantastic projections of greed and need, even as many whites consciously worked towards a new era of equality. This uncanny effect of discovering a buried rhetoric lying just beneath the surface of its supposed retort is perhaps a consequence of taking film as our primary object of analysis. *Song of the South* made concretely visible, and so inescapably public, the affective importance of 'the Negro' in the white collective fantasy of American innocence and benevolence; in 'reminding' white America how much it loved its black folks, and in suggesting that their black folks loved them, too, the film also reminded whites of the unfinished task of creating a country 'in which colored and white mingle throughout'.[8] That *Song of the South* does this reminding by means of a thoroughly discredited reminiscence is certainly disturbing; but it is not, given the US racial history that preceded it (and that continued long afterwards), so terribly surprising.

WHITE NEGROES

The white man is a spoiled child, and when he gets the blues he goes neurotic. But the Negro never had anything before and never expects anything after, so when the blues get him he comes out smiling and without any evil feeling. 'Oh, well,' he says, 'Lord, I'm satisfied. All I wants to do is grow collard greens in my back yard and eat 'em.'

(Mezz Mezzrow, *Really the Blues*, 1946)[9]

The creation of Harris, a white journalist from Eatonton, Georgia, Uncle Remus made his first appearance in the pages of the *Atlanta Constitution* in the autumn of 1876 as 'an elderly ex-slave who occasionally dropped by the *Constitution* offices to beg from the staff and talk his darky talk'.[10] Over the course of about three years this Uncle Remus (whom Robert Hemenway describes as 'little more than a delegate for white Atlanta's views of Reconstruction blacks') evolved into a teller of animal tales: his first tale was published in the *Constitution* on 20 July 1879, and the tar baby story followed some five months later.[11] Within a year of the tar baby's appearance in print, the first 'Uncle Remus' collection – *Uncle Remus: His Songs and His Sayings* – was published to great critical acclaim. The popularity of the tales was such that nine more Uncle Remus volumes were published under Harris's name, two of them posthumously.

Harris once called himself 'an accidental author', and it should be remembered that, even though Uncle Remus was his creation, he never claimed to have invented the stories Remus tells.[12] Rather, Harris attributed the tales to the African-Americans he met while learning the printer's trade at Joseph Turner's *The Countryman*, a newspaper published at Turner's working plantation, Turnwold. Harris went on to use this store of tales as both passport and currency: trading stories with black labourers in Georgia granted him entry into a circle of fellowship not usually permitted between black and white men in the segregated New South even as it provided him with material for publication.[13]

Reading Harris's use of these tales in the light of Eric Lott's 1993 analysis of an economy of 'love and theft' driving the rise of minstrelsy in the antebellum North makes clear the degree to which Harris's creation of the character of Uncle Remus can be seen as a kind of literary minstrelsy, and the two halves of this economy have been offered, individually and in turn, as explanations for Uncle Remus's appeal for white readers.[14] Nineteenth- and early twentieth-century readers of the Remus stories almost certainly saw the tales as informed by, and imparting, a unifying and transcendent love binding together not only black and white but also North and South, regions only recently 'reunited' at the end of Reconstruction via the electoral compromise of 1876 and the withdrawal of Northern troops from the Southern states of the old Confederacy. 'A Story of the War', the tale in the first Uncle Remus collection that comes between 'His Songs' and 'His Sayings', literalises this notion of sectional reunification in the marriage of the Southern 'Miss Sally' (daughter of Remus's mistress, Ole Miss, and sister of the plantation's young master, 'Mars Jeems') and the Northern soldier John Huntingdon. The two meet after Remus shoots young Huntingdon out of a tree; Miss Sally nurses him back to health and into marriage and a post-war life on the plantation.

Huntingdon loses an arm as a consequence of the shooting, but he gains a wife and a faithful servant whom his bride and brother-in-law have always called 'Daddy'.[15] In response to an expression of astonishment from Huntingdon's sister Miss Theodosia (whose Remus nickname, 'Miss Doshy', will be reassigned to the Ole Miss figure in Song of the South) – 'Do you mean to say . . . that you shot the Union solder, when you knew he was fighting for your freedom?' – Remus explains that he shot out of his fear that the soldier was about to kill the homeward-bound 'Mars Jeems'. Guided by love, Remus takes his responsibilities as his white family's protective 'Daddy' far more seriously than his own prospects for freedom.[16]

Thus love was long accepted as the primary motivation for Harris's retelling of these tales, not only Remus's imagined love for his white folks but Harris's love for the Southern black subjectivity that white readers took to be his real subject. Many reviewers believed the books gave the first true portrait of the souls of black folk: the Dial applauded Harris for conveying the 'sentiments and habits of the negroes themselves'; Scribner's Monthly described Uncle Remus as 'true to character and tradition'.[17] Perhaps Harris's own emotional investment in Remus best accounts for this reaction; it is not going too far to say that, through Uncle Remus, Harris rewrote himself as a black man.[18] The notion that identificatory love informed this project of racial mimicry (or, more accurately, racial invention) was not seriously questioned by critics white or black (even Sterling Brown found merit in Harris's portrait[19]) until the years immediately following the Second World War, when the idea that this love might not be 'pure' – that it might stem from a paternalism born of a deeply held sense of black inferiority that blinds white author and white readers to the fury encoded in the Brer Rabbit tales themselves, and so blinds them to the possibility that in fact they are not loved – received its strongest expression in Bernard Wolfe's 1949 essay for Commentary, 'Uncle Remus and the Malevolent Rabbit'. This explosive and important essay (Frantz Fanon drew on its French translation in Les Temps modernes for his Black Skin, White Masks (1952)[20]) raised the possibility that Harris's performance as Uncle Remus was one of theft, not love, a theft motivated by a double desire to censor the revolutionary power of the Brer Rabbit tales (and thereby rationalise racial injustice) and to render as freely given that which actually had been stolen:

> Remus 'gives' with a 'kindly beam' and a 'most infectious chuckle' . . .
> But, if one looks more closely, within the magnanimous caress is an incredibly malevolent blow.
>
> . . .
>
> [In the Brer Rabbit tales of the first Remus collection] there are twenty-eight victories of the Weak over the Strong; ultimately all the

Strong die violent deaths at the hands of the Weak . . . is it too far-fetched to take Brer Rabbit as a symbol – about as sharp as Southern sanctions would allow – of the Negro slave's festering hatred of the white man?

. . .

Harris . . . fitted the hate-imbued folk materials into a framework, a white man's framework, of 'love'. . . . Within this framework of love, the blow was heavily padded with caresses and the genuine folk was almost emasculated into the cute folksy.

Almost, but not quite.[21]

In drawing attention away from the frame and to the tales themselves, Wolfe sought to resituate the site of blackness in the Uncle Remus texts, transferring it from the inauthentic 'plantation darky . . . ego ideal' of Harris's Remus to a Brer Rabbit seen as 'symbol . . . of the Negro slave's festering hatred of the white man'.[22] This reading of the Brer Rabbit tales as coded expressions of black fury over, and strategies for dealing with, racial injustice has become so well known as to require little elaboration here; as Wolfe puts it, 'the Negro slave, through his anthropomorphic Rabbit stories, seems to be hinting that even the frailest and most humble of "animals" can let fly with the most blood-thirsty aggressions'.[23] Harris's theft of these tales is thus motivated by a desire to 'emasculate' the enraged black subject at the centre of his text, and Wolfe's diction here is our first clue to the cultural work being done by this white rereading of Remus, this 're-masculating' rotation from love to theft, this rejection of maternal affection and turn towards manly rage.

Wolfe's essay on Uncle Remus is frequently cited in Harris scholarship; less well known is the unusual 'research' that informed the writing of this essay, research not in black folklore nor in Harris's writings but rather in the psychology of racial mimicry. Wolfe was the co-author of Mezz Mezzrow's *Really the Blues*, the narrative of white-to-black racial conversion published the same year as *Song of the South* that, as Gayle Wald has put it, helped shape the 'hipster ethic' of 'those postwar white male intellectuals whose romanticised appropriations of black culture were . . . instrumental to their development of a critique of the national social and cultural "mainstream"'.[24] Wald describes Mezzrow's book as a kind of passing narrative, partly because it was promoted as such by Random House, but the work is more accurately seen in the tradition of the religious conversion narrative: no one ever mistook Mezzrow for black, except perhaps Mezzrow himself, and the point of the memoir finally is to postulate an essentially black structure of feeling that nonetheless remains accessible to those not lucky enough to have been born into it. *Really the Blues* was a tremendous best-seller, going through six hardcover editions before being released in paperback; and, like Harris's Uncle Remus collections, the book was praised in the white press largely for its racial authenticity, its 'intensity' and 'realness'.[25] As Wald's description of the effect of *Really the Blues* indicates, Mezzrow's memoir deeply influenced white practitioners of the Beat style (Jack Kerouac, Allen Ginsberg, Norman Mailer) who imagined their own 'blackface' performance of hip as motivated by love (of black cultural style), expressive of hate (of white social injustice), and thus culturally and politically liberatory.

Yet 'it would be reckless to attribute to Mezzrow's practice of "voluntary Negro" passing an inherently politically disruptive or subversive agency', Wald notes.

> We cannot simply assume, that is to say, that the extolling of blues or jazz by those for whom, in Mezzrow's . . . words, it was not a 'birthright' was itself necessarily linked to the reduction of the suffering of a racially defined people, or indeed to any direct challenge to the structures of racial division and hierarchy.[26]

From our perspective, coming to Mezzrow's racial conversion via jazz from Harris's racial mimicry through folk tales, Wald's point may seem an obvious one: given that there was little that was politically progressive about Harris's dialect portrait of Uncle Remus, there is no compelling reason to believe, without a significant change in the social and/or political staging of the later performance, that Mezzrow's jive mimicry of Sidney Bechet would significantly differ in its effects (especially since, musically speaking, Mezzrow's copy was a poor one.) The question, then is whether in fact social conditions had changed enough to prompt a reinscription of white adoption of black cultural styles as subversive rather than patronising. Knowing the wrenching changes wrought on the American scene by the Second World War and its Cold War aftermath tempts us to supply an affirmative reply to this question; still, it is worth postponing our answer until we more closely examine Wolfe's Uncle Remus reading. Was Wolfe's critique of Remus shaped by a belief that Harris's blackface enacted a guilty theft, while Mezzrow's proceeded from true love?

In an afterword published in the 1990 reprint edition of *Really the Blues*, Wolfe briefly revisits the circumstances that led him to work with Mezzrow in the 1940s in terms that make clear both his awareness of the uncanny parallels between Mezzrow and Harris (though he never names Harris) and his sense of the complexity of the psychological terrain of blackface performance:

When I first sought [Mezzrow] out in a Greenwich Village jazz club somewhere around 1942, I knew nothing of this personal mythology. I thought he was simply an odd jazz musician who might be the subject for an interesting magazine article. After some nights with him on his home grounds in Harlem, I realized that it would take a lengthy book to do his reincarnation myth full justice. This is the book.

As the job was getting done, it dawned on me that though our ostensible subject was one very particular man it was really about an impersonal matter, a process that sweeps around and through many white American heads: Negrophilia. I began to wonder whether Negrophilia and Negrophobia were . . . polar opposites, or whether to get at the devious psychology of the thing you wouldn't have to see the two mindsets dialectically, in some other relationship than mere opposites. After *Really the Blues* was published, I wrote two essays on the subject, in 1947 and 1948.[27]

One of those essays was 'Uncle Remus and the Malevolent Rabbit', and there Wolfe detects this dialectic enacted in the double structure of Harris's narrative: the warm chuckling Remus is the embodiment of the author's 'Negrophilia', while the lying, violent Brer Rabbit releases his 'Negrophobia'. Wolfe's later analysis of the motivations driving 'Negrophiliac' whites like Mezzrow significantly complicates any effort to isolate a straightforwardly subversive or liberatory effect of post-war, Beat-era blackface. 'Feeling crushed by circumstances themselves,' he writes:

Negrophiliac whites prefer to see the Negro as a pre-social creature in whom the romping subjective is king; the Negro must be defined from 'within' because we feel ourselves so thoroughly puppetized from 'without'. The theory would seem to be that the Negro is *lucky* to be a pariah: banished to the outskirts of the community, he thus evades all the pressures and batterings to which one is subjected at the center and which are lethal to the 'inner spark'.

In this view aestheticism – which here means little more than emotionality, instinct-release, the good time . . . is a luxury of the periphery. It denotes a carefree, pleasure-bound state which must be given up when one becomes 'serious' and enters into the life of the workaday community.[28]

In other words, 'Negrophilia' is motivated largely by nostalgia, by the wish to return to a childlike condition in which a 'carefree, pleasure-bound state' may be enjoyed without end or consequences. Thus we find 'Negrophilia' and 'Negrophobia' in dialectic relation: both involve a use of black form, a projection of black shapes, that has more to do with white needs and anxieties than with black subjectivity; indeed, the Negrophile, in his need for black marginality, inadvertently may hamper civil-rights progress in ways different from, but no less consequential than, those of the Negrophobe. Thus Wolfe ultimately rejects the idea of clearly delineated 'good' and 'bad' blackface performance – of a clear separation of love and theft that would hinge *only* on the surface politics of blackface's moment of articulation – and recognising this dialectic allows us to see more clearly how a reactionary film like *Song of the South* may have a 'brer' relation to ostensibly progressive blackface performances like Mezzrow's. That a white wish to return to an infantile, 'carefree, pleasure-bound state' was keenly felt in the chaotic early Cold War years in the USA seems evident by the proliferation of that wish's effects: not only *Song of the South* and the rediscovery of blackface among Mezzrow and the Beats, but also Leslie Fiedler's postulate, in his reading of *Huckleberry Finn* (a novel begun at the close of Reconstruction and published two years after the appearance of Harris's second volume of Remus tales), of a 'profound child's dream of love in our relation to the Negro' as the founding myth of the American literary tradition, a myth that 'makes no attempt to whitewash our [racist] outrage as a fact; it portrays it as meaningless in the face of love'.[29] For the anxious and uncertain white Beats living in an era marked by shifting and unstable race relations, 'emotionality' and 'instinct-release' came in the form of jazz music; for similarly anxious and uncertain white Americans living through the end of Reconstruction and the installation of Jim Crow, they came in the form of narrative. The historical difference between the two forms of racial performance lies less in determining which is more liberatory (which seems rather obvious) than in accounting for the role of male rage as a newly incorporated and acceptable 'emotion' and 'instinct-release' for early Cold War white consumers of blackface – precisely the 're-masculating' work undertaken in Wolfe's essay. *Song of the South* models one expression of that anger in its construction of 'the laughing place'; Norman Mailer recuperates it for the white negro.

THE LAUGHING PLACE

Something in the argument, or the way Uncle Remus held his head, appealed to the little boy's sense of humor, and he laughed heartily for the first time since Uncle Remus had known him. It was real laughter, too, so real that the old Negro joined in with gusto, and the two laughed and laughed until it seemed unreasonable to laugh any more. To make matters worse, Uncle Remus pretended to become very solemn all of a sudden, and then just as suddenly went back to laughter again. This was more than the little chap could stand. He laughed until he writhed in the old man's arms; in fact, till laughter became painful.

(Joel Chandler Harris, 'The Reason Why', 1955)[30]

Introduced in Harris's fifth Uncle Remus collection, *Told by Uncle Remus*, Brer Rabbit's 'laughing place' signals a point where blackface humour becomes hostile, where pleasure becomes pain, and white acceptance of this disturbance as a kind of comfort becomes a crucial feature of *Song of the South*. Harris's frame narrative describes the brief 'retirement' of Remus from storytelling after 'the little boy to whom he had told his tales grew to be a very big boy' and his return to the business when, 'in the course of time, the man who had been the little boy . . . came to have a little boy of his own'. The Atlanta-based family of 'the man who had been the little boy' comes to visit the now-grandmotherly Miss Sally at the old plantation, and 'it happened in the most natural way in the world that the little boy's little boy fell under the spell of Uncle Remus'.[31] Remus, however, is somewhat disconcerted by this second little boy, who is nothing like his father:

> This latest little boy was frailer and quieter than his father had been; indeed, he was fragile, and had hardly any color in his face. But he was a beautiful child, too beautiful for a boy. He had large, dreamy eyes, and the quaintest little ways that were ever seen; and he was polite and thoughtful of others. He was very choice in the use of words, and talked as if he picked his language out of a book. He was a source of perpetual wonder to Uncle Remus . . .
>
> He was more like a girl in his refinement. All the boyishness had been taken out of him by that mysterious course of discipline that some mothers know how to apply.[32]

Harris makes clear that the boy needs remedial education in proper boyishness, and Remus tells Miss Sally as much when he asks her 'what dey gwine ter do wid dat chile? What dey gwiner ter make out'n 'im?' When she responds, 'I'm sure I don't know,' Remus avers, 'it's a pity – a mighty pity'.[33] The exchange leaves Miss Sally in tears, and in response to Remus's observation she sends the child to him later that very day. Remus begins his schooling of the boy by urging him to eat a potato custard that his mother had forbidden him; when the boy demurs ('mother said it wasn't good for me'), Remus argues that Miss Sally had 'writ wid de dishes' that the child was to eat it. The boy remains doubtful, and so Remus embarks on an explanation of double entendre:

> 'Now, spozin' yo pa wuz ter come 'long 'an say, "Unk Remus, I wanter gi' you a cuff". An' den, spozin' I wuz ter 'low, "Yasser, an' thanky, too, but you better gi' me a pa'r un um while you 'bout it". An' spozin' he'd be talkin' 'bout maulin' me, whiles I wuz talkin' 'bout dem contraptions what you got on yo' shirt-sleeves, an' you ain't got no mo' business wid um dan a rooster is wid britches. Spozin' all dat wuz ter happen, how you speck I'd feel?[34]

It is this disquisition that sends the boy into fits of laughter, the uncontrolled, hysterical laughter that, through Remus's manipulation, 'became painful' and that marks the beginning of his entry into proper boyhood – that is to say, the beginning of an understanding that prohibitions are actually invitations, and that pleasures can be painful.

Harris's rendering of the tale of the 'laughing place' is exemplary in this regard. Brer Rabbit's laughing place is taken by the animals to be a joy-giving source of envy – 'dey wonder an' wonder how Brer Rabbit kin have a laughin'-place an' dey ain't got none' – but it is soon revealed as a place where the joke will always be on them.[35] After leading the curious and eager Brer Fox into a thicket containing a hornet's nest, Brer Rabbit listens to the ensuing drama ('yap, yap, yap, an' ouch, ouch, ouch, an' yow yow yow') 'thumpin' de ground wid his behime foot an' laughin' fit ter kill'.[36] In Harris's narrative, this tale is framed by the boy's telling Remus that his own laughing place 'is right here where you are . . . you are my laughing-place'.[37]

Song of the South revises and dramatically amplifies two aspects of Harris's narrative of the laughing place: the lesson that violence born of anger and revenge can nonetheless be entertaining as well as liberating, and the notion that this lesson, crucial to the proper development of mollycoddled white boys, is best taught by blacks. The film opens with its own set of framing devices in the classic Hollywood 'carry me back' Southern style (a song about cotton, cabins and moonbeams; an establishing shot of an empty rocking chair before a glowing hearth with Remus's chuckle in voice-over) before we see a horse-drawn carriage carrying little Johnny (Bobby Driscoll), his nurse Aunt Tempy (Hattie McDaniel) and his tensely incommunicative parents John and Sally (Eric Rolf and Ruth Warrick) back to the old plantation of Sally's mother, Miss Doshy (Lucile Watson). Moments after their arrival John abandons wife and son to return to Atlanta, and most of the rest of the film is taken up with showing Johnny's grief over the loss of his father being given full compensation in the cabin of Uncle Remus. There he hears three

Brer Rabbit stories: Brer Rabbit in the trap, the story of the tar baby and the tale of the laughing place, all of which appear in animation and which fully exploit the cartoon image's skilful linking of violence with humour. Johnny is so captivated by the tales and the teller that he is moved to announce, in what is both the film's climax and its moment of crisis, that Uncle Remus's cabin is his own laughing place.

Before this moment, however, we see the uptight white Miss Sally growing increasingly troubled by her son's deepening admiration of Remus. Indeed, Johnny's mother looks to be a case study in 'momism', the chief source of American political and cultural weakness according to Philip Wylie's 1942 *Generation of Vipers*. For, rather than acknowledge that Johnny needs his father (an observation Remus makes in the first ten minutes of the film), Sally insists that mother and grandmother are enough; rather than let Johnny catch frogs with Toby (Glenn Leedy), his new black friend (that is, servant), Sally dresses the child up in a green velvet Fauntleroy suit complete with lace collar – an outfit leading to an entirely predictable bout of taunting ('look at the little girlie!') from the poor white Faver boys. She refuses to allow him to keep the hound puppy given to him by the pert, blonde Ginny Faver, true evidence of feminine heedlessness, since viewers know that Ginny rescued the dog after her brothers announced their intention to drown it (thus sending the puppy 'back where it came from' means sending it to its death). Miss Sally is so rigid and foolish, so full of her own ideas, that she very nearly kills her child. Moments after announcing that Remus is his laughing place, Johnny is run down by a bull when he cuts through a pasture in an effort to bring Remus back after the old man, told by Miss Sally to 'stay completely away' from Johnny, decides to leave the plantation. Miss Sally thus emerges as the perfect type of the 'ridiculous, vain, vicious' woman savaged by Wylie as that peculiarly 'American creation', mom:

> Mom is something new in the world of men. Hitherto, mom has been so busy raising a large family, keeping house, doing the chores, and fabricating everything in every home except the floor and the walls that she was rarely a problem to her family or to her equally busy friends, and never one to herself.
>
> Nowadays, with nothing to do, and all the tens of thousands of men . . . to maintain her, every clattering prickamette in the republic survives for an incredible number of years, to stamp and jibber in the midst of man, a noisy neuter by natural default or a scientific gelding sustained by science, all tongue and teat and razzmatazz. The machine has deprived her of social usefulness . . . and man has sealed his own

soul beneath the clamorous cordillera by handing her the checkbook and going to work in the service of her caprices.[38]

This is, of course, in many ways a recognisable version of a misogynistic screed whose roots extend back to antiquity. Wylie's twist of originality (if it can be called that) comes in establishing 'mom' as a particular problem for American freedom and democracy: a fan of Joe McCarthy, she is a kind of Hitler of comfort and conformism, a termagant whose relentless pursuit of bourgeois respectability enslaves the men around her.[39] As a specimen of the type, then, Miss Sally needs to be schooled in the meaning and importance of masculine freedom: she needs to accept her son's emancipation from her side, an emancipation that Remus and his 'laughing place' crucially enable, and she needs to accept her husband's authority. The final minutes of the film accomplish this twinning of emancipation and reunification with dispatch: father John rushes back to the plantation after the accident, but little Johnny refuses to recognise him until Uncle Remus is brought to his bedside. Remus's presence restores the boy to his senses; John pledges to 'stay right here, where I belong'; and Miss Sally promises her son that 'we'll have the laughingest place in the whole wide world'. The film concludes with Remus and the three children – Johnny, Ginny Faver, and Toby – romping in Brer Rabbit's cartoon wonderland, which Johnny is now able to summon up without the help of Remus.[40]

We are now in a position to see that certain aspects of *Song of the South* – most notably its anti-feminism and its imaginative representations of vengeful violence – find themselves rearticulated in Wolfe's re-masculinisation of Brer Rabbit's black rage. This rearticulation reaches a kind of apotheosis in 'The White Negro', Norman Mailer's analysis of the Beat hipster as 'the American existentialist' whose 'decision to encourage the psychopath' in himself derives from his complete absorption of 'the existentialist synapses of the Negro'.[41] In limning the outlines of this new American hero, Mailer expresses nothing but disdain for 'the cameos of security for the average white: mother and the home, job and the family', which emerge here as shackles blacks are lucky not to have:

the Negro (all exceptions admitted) could rarely afford the sophisticated inhibitions of civilization, and so he kept for his survival the art of the primitive, he lived in the enormous present, he subsisted for his Saturday night kicks, relinquishing the pleasures of the mind for the more obligatory pleasures of the body, and in his music he gave voice to the character and quality of his existence, to his rage and the infinite variations of joy, lust, languor, growl, cramp, pinch, scream and despair of his orgasm.[42]

We are recognisably back on the terrain of *Really the Blues*, with the significant addition of misogyny and unapologetic appeals to the 'primitivism' and 'psychopathology' of 'the Negro'. Mailer spills a great deal of ink on this question of the psychopath; understanding the psychopath, he claims, is key to understanding 'the Negro', white or black. But all that needs to be said about the psychopath appears early in the essay in an extract Mailer produces from Robert Lindner's *Rebel without a Cause*: 'The psychopath, *like the child*, cannot delay the pleasures of gratification; and this trait is one of his underlying, universal characteristics.'[43] Mailer's effort to translate this diagnosis along lines of psychic liberation ('In thus giving expression to the buried infant in himself, [the psychopath] can lessen the tension of those infantile desires and so free himself') is unconvincing.[44] Far from revealing the new and threatening urban landscape of the country's homegrown existentialist, Mailer escorts us back to *Song of the South*, specifically to that moment in the film when Johnny, in his rage and despair over losing the puppy, cries out, 'Uncle Remus, you're the best friend I have!'

Mailer's essay was, of course, not allowed to pass unquestioned by black intellectuals: 'The White Negro' drew sharp responses from James Baldwin and Lorraine Hansberry, among others. But the fact that Mailer, a strong supporter of civil rights, insisted, long after his flaws were pointed out to him, on keeping the essay alive through republication in *Advertisements for Myself* (where he called it 'one of the best things I have done') reveals the affective cultural work Uncle Remus continued to do in a Cold War social and political climate ostensibly hostile to his brand of racial mimicry.[45] *Song of the South* touches the chords of a tune that America knows by heart, a tune amenable to endless variation and with more than one verse, but always recognisable and almost tragically catchy.

NOTES

1. Bosley Crowther, 'Spanking Disney', *New York Times*, 8 December 1946, p. 5; 'White Regrets Film', *New York Times*, 28 November 1946, p. 40; Matthew Bernstein, 'Needed: A Negro Legion of Decency', *Ebony* (February 1947), p. 36.
2. Anon., 'White Regrets Film', *New York Times*, 28 November 1946, p. 40; Bosley Crowther, 'Spanking Disney', *New York Times*, 8 December 1946, p. 5.
3. *New York Times*, 14 December 1946, p. 18; *New York Times*, 24 December 1946, p. 12.
4. Matthew Bernstein, 'Needed: A Negro Legion of Decency', *Ebony* (February 1947), p. 36.
5. The Truman Library has made Executive Order 9981 available online at http://www.trumanlibrary.org/9981a.htm
6. See Mary L. Dudziak, *Cold War Civil Rights: Race and the Image of American Democracy* (Princeton: Princeton University Press, 2000).
7. Manny Farber, 'Movies: Dixie Corn', *New Republic*, 115, 23 December 1946, p. 879.
8. Ibid. p. 879.

9. Mezz Mezzrow with Bernard Wolfe, *Really the Blues*, with an introduction by Barry Gifford (New York: Citadel Underground, [1946] 1990), p. 14.
10. Robert Hemenway, 'Introduction: Author, Teller, and Hero' (1982), in Joel Chandler Harris, *Uncle Remus: His Songs and His Sayings* ([1880] 1982; New York: Penguin Classics, 1986), p. 13.
11. Ibid. pp. 13, 14.
12. Paul M. Cousins, *Joel Chandler Harris* (Baton Rouge, LA: Louisiana State University Press, 1968), p. 143.
13. Hemenway, 'Introduction', p. 17.
14. Eric Lott, *Love and Theft: Blackface Minstrelsy and the American Working Class* (New York: Oxford University Press, 1995).
15. Harris, *Uncle Remus: His Songs and his Sayings*, pp. 181–2.
16. For a fuller discussion of Uncle Remus as a figure for reunification, see Hemenway, 'Introduction', pp. 20–1 and John T. Matthews, 'How Remus Frames Race', forthcoming.
17. Hemenway, 'Introduction', p. 14.
18. Ibid. p. 17. See his discussion of Harris's creation of a black persona through his writing (pp. 9–18).
19. See Sterling Brown, *The Negro in American Fiction*, published with *Negro Poetry and Drama*, with a preface by Robert Bone (New York: Atheneum, 1969), pp. 53–8.
20. Frantz Fanon, *Black Skin, White Masks*, trans. Charles Lam Markmann (New York: Grove Weidenfeld, [1952] 1967). See pp. 49–50 n. 7 for the first mention of Wolfe's essay, and pp. 173–6 for Fanon's discussion of its findings.
21. Bernard Wolfe, 'Uncle Remus and the Malevolent Rabbit', *Commentary*, 8/1 (July 1949), pp. 31–2, 35. For a reading of Harris's frame narrative emphasising its connection to the social content encoded in the animal tales, see Matthews, 'How Remus Frames Race'.
22. Wolfe, 'Uncle Remus and the Malevolent Rabbit', p. 40.
23. Ibid. p. 34.
24. Gayle Wald, *Crossing the Line: Racial Passing in Twentieth-Century US Literature and Culture* (Durham, NC and London: Duke University Press, 2000), p. 59.
25. Ibid. p. 58.
26. Ibid. p. 60.
27. Bernard Wolfe, 'Afterword', in Mezzrow and Wolfe, *Really the Blues*, p. 390.
28. Ibid. p. 401.
29. Leslie Fiedler, 'Come Back to the Raft Ag'in, Huck Honey', in Gerald Graff and James Phelan (eds), *The Adventures of Huckleberry Finn*, by Mark Twain (Boston: Bedford Books, 1995), pp. 532, 534. Fielder's essay was originally published in 1948 in *Partisan Review* and expanded into his famous 1960 study, *Love and Death in the American Novel*. For two readings of the essay in the light of recent feminist and gay literary theories, see Christopher Looby, '"Innocent Homosexuality": The Fiedler Thesis in Retrospect', also in Graff and Phelan (eds), *Huckleberry Finn*, pp. 535–50, and Robyn Wiegman, 'Fielder and Sons', in Harry Stecopoulos and Michael Uebel (eds), *Race and the Subject of Masculinities* (Durham, NC, and London: Duke University Press, 1997), pp. 45–68.
30. Joel Chandler Harris, 'The Reason Why', in *Told by Uncle Remus*, in *The Complete Tales of Uncle Remus*, compiled by Richard Chase (Boston: Houghton Mifflin Company, 1955), p. 585.
31. Ibid. p. 579.
32. Ibid. pp. 579–80.
33. Ibid. p. 580.
34. Ibid. p. 585.
35. Harris, 'Brother Rabbit's Laughing-Place', in *The Complete Tales*, p. 608.
36. Ibid. p. 612.
37. Ibid. p. 606.

38. Philip Wylie, *Generation of Vipers* (Normal, IL: Dalkey Archive Press, [1942] 1996), pp. 196, 197, 199.
39. See ibid. p. 206 for the Hitler analogy and p. 209 for the slavery comparison.
40. See James Snead, 'Trimming Uncle Remus's Tales: Narrative Revisions in Walt Disney's *Song of the South*', in Colin MacCabe and Cornel West (eds), *White Screens, Black Images: Hollywood from the Dark Side* (New York: Routledge 1994), pp. 81–99.
41. Norman Mailer, 'The White Negro: Superficial Reflections on the Hipster', in Mailer, *Advertisements for Myself* (New York: G. P. Putnam's Sons, 1959), pp. 339, 341.
42. Ibid. p. 341.
43. Ibid. p. 344; emphasis added.
44. Ibid. p. 346.
45. Mailer, 'Sixth Advertisement for Myself', in Mailer, *Advertisements for Myself*, p. 335.

Chapter Seven

Literature

Policing Dissent: 'Orwell' and Cold War Culture, 1945–2004

Scott Lucas

Since his death in 1950, George Orwell has been widely acclaimed as the greatest English political writer of the twentieth century, exalted for 'his genius . . . his importance for our world, which fails to match his standards of justice and decency in almost every conceivable way'.[1] 'Orwell' is represented as our guide to freedom and our sentry warning of ever-present threats to it. He is invoked as the visionary of totalitarianism and of the betrayal of revolutions. He is revered as the 'contrarian' and the 'dissenter' standing against establishments at home and abroad.

It is the contention of the essay that this 'Orwell' is a mythical figure, created by the author while he was alive and re-created and mobilised by others, notably the state–private network in the United States and Britain, in the cultural battle against Soviet communism in the Cold War. It is the contention of this chapter that, far from being the contrarian, the writing and private sentiments of 'Orwell' were invaluable to the American and British governments. Far from being the defender of dissent, 'Orwell' helped limit and even suppress it through his words, through his relationships with other Cold Warriors, and through his passing of the names of 'crypto-communists' and other suspects to British intelligence services.

Orwell's designated enemies were those on the 'left', irrespective of communist affiliation, who had caused offence by pursuing differing socialisms, differing theories (or even the very notion of economic or social 'theory'), differing perspectives on British foreign policy. In the Manichaean world of the Cold War, Orwell finally left no ground between support of the freedom-loving West and the tyrants of Moscow. For those who tried to occupy such ground, the outcome was a naming and shaming not only in Orwell's essays but also in selection and handover to those whom Orwell could have parodied elsewhere as 'Big Brother'. It was an outcome in harmony with the ideology and strategy of a US government that declared, long before Joseph McCarthy, that the communist subversive lurked everywhere, 'each carrying with him the germs of death for society'.[2]

Orwell had become a vital part of a 'state–private network' developed to fight a total campaign for hearts and minds. Political, economic and military superiority would not suffice in the contest with the Soviet bloc; the American way of life also had to triumph. Both in his direct connection with British intelligence services, when he handed over the names of thirty-eight 'crypto-communists' who were not only unreliable as propagandists but potentially subversive, and in his close relationship with writers like Arthur Koestler who would be the first wave of CIA-supported intellectuals, Orwell the man and Orwell the myth played a vital role in defining the US-led crusade for 'cultural freedom'.

Thus, although Orwell was the archetypal 'English' writer of the twentieth century, he was increasingly projected as the voice of an American-defined 'freedom' to be spread around the world. That freedom was usually defined negatively, however, in terms of the threat of Soviet communism rather than positively in terms of political or economic liberation. Indeed, within weeks of the publication of *Nineteen Eighty-Four*, Orwell was having to insist in a press release that he was a good socialist, countering American newspapers and magazines that exulted in the demolition of English socialism as well as totalitarian communism.

This Cold War framing transcended Orwell's death in 1950 and it would transcend the death of the Soviet foe in 1991. The representation of Orwell in American political culture as the foe of a naïve or dangerous 'left' has been revived after 11 September 2001, labelling and ostracising a 'left' that is now supposedly allied with Islamo-fascists and Saddam Hussein rather than Joseph Stalin. At the end of 2001, Christopher Hitchens warned: 'If one looks closely at the writings of the younger intellectual pacifists, one finds that they do not by any means express impartial disapproval but are directed almost entirely against Britain and the United States.'[3] The allegation is not original: it was first put by George Orwell in his 1945 essay 'Notes on Nationalism'.

The early Cold War was a period in which America would take on the image of 'the age of conformity'. In fact, literature of the period would express disquiet with the tensions of life at home and abroad, be it through the misogynistic tracts of Philip Wylie, the melodrama of Grace Metalious's *Peyton Place*, the detective fiction of Mickey Spillane or the novels of Norman Mailer. Those tensions would not be resolved, but they could be assuaged with the assurance that America's foes represented greater evils.

This assurance most effectively came not from the 'right' but from the 'left'. In 1952 *Partisan Review*, the journal that had travelled from Trotskyist origins to the anti-Communist frontline, set out the manifesto with contributors such as Philip Rahv, Lionel Trilling and Leslie Fiedler defining 'Our Country and Our Culture'. It is perhaps the consummate irony that Orwell, the proponent of Englishness who had sent 'Letters from London' to *Partisan Review* during the war, would be adopted as the icon of an American Oceania that he had never seen first hand.

> My worry has more to do with another thing Orwell warned about – the willingness of people to police themselves, and to believe anything that they're told. Especially the willingness of intellectuals and academics to become worshipers of whomever is in power, or passers-on of whatever the reigning idea is.
>
> (Christopher Hitchens, October 2002)[4]

The centenary has passed. George Orwell, born Eric Blair in Motihari, India, in 1903, has been celebrated as England's greatest political writer. With few troublesome exceptions, he has been hailed for 'his genius . . . his importance for our world, which fails to match his standards of justice and decency in almost every conceivable way'.[5] He is our 'moral force' against unnamed 'orthodoxies . . . wearing yet more elaborate disguises', our saviour from the 'great threats' of 'religious totalitarianism and the rise of global plutocracy'.[6] Journalists retrace his steps to Wigan, which now has a pier for the tourists, one of Britain's leading artists re-creates the 'real' Room 101 in the BBC's Broadcasting House, biographers and essayists pore over photographs and desperately seek a home movie to secure their George.[7]

Meanwhile 'Orwell' continues to be wielded, not necessarily to uphold dissent but to bludgeon it into submission. As I write this in January 2004, Leo McKinstry in the *Daily Telegraph* has invoked Orwell's warning in 'Notes on Nationalism' of 'intellectual pacifists whose real, though unacknowledged, motive appears to be a hatred of western democracy and an admiration for totalitarianism'.[8] In the American journal *Dissent*, Joann Barkan tried to stifle the concept, used the same Orwellian essay as an epiphany: 'Coming across the notion of "negative nationalism" again has been useful for thinking about the blame-America-first leftists with their obsessiveness, resentments, and ability to shut out inconvenient realities.'[9] British Prime Minister Tony Blair echoed Orwell's Second World War call to arms, *The Lion and the Unicorn*, to swat away opposition and claim a 'foreign policy, robust on defence and committed to global justice. [This idea enables] us to espouse positions that in the past the left had regarded as impossible to reconcile: patriotism and internationalism'.[10]

'Orwell' lives on, yet his survival is far from the simple exaltation of 'freedom' claimed by those who invoke him. In their polemics, they use the author to silence those who dare question the foreign policy of Washington and London and, in so doing, expose an Orwellian relationship with Cold War culture that continues to this day. Whatever the merits of the author's writing and observations, he cannot be separated from his central place in a contest in which the American and British states overtly and covertly tried to define the battle for hearts and minds both at home and abroad. As the *New York Times* review of *Nineteen Eighty-Four* summarised: 'No other work of this generation has made us desire freedom more earnestly or loathe tyranny with such fulness.'[11]

I

In early 1999 Christopher Hitchens, British born but now a fixture on the American intellectual and literary stage, offered an affidavit to Republican Congressmen prosecuting the impeachment of Bill Clinton. While his ultimate target was the President, his specific complaint was that Sidney Blumenthal, Hitchens's close friend since the 1980s and now an aide to Clinton, had revealed that the President had described Lewinsky as a stalker. If true, the remark could put Blumenthal in jail for perjury, as he had just denied to the congressional investigators that he made any such remark.

Within days, Hitchens was being labelled by New York and Washington columnists as 'Christopher Snitchens'. Alexander Cockburn, Hitchens's colleague at *The Nation*, declared: 'As a Judas and a snitch, Hitchens has made the big time.' The immediate *casus belli* might be a domestic political storm, years after the fall of the Soviet Union; however, the rhetoric and substance of the charge were from the America of the early Cold War, when intellectuals took sides over the ethics and morality of testifying to the FBI and the House Un-American Activities Committee (HUAC). Navasky made the historical link: 'To cooperate with opportunistic prosecutors or prosecutorial operations raises real questions, as it did in the Fifties when people who cooperated legitimized these operations.'[12]

Indeed, both sides in the Hitchens–Blumenthal affair could claim a direct descent from a specific incident of a 'decent' writer, perhaps the most decent of all, naming names in Cold War Anglo-America. A year before Hitchens's affidavit, he and Alexander Cockburn had debated whether George Orwell was a 'snitch'.[13]

On 29 March 1949 Orwell, reclining gaunt and tubercular in a Gloucestershire sanatorium, less than a year from his death, received a special guest. Celia Kirwan, the sister-in-law of Arthur Koestler and a former editorial assistant at the journals *Horizon* and *Polemic*, both outlets for Orwell's essays, had been one of the objects of Orwell's infatuations after the death of his wife in 1945. The author had quickly proposed marriage; Kirwan 'gently refused him' but they remained close friends.[14]

By 1949 Kirwan had a professional as well as a personal interest in seeing Orwell, for she was working for the top-secret Information Research Department (IRD). Created in January 1948 by a Labour government trying to manoeuvre between Stalin's Soviet Union and the capitalism of the United States, the IRD was working with the Foreign Office and MI6 to generate and distribute pro-British and anti-Communist propaganda at home and overseas. The department's standard operating procedure was to pass useful 'information' to journalists, authors, trade unions and voluntary associations, who then disseminated the material under their own names.[15]

During her visit, Kirwan just happened to 'discuss some aspects of [IRD's] work' with Orwell. She reported: 'He was delighted to learn of them, and expressed his wholehearted and enthusiastic approval of our aims.' Unable to write for IRD because of his health, the author eagerly suggested the names of others who could be helpful.[16] And there was more: Orwell had a blue notebook of 135 'crypto-communists' and other suspects whom he thought would be of interest to Kirwan and her colleagues; he duly dispatched his friend and future literary executor Richard Rees to retrieve the notebook from his London flat. A week later, after pondering, 'The whole difficulty is to decide where each person stands, & one has to treat each case individually', Orwell sent Kirwan the thirty-eight names that merited the IRD's further attention.[17]

Beyond the celebrity of a Chaplin, a Priestley, a Michael Redgrave being proffered to British intelligence, the suspects were bland fare. There were two Soviet agents, the jailed physicist Alan Nunn May and Peter Smollett of the wartime Ministry of Information, who had intervened to stop Jonathan Cape publishing *Animal Farm* (1945) as an anti-Soviet fable. There was Tom Driberg, the flamboyant Member of Parliament who was in contact with MI5 as well as officials from the Soviet Embassy. Then, however, it was a case of the *Daily Express*'s correspondent Alaric Jacob, who dared to think during the Second World War that the Soviet society was 'basically a just one', of *Guardian* reporters and editors who did not sufficiently criticise Moscow, of a prominent historian like E. H. Carr whose interpretation was the 'wrong' one, of a novelist like Naomi Mitchison who apparently was a 'silly sympathiser', or a Nobel Prize-winning physicist like Patrick Blackett whose transgression is still unclear.[18]

For those carrying the mantle of Orwell into the twenty-first century, the incident has been a recurrent distraction. It was first revealed to a general audience in 1996, after some files of the IRD were finally released at the British Public Record Office. There was a refrain two years later, when Peter Davison published a censored version of the notebook in his twenty-volume catalogue of Orwell's life and work, and another resurgence in 2003 when Timothy Garton Ash obtained the thirty-eight names. (Garton Ash was shown a copy of an IRD report by Celia Kirwan's daughter; in a sudden declaration of openness, the British government declassified the document.)[19]

Far from giving any ground in the portrayal of Orwell as unblemished champion of liberty, his supporters compiled volumes of explanations and dismissals. Foremost amongst them was the depiction of the event as trivial. Hitchens tried to fend off Perry Anderson's careful recitation of the facts by claiming that this was no more than a bit of fun between Orwell and Rees: 'It is quite possible to respect [Orwell's] memory . . . without approving his service to the secret state,' with the same decoy of a 'game [that] consisted of guessing which public figures would, or would not, sell out in the event of an invasion or a dictatorship'.[20]

For those who saw that this thin line might not hold, there were other rationales. Orwell was 'depressed and mortally ill'. He had 'continued strong feelings for a particularly attractive, warmhearted, and cultured woman'. There was the false representation that the IRD had little to do with British intelligence services, and the breezy assertion that none of this ultimately mattered: 'Nothing bad happened to' those on 'the List'.[21]

Yet, in many of these protests, there was the (unacknowledged) admission that the contradictions of Orwell's could not be resolved. There was no possibility of squaring the circle of the creator of Big Brother cooperating with a British Big Brother 'to discover which individuals are honest and which are not'.[22] In the 1990s and into the twenty-first century, it was only in the sanctuary of a 'Cold War culture' that 'Orwell' could be rescued.

In that culture, both then and now, 'freedom' had to sit side by side with 'security', the rhetorical claim that Orwell was right to identify the enemy within. 'He, unlike some liberals of a later generation (or old fellow travellers who never can forgive him for "premature anti-Stalinism"),' pronounced Bernard Crick, 'took the communist threat seriously'. Timothy Garton Ash added, 'He thought there was a war on, a "cold war", and he feared that the Western nations were losing it', partly because of 'the work of a poisonous array of naive and sentimental admirers of the Soviet system, declared Communist Party (CP) members, covert ("crypto-") communists, and paid Soviet spies'. Hitchens, after a series of contradictory explanations for 'this relatively trivial episode', finally jettisoned the game for 'a confrontation with the poisonous illusion that the Soviet system had a claim on the democratic Left'.[23] Long before the New America of the twenty-first century, Orwell was exonerated with the language of 'with us or against us'.

II

Certainly Orwell's political activity, as well as his writing, was closely concerned with 'freedom'. In 1945 he and his good friend Arthur Koestler promoted a Freedom Defence Committee, formed after the prosecution of an anarchist newspaper for anti-militarist propaganda. He fretted about the treatment of real and prospective foes, criticising the treatment in liberated France of 'collaborators' and expressing concern that the ten-year sentence on the scientist Alan Nunn May, convicted of passing secret information to the Soviet Union, was too harsh.[24] On more than one occasion, he opposed a ban on the Communist Party.[25]

However, this positive projection of 'freedom' was always intertwined with and even constricted by a vision of the enemy that might extinguish it. By 1943 Orwell had turned away from the challenge of 'fascism' to the spectre of the 'revolution betrayed', drafting the 'little squib' that would become *Animal Farm*. He worried that 'the English left-wing intelligentsia worship Stalin because they have lost their patriotism and their religious belief without losing the need for a god and a fatherland'.[26]

Even more important than Orwell's allegory of Soviet history was the issue of 'freedom' within. Stephen Sedley's case that *Animal Farm* 'does not begin to cast light on what for any socialist is the real question: what has gone wrong and why?' is well made but tangential.[27] Orwell was not analysing but sounding a warning. As early as 1938, Orwell had decided that 'the very important question . . . is whether a western country can in practice be controlled by Communists acting under Russian orders'; so, long before the end of the war with Germany, he 'consider[ed] that willingness to criticise Russia and Stalin is the test of intellectual honesty'.[28] From here it was only a short jump to claim, in 1947, that those who advocated cooperation rather than confrontation with Moscow were 'crypto-Communist . . . pursuing a policy barely distinguished from that of the CP [Communist Party] and . . . are in effect the publicity agents of the USSR in this country'.[29]

Orwell's position was not a product of the Cold War. As early as 1936, he had staked out his differences from the 'left' through the diatribe in Part Two of *The Road to Wigan Pier* against the 'warm-hearted, unthinking' socialist of the working class or the middle-class socialist, 'intellectual, book-trained . . . out of touch with common humanity . . . [with his] soggy half-baked insincerity and his pullover, his hair, and his Marxian quotation'.[30] His experiences in the Spanish Civil War bolstered his hatred of 'hack-journalists and the pansy Left, parlour Bolsheviks, and sleek little professors', and his sudden conversion to the 'English' war effort in 1940 was highlighted by the denunciation of 'the people whose hearts have never leapt at the sight of a Union Jack [and] who will flinch from revolution when the time comes'. Readers could rest assured that 'the direct, conscious attack on intellectual decency comes from the intellectuals themselves'.[31]

In Orwell's changing political scenarios, the 'left' could never be on the correct side. When the author embraced pacifism on his return from Spain, it was the 'left' that was advocating a 'war against Germany' in which its members would 'associate themselves with the fascising process'. However, when Orwell trumpeted the 'English patriotism' of a fight against Hitler, it was the pacifists of the 'left' who were 'objectively pro-Fascist'.[32] Any protest of the 'left' against imperialism was a sham 'since its adherents 'earn[ed] their living by demanding something that they don't generally want', even as Orwell the anti-imperialist was explaining that 'it was still possible to be an imperialist and a gentleman'.[33]

There was no need then to co-opt or manipulate Orwell into service for the Cold War campaign of the US government. His long-established, if ill-defined, antipathy to all groups 'left' was ideal for the general pursuit of 'anti-communism', one in which not only communists but also 'fellow travellers' and even those with suspect views of American foreign policy had to be policed and curbed. After all, for Orwell, 'it [was] a fact that the Communists are at present the main danger to the Government and might become a real political force if some calamity abroad – for example, large-scale fighting in India – made the Government's foreign policy acutely unpopular'.[34] Meanwhile, his summoning of 'freedom' could serve as the positive dimension of the state-private network

As early as 1943 Orwell had begun writing to correspondents about a possible mobilisation of British and European writers. Not all the authors were in Orwell's political camp – he included the 'crew' of Alex Comfort, the pacifist and anarchist poet with whom he had sharply clashed a year earlier – but most were already doing wartime service at the BBC. In 'As I Please', his column for the *Tribune* newspaper, Orwell went further by touting Ignazio Silone, André Malraux, Franz Borkenau and the Belgian Victor Serge, all of whom were fervent anti-communists, and contrasting them with 'suspect' counterparts such as Harold Laski.

A central place in this network was reserved for Arthur Koestler. As the ex-communist who had nobly exposed the cruelties of his Soviet masters in *Darkness at Noon* (1940), Koestler was establishing a special place in the

Anglo-American political culture even as he stepped foot in Britain. A year before Moscow turned from enemy to ally against Hitler, *Darkness at Noon* had exposed the evil that 'decent' democracies should fight. And, as soon as Moscow turned from ally to enemy in 1945, Koestler's condemning work would be cited with renewed vigour on both sides of the Atlantic.

Soon after his arrival in Britain in 1940, Koestler had visited Orwell. By the end of the war, the relationship was reversed, with Orwell a frequent guest at Koestler's home in north Wales, staying over Christmas and New Year of 1945–6. The two men had already formed the Freedom Defence Committee and proposed 'psychological disarmament', with free distribution of British newspapers, books and other materials within the Soviet Union, when in March 1946 Orwell responded to an approach by an American trade unionist with the proposal that Koestler contact the International Relief and Rescue Committee. The IRRC was soon asking Koestler to carry out a lecture tour of the USA.

This was far more, however, than cooperation with a benevolent 'private' organisation. The IRRC had close links with the US government, eventually receiving most of its funding from the CIA, and the State Department endorsed Koestler's tour 'as highly desirable in the national interest'.[35] Over three months in spring 1948, Koestler met the leadership of the anti-communist intelligentsia, including Philip Rahv, Daniel Bell, Lionel Trilling, Sidney Hook, Mary McCarthy and James Burnham, as well as the wartime director of US intelligence services, William Donovan. Through the influential journal *New Leader*, which was also covertly supported by the US government, Koestler was introduced to the ex-communist Max Eastman, union leader (and CIA contact) David Dubinsky, Eugene Lyons and Dwight McDonald.[36] Most of these new friends joined Koestler as founding members of the Congress for Cultural Freedom, developed with the cooperation of the US government in 1949 and funded by the CIA as the intellectual vanguard of the 'free world'.

Reduction of Orwell's last novel, *Nineteen Eighty-Four*, to an anti-communist polemic risks simplicity, even crudity. As the author argued, the book was a broader presentation of 'totalitarian ideas [that] have taken root in the minds of intellectuals everywhere' and an attempt to 'draw these ideas out to their logical consequences'.[37] Totalitarianism did not arise solely from communist ideology and systems; centralised authority and the extension of technology to control, rather than liberate, the population could be features of any society. When confronted by interpretations in American magazines such as *Time* and *Life* that he was identifying threats such as Britain's governing Labour Party, Orwell responded: 'My recent novel is NOT intended as an attack on Socialism or on the British Labour Party (of which I am a supporter) but as a show-up of the perversions to which a centralised economy is liable and which have already been partly realised in Communism and Fascism.'[38]

The problem, however, was that Orwell had left himself open to such interpretations, with his long-term antipathy to others on the 'left' finding specific expression in *Nineteen Eighty-Four*'s representations not only of communism but of the system of 'Ingsoc' (English Socialism). Orwell's publisher, Fredric Warburg, commented when he first read the manuscript:

> This I take to be a deliberate and sadistic attack on socialism and socialist parties generally . . . It seems to indicate a final breach between Orwell and socialism, not the socialism of equality and human brotherhood which clearly Orwell no longer expects from socialist parties, but the socialism of Marxism and the managerial revolution.[39]

Orwell may have entered into, and even laid the foundation for, the definition of a new concept of power and society; two years later, Hannah Arendt would publish her seminal book on the *Origins of Totalitarianism*. However, where Arendt's work was a critique of the phenomenon, which did not define itself through attention to 'right' or 'left', Orwell's ideas were taken in only one direction. As Philip Rahv of *Partisan Review* announced:

> This novel is the best antidote to the totalitarian disease that any writer has so far produced . . . I recommend it particularly to those liberals who still cannot get over the political superstition that while absolute power is bad when exercised by the right, it is in its very nature good and a boon to humanity once the left, that is to say 'our own people', takes hold of it.

A newspaper vendor was more concise when he told Isaac Deutscher, a member of 'Orwell's List' and future critic of *Nineteen Eighty-Four*, 'You must read this book, sir. Then you will know why we must drop the atomic bomb on the Bolshies.'[40]

'The List' not only made manifest that Orwell's specific concerns were with 'left' rather than 'right'; it confirmed that he was willing to cooperate with the state in the monitoring and possible suppression of such suspects. In one sense, however, 'the List' is a distraction, for it was the 'positive' projection of 'Orwell' that would soon occupy the state.

Orwell had already provided some assistance in 1947 when he wrote a special introduction for an edition of *Animal Farm* for Ukrainian displaced persons, a key audience for American agencies seeking to foment 'nationalist' insurgency against Moscow. After his burial, however, there were greater opportunities for exploitation. The CIA moved quickly to obtain the film rights to *Animal Farm* from Orwell's widow, Sonia; according to the covert operator, E. Howard Hunt (later of Watergate infamy), Sonia's price was an introduction to Clark Gable. When *Animal Farm* was released in 1954, the FBI declared that it 'hit the jackpot'. Two years later the film version of *1984*, which received similar encouragement from the US government, was distributed. The American Committee for Cultural Freedom, another 'private' organisation funded by the CIA, offered advice on the screenplay. (Once more 'the List' offered an irony; one of its most famous members, Michael Redgrave, played O'Brien.)[38]

British intelligence services also played their part in the promotion of England's greatest political writer. Burmese, Chinese and Arabic editions of his *Animal Farm* were distributed, and the IRD developed a comic-strip version of the book for countries such as India, Burma, Eritrea, Thailand, Mexico, Venezuela and Brazil. In 1954, when a new edition of *Animal Farm* appeared alongside the release of the film, Christopher Woodhouse gave a glowing endorsement in the *Times Literary Supplement*:

> *Animal Farm* will not, like *Uncle Tom's Cabin*, contribute to changing history within a decade or so, but it probably has as good a chance as any contemporary work of winning its author a place – unacknowledged, of course – among Shelley's legislators of the world . . . If the worst comes to the worst and [Orwell] fails as a legislator, he is then virtually certain of immortality as a prophet.

Woodhouse's credit at the end of the review did not mention that he was an officer in MI6.[42]

The direct use of Orwell by the state, however, was only a manifestation of a much wider appropriation of 'Orwell' for Cold War culture. In the USA, his death was opportune for those looking for an icon against perceived enemies at home and abroad. He was the personification of Arthur Schlesinger's 'vital center', a bastion of common sense sustaining Daniel Bell's 'end of ideology' and embodying Irving Howe's 'dissent'. (This 'vital center' was not limited to the page; both Schlesinger and Bell were important activists in the CIA-backed Congress for Cultural Freedom.)[43]

Orwell's exaltation was led by Lionel Trilling, a self-professed pioneer of the moral middle way. Trilling anointed Orwell as the 'St George' of common sense:

> It is hard to find personalities in the contemporary world who are

analogous to Orwell. We have to look for men who have considerable intellectual power but who are not happy in the institutionalised life of intellectuality; who have a feeling for an older and simpler time, and a guiding awareness of the ordinary life of the people, yet without any touch of the sentimental malice of populism; and a strong feeling for the commonplace; and a direct unabashed sense of the nation, even a conscious love of it.[44]

Just as Orwell had used 'decency' in the 1930s to berate those socialists who set out a theoretical approach to economic and social issues, so the illusion of a common-sensical pragmatism and the 'center' was directed primarily against the supposed 'left'. Orwell was 'the wintry conscience of a generation which in the thirties had heard the call to the rasher assumptions of political faith', of 'the intellectuals who would not revert to [his] sense of decency', and of the intelligentsia who apparently desired 'a breakdown of law and order which would produce a situation in Britain comparable to that in St Petersburg in 1917'.[45]

Of course Orwell would not remain the undisputed property of a state–private network directed against communism. The breadth of his writing allowed others to claim him for other battles, including those fighting the 'propaganda' and policies of the British and US governments. After all, Orwell had been a trenchant critic of American culture, and his vision of a world divided between three great empires was not an oath of allegiance to the United States and 'Airstrip One', its British ally. Noam Chomsky, as he wrote of the 'new mandarins' serving the American state in 1969, could consider Orwell the model of the 'responsible intellectual'.[46]

Still the Cold War construction of 'Orwell' as the sage who 'demanded publicly that his own side should live up to their principles' would always be converted into a cudgel against a 'left' that was naive or dangerous.[47] Some stalwart anti-communists tried in the 1980s to appropriate St George. Norman Podhoretz announced, 'If Orwell were Alive Today, He'd be a Neo-Conservative', while *The Sun* trumpeted, 'As 1984 opens, we have been spared the Orwell nightmare. We have liberty under Margaret Thatcher.'[48] More effective, however, were the uses of Orwell by those claiming to protect the 'left' by damning it. Here was the ' "true" intellectual . . . [who] flayed the Left intelligentsia in order to fortify it, not to weaken it'.[49] It would be a twenty-first-century Labour Home Secretary who would call forth Orwell's argument from *The Lion and the Unicorn* and the Second World War: 'Given the Left's tendency to wash their hands of the notion of nationhood, it's unsurprising our perception of Britishness became a conservative one.'[50]

If supposed victory in the Cold War threatened to make this Orwell marginal or, at best, a clichéd benchmark for every phenomenon from closed-circuit cameras to 'reality' television, 11 September 2001 restored him to prominence. Yet, true to the construction of 'Orwell' from the 1930s, he was used to pillory those who questioned a rush to war in Afghanistan and beyond. Christopher Hitchens, who was already penning a short defence of Orwell so he could don the writer's 'contrarian' mantle, was railing a left 'too stupid', 'too compromised' or too 'twisted' to recognise Orwell's (and Hitchens's merits);[51] now he insisted that '[Orwell] would have seen straight though the characters who chant ' "No War On Iraq" ' and recycled 'Notes on Nationalism':

> There is a minority of intellectual pacifists, whose real though unacknowledged motive appears to be hatred of western democracy and admiration of totalitarianism. Pacifist propaganda usually boils down to saying that one side is as bad as the other, but if one looks closely at the writings of the younger intellectual pacifists, one finds that they do not by any means express impartial disapproval but are directed almost entirely against Britain and the United States.[52]

Days before the first American bombs fell on Kabul, Michael Kelly, the editor of *The Atlantic* and columnist for the *Washington Post*, used Orwell's 1942 diatribe against 'Fascifists' to proclaim: 'The American pacifists . . . are on the side of future mass murders of Americans. They are objectively pro-terrorist . . . That is the pacifists' position, and it is evil.' Days after they fell on Baghdad, the *Daily Telegraph* passed sentence on what 'George Orwell once called . . . "the peculiar masochism of the English Left": a readiness to side with all manner of villains – the IRA, the Soviet Union, Saddam – provided they are anti-British'.[53]

III

In March 1947 Orwell wrote: 'There is no kind of evidence or argument by which one can show that Shakespeare, or any other writer, is "good" . . . Ultimately, there is no test of literary merit except survival, which is itself an index to majority opinion.'[54]

Yet the veneration of the 'good' Orwell depended on this illusion of objectivity, albeit through political rather than literary credentials. That veneration in turn came not from some detached measurement of 'freedom' or 'democracy' or any other abstract concept in Orwellian essays and novels but from the demands and circumstances of a Cold War culture. In short, whether or not the decent 'Orwell' existed, he had to be created.

Timothy Garton Ash has proclaimed this creation as the ultimate victor over 'the three dragons against which Orwell fought his good fight – European and especially British imperialism; fascism, whether Italian, German or Spanish; and communism, not to be confused with the democratic socialism in which Orwell himself believed'.[55] On closer examination, however, Orwell's good fight against imperialism was far from constant, with his praise for Kipling, his 'shout[ing] with laughter to hear, for instance, Gandhi named as an example of the success of non-violence', and his response to Nehru's question 'Who dies if India lives?': 'How impressed the pinks will be.'[56] He fought against fascism in Spain in 1937 and in the Home Guard from 1940, but in between he opposed confrontation with Hitler's Germany. And, while his position against communism was constant, he not only confused but conflated it with a fight against those democratic socialists whom he considered suspect.

None of this makes Orwell a 'bad' writer or, for that matter, a 'bad' person, any more than his writing and political positions make him objectively 'good'. As Raymond Williams concisely argued more than thirty years ago: 'Soon after his death Orwell became, in effect, a symbolic figure.'[57]

What must be acknowledged, however, is that the objective, decent, common-sense 'Orwell' has been created in part as a cudgel to beat those who may put forth opposing views. Much of Orwell's venom was directed not at the government of the day but at a supposed 'left' that was transformed from a range of social, economic and political perspectives into a threatening bloc; part of his writer's strategy in this transformation was to fashion himself as the 'contrarian', converting 'socialists' and 'fellow travellers' from dissenters into a centre of power to be confronted.

Whether or not Orwell intended this strategy to become part of a Cold War cultural battle, it was ideal for confrontation with Moscow. The US government's blueprint for the campaign against communism, NSC-68 (1950), permitted no middle ground:

Unwillingly our free society finds itself mortally challenged by the Soviet system. No other value system is so wholly irreconcilable with ours, so implacable in its purpose to destroy ours, so capable of turning to its own uses the most dangerous and divisive trends in our own society, no other so skillfully and powerfully evokes the elements of irrationality in human nature everywhere . . .[58]

Orwell had offered his own division in 1947:

there is one question that should be answered plainly. It is: 'If you had to choose between Russia and America, which would you choose?' . . . And in spite of all the fashionable chatter of the moment, everyone knows in his heart that we should choose America.[59]

Orwell's 'with us or against us' position may have been adopted reluctantly – he was far from a fan of American culture – but he had embraced it. Those of the 'left' who had not carried out the same embrace risked identification in his 'List', in his contact with the British state, and in his legacy in American culture.

The man who once wrote of the 'ever-present danger of becoming simply anti-Communist . . . which is completely sterile even if it isn't harmful' was dead; now he was to be exalted as the icon of 'freedom', even if that meant containing the freedom of others to question the US and British states and their foreign policies. More than fifty years before George W. Bush would declare, 'You are either with us or you are with the terrorists', another George would set out the clear distinction of us and them: 'Don't imagine that years on end you can make yourself the boot-licking propagandist of the Soviet regime, or any other regime, and then suddenly return to mental decency. Once a whore, always a whore.'[60]

Notes

1. John Carey, 'The Invisible Man', *Sunday Times*, 18 May 2003, Culture, p. 35.
2. The quote is from President Truman's Attorney General, Tom Clark, in 1947, http://www.people.memphis.edu/sherman/chronoColdWar.htm. See Richard Freedland, *The Truman Doctrine and the Origins of McCarthyism* (New York: Knopf, 1971).
3. Christopher Hitchens, *Orwell's Victory* (London: Allen Lane, 2002), p. 9.
4. Quoted in Elizabeth Wassermann, 'The Power of Facing', *Atlantic Unbound*, 23 October 2002, http://www.theatlantic.com/unbound/interviews/int2002-10-23.htm
5. John Carey, 'The Invisible Man', *Sunday Times*, 18 May 2003, Culture: p. 35.
6. D. J. Taylor, *Orwell* (London: Chatto and Windus, 2003), pp. 2–3; Gordon Bowker, *George Orwell* (London: Little, Brown, 2003), p. 434.
7. Paul Vallely, 'On the Road Again', *The Independent*, 30 April 2003, http://news.independent.co.uk/uk/this__britain/story.jsp?story=401640; Richard Brooks, 'Orwell's Room 101 to be Work of Art', *Sunday Times*, 23 March 2003, p. 14; Taylor, *Orwell*, pp. 235–7; Thomas Pynchon, 'The Road to 1984', *The Guardian*, 3 May 2003, http://books.guardian.co.uk/review/story/0,12084,948203,00.html
8. Leo McKinstry, 'Why isn't CND cheering Bush?', *Daily Telegraph*, 11 January 2004, http://www.telegraph.co.uk/opinion/main.jhtml?xml=%2Fopinion%2F2004%2F01%2F11%2Fdo1102.xml&secureRefresh=true&__requestid=6212. The quote is originally from George Orwell, 'Notes on Nationalism', *Polemic* (October 1945), reprinted in *The Collected Essays, Journalism and Letters of George Orwell* hereafter *CEJL*, vol. 3: *As I Please, 1943–1945*, ed. Ian Angus and Sonia Orwell (London: Secker and Warburg, 1968), pp. 361–80. (All subsequent references to the *CEJL* volumes retain the same publication details.)

9. Joann Barkan, '"My Mother, Drunk or Sober": George Orwell on Nationalism and Patriotism', *Dissent* (Winter 2003), http://www.dissentmagazine.org/menutest/archives/2003/wi03/barkan.htm

10. Tony Blair, 'The Left should not Weep if Saddam is Toppled', *The Guardian*, 10 February 2003, http://www.guardian.co.uk/comment/story/0,3604,892331,00.html

11. *New York Times*, 2 June 1949, reprinted at http://www.angelfire.com/pop/orwell/essay.html

12. Maureen Dowd, 'Streetcar Named Betrayal', *New York Times*, 24 February 1999, http://www.nytimes.com/library/opinion/dowd/022499dowd.html; Alexander Cockburn, 'Hitch the Snitch', *Counterpunch* (February 1999), http://www.counterpunch.org/snitch.html; Victor Navasky, quoted in Susan Lehman, 'Et Tu, Christopher?', *Salon*, 11 February 1999, http://archive.salon.com/media/lehm/1999/02/11lehm2.html

13. Christopher Hitchens, 'Orwell – A Snitch?', *The Nation* (February 1998), p. 3; Alexander Cockburn, 'Orwell and Koestler', *The Nation* (April 1998), p. 7.

14. *The Complete Works of George Orwell*, ed. Peter Davison, vol. 20: *Our Job is to Make Life Worth Living* (London: Secker and Warburg, 1998), p. 318. Celia Kirwan, later Goodman, died in October 2002. See the obituary in *The Independent*, 25 October 2002, http://news.independent.co.uk/people/obituaries/story.jsp?story=345693

15. See Scott Lucas and C. J. Morris, 'A Very British Crusade: The Information Research Department and the Cold War', in Richard Aldrich (ed.), *British Intelligence, Strategy, and the Cold War* (London: Routledge, 1992), pp. 85–111.

16. Quoted in, *The Complete Works*, vol. 20, p. 319.

17. Ibid. vol. 20, p. 240.

18. The abridged 'List' from the notebook, minus the thirty-eight names passed to the IRD, is in ibid. vol. 20, pp. 242–58. The thirty-eight names were finally published in anon., 'Orwell's List', *The Guardian*, 21 June 2003, Review, p. 7.

19. See anon., 'Orwell's List', *The Guardian*, 21 June 2003, Review, p. 7; John Ezard, 'Blair's Babe', *The Guardian*, 21 June 2003, http://www.guardian.co.uk/uk_news/story/0,3604,982159,00.html; Timothy Garton Ash, 'Love, Death, and Treachery', *The Guardian*, 21 June 2003, Review, pp. 4–7.

20. Perry Anderson, 'A Ripple of the Polonaise', *London Review of Books*, 21, 22 November 1999, p. 6 and subsequent letters from Christopher Hitchens (6 January 2000), http://www.lrb.co.uk/v22/n01/letters.html#10, Perry Anderson (20 January 2000), http://www.lrb.co.uk/v22/n02/letters.html and Christopher Hitchens (3 February 2000), http://www.lrb.co.uk/v22/n03/letters.html; Christopher Hitchens, *Orwell's Victory* (London: Allen Lane, 2002), p. 112.

21. See Frank Johnson, 'Orwell Was Right to Spy for Britain', *Daily Telegraph*, 12 July 1996, p. 26; Bernard Crick, 'Blair vs. the Left', *The Guardian*, 12 July 1996, p. 14; Mervyn Jones, 'Fears that Made Orwell Sneak on his Friends', *The Guardian*, 13 July 1996, p. 26; Geoffrey Wheatcroft, 'Big Brother with a Moral Sense', *Independent on Sunday*, 28 June 1998, reprinted at http://www.netcharles.com/orwell/ctc/docs/defence.htm; Christopher Hitchens, letters to *London Review of Books* (6 January 2000); (3 February 2000); Timothy Garton Ash, 'Orwell for our Time', *The Guardian*, 5 May 2001, http://www.guardian.co.uk/saturday_review/story/0,3605,485972,00.html

22. Orwell, 'As I Please', *Tribune*, 8 December 1944, in *CEJL*, vol. 3, pp. 288–91.

23. Bernard Crick, 'Orwell's "Premature Anti-Stalinism"', *The Guardian*, 24 June 2003, http://www.guardian.co.uk/letters/story/0,3604,983788,00.html; Timothy Garton Ash, 'Orwell's List', *New York Review of Books*, 25 September 2003, http://www.nybooks.com/articles/16550; Hitchens, *Orwell's Victory*, p. 113.

24. Orwell, 'As I Please', *Tribune*, 8 August 1944, reprinted at http://orwell.ru/library/articles/As_I_Please/e/e_aip_3.htm; Orwell to Frank Richards (6 August 1946), in *CEJL*, vol. 4: *In Front of your Nose, 1945–1950*, p. 197.

25. Orwell, 'Burnham's View of the Contemporary World Struggle', *New Leader*, 29 March

1947, in *CEJL*, vol. 4, p. 313.

26. Orwell to Gleb Struve (17 February 1944), in *CEJL*, vol. 3, p. 95; George Orwell, 'London Letter', *Partisan Review* (July–August 1943), in *CEJL*, vol. 2: *My Country Right or Left, 1940-1943*, p. 286.

27. Stephen Sedley, 'An Immodest Proposal: *Animal Farm*', in Christopher Norris (ed.), *Inside the Myth – Orwell: Views from the Left* (London: Fontana, 1984), p. 159.

28. George Orwell, review of S. Casado's *The Last Days of Madrid*, *Time and Tide*, 20 January 1940, in *CEJL*, vol. 1: *An Age Like This, 1920-1940*, p. 411; Orwell to John Middleton Murry (5 August 1944), in *CEJL*, vol. 3, p. 202.

29. Orwell letter to *Tribune* (17 January 1947), in *CEJL*, vol. 4, pp. 407-14.

30. See George Orwell, *The Road to Wigan Pier* (London: Penguin, [1937] 1962), pp. 139, 149-52, 156, 159.

31. George Orwell, *Homage to Catalonia* ((Harmondsworth: Penguin, [1938] 1989), pp. 64-5; George Orwell, 'My Country, Right or Left', *Folios of New Writing*, in *CEJL*, vol. 1, pp. 535-40; George Orwell, 'The Prevention of Literature', *Polemic* (March 1946), in *CEJL*, vol. 4, pp. 59-72.

32. Orwell to Herbert Read (5 March 1939) in *CEJL*, vol. 1, p. 387; George Orwell, 'A Controversy', *Partisan Review* (September–October 1942), in *CEJL*, vol. 2, pp. 227-30.

33. George Orwell, 'Not Counting Niggers', *Adelphi* (Christmas 1939), in *CEJL*, vol. 1, p. 394; George Orwell, 'On Kipling's Death', *New English Weekly*, 23 January 1936, in *CEJL*, vol. 1, p. 159.

34. George Orwell, 'London Letter', *Partisan Review* (Summer 1946), in *CEJL*, vol. 4, pp. 184-91.

35. Eric Thomas Chester, *Covert Network: Progressives, the International Rescue Committee, and the CIA* (Armonk, NY: M. E. Sharpe, 1995); David Cesarani, *Arthur Koestler: The Homeless Mind* (London: William Heinemann, 1998), pp. 305-10.

36. Cesarani, *Arthur Koestler*, pp. 305-10.

37. Orwell to Francis Henson (16 June 1949) in *CEJL*, vol. 4, p. 502.

38. Orwell to Henson (16 June 1949) in *CEJL*, vol. 4, p. 502.

39. Warburg memorandum, 1948, cited in Bernard Crick, *George Orwell: A Life* (Harmondsworth: Penguin, 1982), p. 567.

40. Philip Rahv, 'The Unfuture of Utopia', *Partisan Review* (July 1949), reprinted in Jeffrey Meyers, *George Orwell: The Critical Heritage* (London: Routledge and Kegan Paul, 1975), p. 267; Isaac Deutscher, '1984 – The Mysticism of Cruelty', in *Russia in Transition and Other Essays* (London: Hamish Hamilton, 1957), p. 245.

41. Frances Stonor Saunders, *Who Paid the Piper? The CIA and the Cultural Cold War* (London: Granta, 1999), pp. 293-301; David Hencke and Rob Evans, 'How Big Brothers Used Orwell to Fight the Cold War', *The Guardian*, 30 June 2000, http://www.guardian.co.uk/international/story/0,3604,338230,00.html; Scott Lucas, *Freedom's War: The US Crusade against the Soviet Union, 1945-56* (New York: New York University Press, 1999), pp. 64-5.

42. Richard Norton-Taylor and Seamus Milne, *The Guardian*, 11 July 1996, http://www.guardian.co.uk/international/story/0,3604,338230,00.html; C. M. Woodhouse, 'Animal Farm', *Times Literary Supplement*, 6 August 1945, pp. xxx-xxxi. Woodhouse was one of the key MI6 personnel involved in the planning and execution of the 1953 overthrow of the Mossadegh government in Iran, which had offended Britain with the nationalisation of the Anglo-Iranian Oil Company. See C. M. Woodhouse, *Something Ventured* (London: Granada, 1982).

43. See the chapters on the CCF in Stonor Saunders, *Who Paid the Piper?*, pp. 75-84, 302-13.

44. Lionel Trilling, 'George Orwell and the Politics of Truth', in Trilling, *The Opposing Self* (London: Secker and Warburg, 1955), pp. 151-72.

45. V. S. Pritchett quoted in David Pryce-Jones, 'Orwell's Reputation', in Miriam Gross (ed.), *The World of George Orwell* (London: Weidenfeld and Nicolson, 1971), p. 150; John

Atkins, *George Orwell* (London: Calder and Boyars, 1945), p. 1; Richard Rees, *George Orwell: Fugitive from the Camp of Victory* (London: Secker and Warburg, 1961), p. 45.

46. Noam Chomsky, 'Objectivity and Liberal Scholarship', in *American Power and the New Mandarins* (London: Chatto and Windus, 1969), pp. 65-98.

47. Crick, *George Orwell*, pp. 17-18

48. Norman Podhoretz, 'If Orwell were Alive Today, He'd be a Neo-Conservative', *Harper's* (January 1983), pp. 30-7; *The Sun* (leader), 1 January 1984, quoted in Malcolm Evans, 'Text Theory, Criticism: 20 Things You Never Knew about George Orwell', in Norris (ed.), *Inside the Myth*, p. 15.

49. John Rodden, 'Orwell and the London Left Intelligentsia', in Graham Holderness, Bryan Loughrey and Nahem Yousaf (eds), *George Orwell* (London: Macmillan, 1998), pp. 177-8.

50. Jack Straw, 'Blame the Left, Not the British', *The Observer*, 15 October 2000, http://observer.guardian.co.uk/comment/story/0,6903,382758,00.html

51. Hitchens, *Orwell's Victory*, p. 33.

52. 'The E-Mails Pour In', *AndrewSullivan.com*, 30 October 2002, http://www.andrewsullivan.com/ book_club.php?book_num=book_club_blog.html; Hitchens, *Orwell's Victory*, p. 9.

53. Michael Kelly, 'Phony Pacifists', *Washington Post*, 3 October 2001, p. A31; 'War on the Home Front', *Daily Telegraph*, 10 March 2003, http://www.telegraph.co.uk/opinion/main.jhtml?xml=%2Fopinion%2F2003%2F03%2F10%2Fdl1001.xml&secureRefresh=true&_requestid=9649

54. George Orwell, 'Lear, Tolstoy, and the Fool', *Polemic* (March 1947), in *CEJL*, vol. 4, p. 290.

55. Timothy Garton Ash, 'Orwell for our Time', *The Guardian*, 5 May 2001,http://www.guardian.co.uk/saturday_review/story/0,3605,485972,00.html

56. Orwell, 'A Controversy', *Partisan Review* (September–October 1942), in *CEJL*, vol. 2, pp. 227-30; Orwell's diary (10 April 1942), in *CEJL*, vol. 2, p. 418.

57. Raymond Williams, *Orwell* (London: Fontana, 1971), p. 83.

58. NSC-68, 'United States Objectives and Programs for National Security', 14 April 1950, reprinted at http://www.fas.org/irp/offdocs/nsc-hst/nsc-68.htm

59. George Orwell, 'In Defence of Comrade Zilliacus', unpublished (Autumn–Winter 1947), in *CEJL*, vol. 4, pp. 395-400.

60. George Bush address to Congress, 20 September 2001, reprinted at http://www.whitehouse.gov/news/releases/ 2001/09/print/20010920-8.html; Orwell, 'As I Please', *Tribune*, 1 September 1944, in *CEJL*, vol. 3, p. 224.

CHAPTER EIGHT

Television

Cold War Television and the Technology of Brainwashing

Alan Nadel

The complex legislative and industrial negotiations that preceded the advent of American broadcast television and determined its industrial, commercial and technological shape have been extensively discussed, most notably by Erik Barnouw, William Boddy and Lynn Spigel.[1] Among the factors at stake were the technical norms that would standardise broadcasting and the concomitant technology that would meet those standards, the methods by which television broadcasting would be financed and the role, nature and level of government participation in the medium. While these factors all helped configure television as a cultural phenomenon, the moment of the medium's reception, which will be the focus of this chapter, also profoundly affected the meanings of television in American culture.

Television, in this context, is not so much a 'thing' as a rubric that unites several separate albeit interdependent meanings. It is both an appliance – a 'box' – and an intricate technology outside the box, which gives that appliance its function. The technology comprises not only the broadcast apparatus but also the social machinery that produces the 'material' that the apparatus transmits. Television is also the material itself, the flow – as Raymond Williams called it – of images and narratives.[2] One does not, after all, watch the appliance but rather what the appliance shows. Television denotes an activity, moreover, separate from the specific shows, an evening's pastime. Finally, television represents a source of authority, a definitive conduit to an external reality.

Although this last role has changed greatly since 1980, American television, during the height of the Cold War, despite being an extremely contrived and heavily censored medium, spoke in the public imaginary as the apparatus *sine qua non* of unmediated reality. It seemed to unite without contradiction the descriptive and the proscriptive, the spontaneous and the normative, the fabricated and the real.

But television was not initially intended to be a product of the Cold War. The technology for broadcast television was developed during the 1930s, and, had things gone according to plan, 1939 would have marked the beginning of the television era. Indeed, the first television broadcast was made from the 1939 World's Fair in New York, but the outbreak of the Second World War diverted both materials and expertise into the arms industry and the war effort. As a result, from 1939 to 1948, American broadcast television was limited to a few hours daily in only six cities.

Thus the social and cultural phenomenon that the American public would know as television arrived a decade later than initially intended. During the course of that hiatus, however, the anticipation and image of television steadily grew in the national consciousness, such that before even five per cent of all Americans had ever seen a television show the technology had acquired an aura: television, its intended audience was encouraged to believe, would master the distant and the temporal so as to put all Americans in immediate, direct touch with everything.

This prolonged build-up culminated, however, in the midst of a Cold War the characteristics of which could not have been predicted a decade earlier. American television thus would have impacted on Americans' beliefs and attitudes differently, had it arrived under a different set of historical circumstances, circumstances that, in the name of security and prosperity, did not mandate normality and privilege surveillance.

In this context, television's role as the apparatus of reality merged with its role as a technology of the surveillance state. It was an external power – a mysterious science – that let invisible waves enter the home to produce images, potentially both facilitating and controlling individual freedom. As such it restaged an American concern with the subversive power of the demonic Other that dated to the colonial period, and found its contemporary apotheosis in the concept of 'brainwashing', a motif of Western Cold War propaganda attributed to the Korean War. Like television, brainwashing represented a technological breakthrough in the science of perception, in the comprehension of reality and in the notion of citizenship. Both television and brainwashing used technology to invert and confuse, without detection, the relationship between inside and outside, producing a psychological (and, perhaps, characterological or even spiritual) manipulation. This same struggle with the potential of technology to alienate Americans from themselves can be seen manifested in such diverse products of the 1950s as the famous sociological study *The Lonely Crowd*, the sci-fi cult film *Invasion of the Body Snatchers* and the best-selling book on motivational research *The Hidden Persuaders*. All of these works fear some version of brainwashing that unites the contradictions endemic to the concept of televisual reality that infused the period of the medium's initial reception.

My childhood was not a happy one. While not scarred by the extremes of deprivation or abuse, it was lonely, full of the anxieties, rejections and insecurities endemic, we now know, to growing up. My parents, well intentioned, late to have married, seemed to come from an entirely different universe – my father, in fact, was born in Victorian London – a different universe with which I could communicate only through the dense static of mutual frustration, anger and disappointment. Although the term 'dysfunctional' was not part of my vocabulary, I did have the acute sense that my home life was abnormal in that it differed so drastically from the contented American family life that was – as television relentlessly assured me – the norm.

I remember in that context very specifically wondering as I reached puberty what it felt like to be 'well adjusted', to be what I thought of as 'normal'. There was at that moment a presidential election taking place, the first presidential election in which I took a serious interest. Since being normal was inextricably wed, in the lexicon of Cold War American culture, to success, I accepted as *prima facie* that the two most successful people in the nation – the presidential nominees of the Democratic and Republican parties – must epitomise normality. And I remember wondering at age thirteen whether I would ever know what it felt like to be as well adjusted as John Kennedy or Richard Nixon.

I have started with this anecdote to introduce two central points: one, that Cold War brainwashing was *not* a myth, and, two, that it was fundamentally connected to understanding the world televisually. In regard to that second point, let us remember that the word 'television' has numerous, discrete meanings. A television is both an appliance and a set of programmes; the thing one watches when one watches television, after all, is not the television set, but the signals that the appliance receives and decodes, signals produced outside and independent of it. Television is also an activity outside of and independent of the programmes, such that one can decide to spend the evening watching television without having any specific programme in mind. Television is also a medium, a mode of organisation and presentation. Finally, and most subtly but also most pervasively, it is a way of knowing the world, a mediation between knowledge and identity, a way of fixing the self in the matrices of time, space, distance, history and the myriad nodes of personal affiliation.

My examination of the Korean War, in this context, will thus serve as a way of focusing, specifically, on this last sense of television in order to explore the concept of brainwashing as the evil Other of the national conformity promoted by American television and at the same time the embodiment of that conformity. I want to suggest, therefore, that the Korean War and television both helped give credibility to brainwashing as a perpetuation of the narrative of the demonic that has infused American culture in numerous forms since the colonial period. Whatever methodologies of cultural history may help clarify aspects of television's appearance on the American scene, it is important to remember that the way it was organised and construed followed from specific industrial and legal outcomes produced in conflict, not consensus, and certainly not preordained. Equally we must recognise that these conflicts and their resolutions occurred under historically specific conditions, as did the televisual product produced by those resolutions. American television's impact thus necessarily would have been different, had it not entered the public imaginary at roughly the same time as the atomic bomb, the baby boom, McCarthyism, suburbia and the Korean War; had it not entered the lives of a nation fixated on politically mandated normality and obsessed with uprooting nonconformists; had it not become the unifying common experience of a nation constantly on the watch, lest it blink and its unprecedented prosperity be stolen, unobserved, by subversives.

American television as we know it was thus the apparatus *sine qua non* of people who thought they had better watch out. For reasons extensive and profound, even in its barest incipience it was set to become the definitive apparatus of American reality, conveying in a manner simultaneously unique and traditional a notion of the American *e pluribus unum* as a variegated but nonetheless relentless set of lessons in nationalism, 'living room lectures', as Nina C. Leibman has generically named them.[3]

In this context, television had a fundamental role in defining 'un-American' activities, not only in that, through blacklisting, it helped mark subversives but also in that it presented messages about non-subversive behaviour and the role models who exemplified it. In order to help meet its Federal Communications Commission (FCC)-mandated public service function, for instance, television broadcast religious programmes. It also presented public service messages such as 'the family that prays together stays together'. In the 1950s, the term 'togetherness' became an informing motif of American television that united sitcoms, religious service shows and public service announcements. Even talk shows, such as *Today*, manifest 'togetherness' by bringing the world to the viewer, filtered through an ersatz family of hosts and assistants. One early *Today* host, Ernie Kovacs, used his wife, Edie Adams, as part of the cast, and another host, Dave Garroway, included in his morning family J. Fred Muggs, a chimp who vividly merged the traits of the viewers' diapered babyboomer infants and their adored house pets.

Thus at every turn television differentiated American acts and values from un-American activities and objectives. People who did not consider religious broadcasts a form of public service, people who had not allowed their families to pray or stay together, people who espoused controversial positions or associated with those who did (or were even accused of associating with them): these people were suspect.

With the outbreak of the Korean War, suspicion became an even more overt obligation. American soldiers, after all, were in the line of fire or interred behind enemy lines, so no one – especially a sponsor whose sales depended in part on the image that television promoted – wanted to be charged with employing fellow travellers or even inadvertently airing communist perspectives. Thus *Red Channels*, a magazine operating with little scrutiny of its less than reliable information, widely influenced network employment practices.

As part of the Korean War effort, moreover, NBC presented in 1950 *Battle Report Washington*, a government-controlled show, and the now defunct DuMont network ran *Our Secret Weapon – The Truth*, a counter propaganda show. CBS fuelled nuclear frenzy with 'What to Do During a Nuclear Attack', a documentary hosted by Walter Cronkite. Like the widely shown 1950s public service short 'Duck and Cover', 'What to Do During a Nuclear Attack' conveyed a dual message – that nuclear assault could occur at any moment and that with the right preparation Americans could avoid serious personal harm. This odd mixture of universal paranoia and mundane pragmatism, simultaneously apocalyptic and optimistic, provided a thematic blend ideally suited to affirming television's role as avatar of the American surveillance state, a cultural model that invested surveillance with an aura of civic pride rather than the fear of secret police. In the cultural lexicon, the FBI protected rather than threatened personal liberty; it uprooted communists and their sympathisers – those people who valued the interests of the state over the rights of the individual. Hypervigilance thus combined duty and pleasure, for, in assisting the surveillance state, the private citizen was preserving his or her own freedom. This mindset required, of course, delimiting freedom within very narrow parameters. It eliminated from the realm of legitimate debate what could, with intellectual validity, be seen as an inherent conflict between surveillance and freedom.

Television, in other words, supported a way of knowing the world consistent with the principles attributed to communist brainwashing, the chief common characteristic being a relentless indoctrination into a set of homogeneous norms. The goal of brainwashing is to create in the subject a different understanding of reality, an outcome made possible only through a set of scientific advances, allegedly based on the work of the Russian psychologist Ivan Pavlov. In his classic 1956 study of brainwashing in Korea (a sequel to his 1951 book on brainwashing in China), Edward Hunter portrays Pavlov as an old man duped by the Soviets.[4] Hunter found most threatening the implication in Pavlov's work that humans are animals. He describes a central scene in a Russian film, titled *The Nervous System*, demonstrating that a dog could be *taught* to salivate. Hunter viewed the film with novelist Ayn Rand and another friend named Dr Leon Freedom. (Dr Freedom, according to Hunter, was a professional 'neuropsychiatrist', not, as one might assume from his name, a professional wrestler.) For this sage triumvirate – Hunter, Rand and Dr F – the scene revealed something 'unnatural', as signified by what they regarded as an oxymoron: the phrase 'conditioned-reflex'.

The version of the film they saw, moreover, contained edits that hid the Soviets' sinister designs. In the uncut version: 'The incriminating scene began with a young man sitting in a chair, attached to it like the dog in a harness . . . A rubber suction tube was stuck into the boy's mouth to measure his saliva.'[5] After some conditioning a subsequent scene resembling a B horror flick shows 'the lad stretched out on a hospital cot like a patient awaiting an appendectomy, except that he was fully dressed. The rubber tube was still inserted into his mouth, its other end projecting in the thin glass receptacle.' In this setting, we witness the boy reduced to an animal when 'the light flashed without any biscuits falling from the cone. The boy's saliva flowed just the same. He was reacting exactly like a dog.'[6] The appalled Hunter goes on to explain:

> This was the part that made the film of such vital importance to the training laboratories operated by Soviet Secret police. Conditioned reflexes could conceivably be produced to make this youth react like the dog that rolled over at its trainer's signal. Only instead of a light, the Kremlin could use words as signals – any words would do – *imperialism, learning, running dog of the imperialists, people, friend of the people, big brother*, without relationship to the actual meaning. The Kremlin's plan was to make these reflexes instinctive, like the reactions of the animals – and boy – shown in the movie. When we appreciate the fact that this film was produced in 1928, the long-term planning of the communist hierarchy becomes frighteningly evident.[7]

Equally ominous portents, at least in theory, could have been attributed to the 1927 first public demonstration of television. If, as Hunter believes, 'the scene with the harnessed boy could have warned the Free World that these experiments really had human beings in view', the great fear is connected to the uncanny, that is, to the uncomfortable relationship between the scientific and the natural.[8] Science reveals natural laws: it is the technology of the possible; science subverts nature: it is the technology of the impossible. Permeating Hunter's book is the terrible ambivalence towards science that informed the atomic age, such that, as I pointed out in my book *Containment Culture*, there were even government documents pondering how to deal with the atom's 'dual nature'.[9]

Like Pavlovian science, television technology evoked an uncanny power of the real, which to a large degree drew upon a faith in visual representation. Noting the commercial value of television, a 1947 article explained about it that 'by *visual* demonstration *actual proof* can be submitted of many things that now must be accepted on mere statement'.[10] Television's power was further enhanced by its potential for immediacy. It was the instrument of truth because it showed reality before it could undergo alteration. As early as 1942, when certainly less than one per cent of the American population had ever seen a television broadcast, one author predicted that 'television is destined to bring into the home total means for participation in the sights and sounds of the entire world'.[11]

Since television brought reality into the home, implicitly 'real life' existed elsewhere, and television thus threw into unstated comparison the 'land of plenty' and the meagre living rooms into which the nation's plenitude was electronically channelled. Access to that plenitude, moreover, rendered television invaluable to citizenship, for, as the word 'participation' implied, television was being imagined as an instrument of participatory democracy, allowing citizenship, undaunted by distance, unobstructed by topography, untainted by rhetorical manipulation.

If by 1949 television was still very far from fulfilling its panoptic promise, that promise, nevertheless, remained the privileged criterion by which the medium would be measured. Gilbert Seldes, one of the most articulate early critics of the medium, wrote in that year:

> The fact that television can transmit actuality is of prime psychological importance. It invites us to 'the conception of things as they are'; it sets us on the way to maturity . . . The essential thing is to determine that television will satisfy the deep human desire to look, at times, on the face of reality.[12]

Perhaps the most powerful expression of this perception came in 1952 from Pat Weaver, who would shortly become the head of NBC programming. 'It is because', he wrote, having the all-family, all-home circulation through a planned radio–television schedule, we can create a new stature in our citizens. The miracles of attending every event of importance, meeting every personality of importance in your world, getting to observe members of every group, racial, national, sectional, cultural, religious; recognizing every city, every country, every river and mountain on sight; having full contact with the explanations of every mystery of physics, mechanics and the sciences; sitting at the feet of the most brilliant teachers, and being exposed to the whole range of diversity of mankind's past, present, and the aspirations for mankind's future – these and many other miracles are not assessed yet. But I believe that we vastly underestimate what will happen.[13]

In Weaver's conception, television functions as the *über*-citizen whose universal scope could elevate the ordinary American. Televisual citizenship, superior to more ignorant, limited, pedestrian, citizenship, comprised the ideal, so that television, by setting the standard and providing the means for achieving it, represented the perfection of American ideology.

At least in theory. But constantly television belied its theoretical promise, functioning less as a conduit to all knowledge and experience than as a relentless rhetorical machine geared to represent its impossible promise as a fait accompli. A significant pillar of the argument rested on underscoring 'spontaneity'. 'Preparation for the unexpected', James Caddigan noted in 1945,

seems like a larger order to fill, yet, that is exactly the job that must be handled if the special event or news incident is to be produced with the 'immediacy' that television promises. The television audience of the future is being educated at the present time to expect sight of an incident 'as it happens'.[14]

This symbiotic relationship between the planned and the unpredictable, moreover, implicitly identified television with the surveillance state mentality pervasive at the time of the medium's proliferation. 'Television's surveillance potential', Jeanne Allen points out, 'was quickly associated with aircraft intelligence gathering'.[15] Army intelligence, in fact, was the model Caddigan recommended for television news gathering. News divisions, he believed, should set up for each area a 'television intelligence file' that would include notification contacts, topographic data, weather reports and correct credentials, because, 'at the time of an incident, intelligence from the field will be most important to the production staff . . . at the station'. The need for this form of military-style intelligence gathering, moreover, was 'a never ending job as each new production will provide added information that can be used to advantage on some future show'.[16]

The sense of a world under surveillance was hardly an anathema to the post-Second World War American populace. Throughout the mounting search for subversion that characterised the late 1940s and much of the 1950s, television proved significant in several ways. Quickly recognised for its capacity to reveal the obscure, it helped support the idea that America might successfully become a place of universal scrutiny, which would require significant homogeneity. Identifying deviance, after all, requires norms against which to measure the deviation, and nothing was more deft or prolific at supplying them than television. 'The aim of television', as David Marc so aptly puts it, 'is to be normal. The industry is obsessed with the problem of norms.'[17]

During the Second World War, for example, television was used in New York City to train air raid wardens, based on the idea that, as Orin Dunlap stated, 'there is always a best lecturer for any subject and through television he can actually instruct all the parties instantly and uniformly'.[18] This concept of a 'best lecturer' associated television with the idea of American exceptionalism, in that the technology of television allows all Americans to receive the 'best'. 'In this war program', Dunlap explained, 'light has been shed on the ability of television to put into practical use the unlimited possibilities envisaged for it after the war'.[19] After the war, through television, the 'best' would become the standard, and the standard would be available universally.

Far from deploying the best of American art, performance or reportage, however, in practice television presented the nation's lowest common denominators. With two networks monopolising the competition for viewers, the safe, the clichéd and the uncontroversial had enormous advantage over the experimental, the original and the challenging. This economic mandate when applied to the concept of citizenship obviously effected a very conservative citizen. Television could thus function as the site of 'democracy' to the extent that 'democracy' – representing what the most people had in common – was defined in opposition to 'idiosyncrasy'. Broadcasting nationalised the common person in every way that his or her values were common rather than unique, clichéd rather than original, status quo rather than progressive.

At the same time, of course, early television also told us that reality could be apprehended only through elaborate distortions, shrunk to 13 inches, muted to black and white tones (themselves usually reduced to shades of grey), filtered through static, snow and fuzz, subject to horizontal warping and vertical rolling. In every direction, the face of reality experienced invidious subversion. Television thus signified both the power and the fragility of unmediated truth. That power – to present a world greater than the apparatus that contained it or the viewer who owned that apparatus – aligned television with the supernatural. Its way of knowing the world collapsed the distinctions between inside and outside, between subject and object, between part and whole.

Beyond that, early television was perhaps the most censored mass entertainment in modern history, even more than the film industry that had been, from the early 1930s on, rigorously censored at every level of production, and with the outbreak of the Second World War even further scrutinised by the Office of War Information. After the Second World War, the House Un-American Activities Committee (HUAC) applied yet another microscope to the film industry, attempting to determine whether some films might contain subversive messages, that is, messages so subtle and deeply closeted as to slip past the censors but at the same time blatant enough and powerful enough to subvert the more innocent general population. At work here is a fear of – what else can we call it? – fear of the Devil, that is, of a guile so potent as to evade all ordinary precautions and, as well, every extant form of hypervigilance. The surveillance state, after all, is a testimony to the inadequacy of surveillance. Like much Puritan dogma, the surveillance state constantly reminds us that we have to be ever watchful, *more* watchful, *ever more* watchful.

And if we had to be ever more watchful about films, then naturally we had to be even more ever watchful about the medium that everyone was watching. A rabbi, a priest and a minister were present on the set for the filming of each of the *I Love Lucy* episodes dealing with Lucy's pregnancy. The clergy could thus vouchsafe against some indecency that went undetected by the actors, writers, producers, directors, that is, by the normal mechanisms of television production. These clergy, serving as invited agents of the *ultimate* surveillance state, would make impossible even the inadvertent subversion of American mores.

At the very moment that those episodes were being filmed – Lucy, both the character and the actress, gave birth the day before President Eisenhower's inauguration – the Devil so carefully banished from Desilu Studios was finding a fertile home in North Korean prisoner-of-war camps, on the edge of the Manchurian border, where, with the aid of communist interrogators and twentieth-century technology, he was washing the brains of American GIs.

I want to make clear, at this point, that the experience of American prisoners of war was extremely brutal, cruel and tortured. But brainwashing is not torture; in fact, it is exactly the opposite of coercion, for coercion requires threat and force to evoke actions that the victim wilfully opposes. Torture is a treatment necessitated by the inability to change the will, to wash the brain. Thus throughout Hunter's discussion of Korean War brainwashing, we see the Pavlovian methods constantly failing, always requiring increased threat, deprivation, physical and mental torture.

Hunter starts by explaining the concept of brainwashing using the unmistakable language of alien invasion and conspiracy:

> The new word *brainwashing* entered our minds and dictionaries in a phenomenally short time. This sinister political expression had never been seen in print anywhere until a few years ago. About the only times it was ever heard in conversation was inside the tight, intimate circle of trusted relatives or reliable friends in Red China during the short honeymoon period of communism. The few exceptions were when a Red indoctrinator would lose his temper and shout out, 'You need a brainwashing.'[20]

Like the mysterious stranger found in American literature, moreover, 'brainwashing' drew on the unnamed powers of darkness. The word, Hunter explained, 'described a strategy that had yet no name'.[21] Worked on the Chinese people, it resembled 'in many peculiar ways . . . a medical treatment', but Hunter assures that 'what they had undergone was more like witchcraft, with its incantations, trances, poisons, and potions, with a strange flair of science about it all, like a devil dancer in a tuxedo carrying his magic brew in a test tube' (an image no doubt meant to hint at communist infiltration of Mardi Gras).[22]

Since America's technological supremacy depended on the effectiveness of science, true science could not easily be rebuffed. Thus, if brainwashing were absolutely scientific, it could not be resisted by a triumph of the will. But that, according to Hunter, is exactly what was called for. Although brainwashing, according to the experts, was a demonic mixture of science and pseudo-science, of Pavlovian conditioning and overt torture, of direct indoctrination and indirect subversion, this well-honed and virulent technique was nevertheless completely ineffective when used against Americans with adequate strength of character. The fight against brainwashing, in other words, was internal, a struggle not with the forces of evil but with the temptation to succumb to one's own weakness.

Like televisual reality, it represented a breakdown of the boundary between inside and outside. Hunter's accounts of Korean brainwashing 'and the men who resisted it' read like a science fiction novel in which an overwhelming external power – that of the all-powerful captor – eventually fails in the face of the will, spirit and character of his captive.

I believe, as I have noted, that this narrative of the struggle between true character and superhuman power was at work in HUAC's relentless search to discover what American activities were *un*-American. The narrative also informed one of the most influential books of the post-war period, *The Lonely Crowd*. This 1951 study written by Yale sociologist David Reisman resembles a somewhat plodding piece of science fiction. Although the work achieved textbook status and is still frequently cited by social historians and cultural critics, its subtitle, 'A Study of the Changing American Character', reveals its quasi-fictional foundation.

As Reisman makes clear at the outset, he does not 'plan to delay over the many ambiguities of the concept of social character' even over 'whether there is any empirical proof that it really exists'.[23] In the place of empirical proof he provides what Henry James would call the donnée – a fiction's given premise: 'The assumption that a social character exists has always been a more or less invisible premise of ordinary parlance and is becoming today a more or less visible premise of the social sciences.'[24] If the source of this invisible character is the equally invisible premiss of ordinary parlance, then any alterations to that 'character' of course might escape general notice, even in the age of post-war hypervigilance. *The Lonely Crowd* attempts, therefore, to alert the public to an as-yet-unnoticed mutation. The book, as Reisman makes clear, is 'about the way in which one kind of social character, which dominated America in the nineteenth century, is gradually being replaced by a social character of quite a different sort'.[25]

That 'character' is changing from being what Reisman calls 'inner-directed' to what he calls 'other-directed', that is, motivated by peer pressure rather than internal values. The inner-directed person, Reisman explains, in terms worthy, perhaps, of either Ray Bradbury or *Popular Mechanics*:

has early incorporated a psychic gyroscope which is set going by his parents and can receive signals later on from other authorities who resemble his parents. He goes through life less independent than he seems, obeying this internal piloting. Getting off course, whether in response to inner impulses or to the fluctuating voices of his contemporaries, may lead to the feeling of guilt.[26]

For the inner-directed person a scientific device, the 'psychic gyroscope', keeps him on course, gives him balance, and this pinnacle of nineteenth-century American individualism is built fully equipped with a self-correcting mechanism: guilt. 'Contrasted with such a type as this', Reisman explains, 'the other-directed person learns to respond to signals from a far wider circle than is constituted by his parents. The family is no longer a closely knit unit to which he belongs but merely part of a wider social environment to which he early becomes attentive.'[27] Without a psychic gyroscope, in other words, this new mutation of the American character is receptive to alien signals. Guidance from mother has been replaced with messages from the mother ship. As a result, the other-directed person becomes odd, almost, Reisman's language implies, eerie: 'For him, the border between the familiar and the strange . . . has broken down.'[28] The amorphous, spongelike receptivity of this mutant, furthermore, effects an inverted reality: 'As the family continuously absorbs the strange and so reshapes itself, the strange becomes familiar.'[29]

Americans, like the citizens of Santa Mira California, in the 1955 film classic *Invasion of the Body Snatchers*, have undergone a strange, barely noticeable change: their emotions and their individuality have disappeared.[30] In the film, the hero, Dr Myles Binell, after returning from a business trip, notices that his patients as well as residents of Santa Mira are odd. One woman, Wilma, tells Myles that her Uncle Ira does not seem to be himself, even though he seems to be able to answer all the germane questions about his personal history. With a distressed look on her face, Wilma tells Myles: 'I've talked to him about them all. He remembers them all down to the last detail, just like Uncle Ira would. But Myles . . . there's no emotion – none, just the pretense of it: the words, the gesture, the tone; everything else is the same but not the feeling. Memories or not, he isn't my Uncle Ira.'

Later, when Myles and his girlfriend Becky are confronted by former friends whose bodies have been 'snatched', the following interchange occurs:

Dr Coffman: Myles, you and I are scientific men. You can understand the wonder of what's just happened. Now just think. Less than a month ago, Santa Mira was like any other town. People were nothing but problems. Then out of the sky came a solution. Seeds drifting through space for years took root in a farmer's field. From the seeds came pods which have the power to reproduce themselves in the exact likeness of any form of life.

Myles: So that's how it began – out of the sky.

Dr Coffman: Your new bodies are growing in there and taking you over, cell per cell, atom per atom. There's no pain. Suddenly while you're asleep, they'll absorb your mind, your memories, and you're reborn into an untroubled world.

Myles: Where everyone's the same?

Dr Coffman: Exactly.

Myles: What a world. We're not the last humans left. They'll destroy you.

Dr Coffman: Tomorrow you won't want them to. Tomorrow you'll be one of us.

Myles: I love Becky. Tomorrow will I feel the same?

Dr Coffman: There's no need for love.

Myles: No emotion? Then you have no feelings, only the instinct to survive. You can't love or be loved. Am I right?

Dr Coffman: You say it as if it were terrible. Believe me, it isn't. You've been in love before. It didn't last. Love, desire, ambition, faith – without them life's so simple. Believe me.

Myles: I don't want any part of it.

Dr Coffman: You're forgetting one thing.

Myles: What's that?

Dr Coffman: You have no choice.

Although this dialogue is supposed to be a cautionary dramatisation of the freedoms at risk through a subversion of reality, that is, though a corruption of the freedom of will, choice and knowledge portended by and associated with television, it is an even more cogent expression of the anxiety about submitting to the pervasive technology of normal life that television embodied. The solution to interpersonal problems came, like a broadcast signal, 'out of the sky' to produce alternate replicas 'cell per cell, atom per atom', deviating from the citizens only in terms of its levelling normality, its emotional homogeneity. If the body snatchers promise to rid the citizens of love and hate, television more modestly promises to contain those feelings at a safe distance, modify their amplitude and allow the tensions between them to find safe resolutions within equally predictable moral and temporal parameters.

Although the film's title connects these traits to the body, bodies, in fact, are exactly the parts that that the aliens bring with them, in huge pods. Like the brainwashers of whom Hunter warns us, they snatch minds and, like those brainwashers, they can succeed only if their victim weakens, in the film represented by going to sleep.

Going to sleep in this sense is similar to what happens, for Reisman, when one loses his gyroscope. In *The Lonely Crowd* the new American character retains its balance by relying not on its own normalising mechanisms but on norms that it acquires externally. The relatively stable pursuits of the inner-directed person, Reisman explains, 'are today being replaced by the fluctuating tastes which the other-directed person accepts from his peer group', and this shift produces an 'objectless craving'.[31]

Reisman is describing what I have briefly outlined as televisual citizenship, a citizenship that relies on a powerful external technology to put the citizen in touch with the face of reality. Perhaps the most frightening aspect of *The Lonely Crowd* is that it allows no logical position from which the power of this external force can be overcome, because, no matter how much Reisman fears the imposition of external norms, he nevertheless must rely on them to posit a concept such as a 'social character' upon which his story entirely depends. To put it another way, because other-directedness is the position necessary for constructing the concept of inner-direction, the inside and outside of Reisman's chronology collapse, revealing the inner-directed character to be the product of an other-directed narrative. Reisman is speaking from a world of inverse causality.

He is behaving, in other words, like one of Hunter's brainwashers who constantly invert cause and effect in order to distort our understanding of reality. Just as television does. Clearly we can see now that, like Reisman's narrative of the mutating American character, television's obsessively normative reality was a projection *onto* the American landscape, not a reflection *of* it. What passed as television's outside world was just someone else's internal vision. Both television and brainwashing depended upon faith in the idea of a technically enhanced reality. In juxtaposition, these two technologies of the real remind us of the dangers inherent in looking on the face of reality, since reality, like science, is two-faced and not everyone has the strength of character to sort the rightful from the sinister.

This collapse of the inside and the outside was also being enacted on the Korean geographical and political terrain, where civil war and the international conflict were indistinguishable from each other; where terms such as 'start' and 'finish' were dislodged from their standard usage; where, as with the television of the period, 'definition' and 'resolution' were not objective terms, but relative qualities of distortion amid an ever-shifting mix of signals. In the end – a period of fighting that lasted longer than the war that led up to 'the end' – the *reason* America fought the Korean War, according to some official statements, was to determine the disposition of the prisoners of war created by it.

Korea is the place where the dependent and the independent, the inside and the outside, merge. It is the real war of the Cold War and the cold reality of containment's permeability. Inside Korea, all the world's struggles, all its superpowers, were contained, but only barely. At each stage, they threatened simultaneously to pour in and to pour over. Korea was an impoverished country that was inundated by excess: states and troops exceeding borders, exceeding truces; MacArthur exceeding his authority, not to mention his supply lines; treatment of prisoners of war on both sides exceeding international conventions and exceeding even the temporal margins of repatriation, as some of the American prisoners refused to return to America and others became prisoners again when they did. Countless others returned to their homes, their minds, many suspected, still enslaved by the dark science. The alien had snatched their brains, it was feared, and they were still directed by some Other, an undefined combination of the demonic, the communistic and the Asian. Secretly manifesting this other direction, this new orientation, they might undermine the normative nuclear family and with it the American resolve that resided in the vestiges of Reisman's national 'social character'.

In an other-directed society, after all, one always has to be careful about one's peers, since they provide the society's values. To put it another way, conformity was vital to the national interests; deviance was suspect. At the same time, as the Chinese had shown, conformity was deviant, a relinquishing of the normal self to scientific manipulation. To this end, we had to rely on science – the miracle of television – to put us in touch with appropriate norms, but science, as the Korean experience demonstrated, was not reliable; it could establish inappropriate norms; it could make deviance seem normal. Only strength of character could resist the subversion of insidious, inscrutable science, but such strength, Reisman fearfully warned, was disappearing.

Later in the decade, Vance Packard would, in *The Hidden Persuaders*, again powerfully articulate the intersection between brainwashing and televisual citizenship. In describing the post-Second World War shift to a consumer society, Packard too adapted the idea that Americans could, without their knowledge, be forced to internalise an alien Other. This battle for the will of the American character once again merged the demonic, the technological and the psychological in Packard's attempt 'to explore a strange and rather exotic new area of American life', startlingly like that portrayed in *Invasion of the Body Snatchers*, in which 'many of us are being influenced and manipulated, far more than we realize, in the patterns of our everyday lives'. [32] Repeatedly Packard refers to the 'probers' and the 'probed', and the 'psychiatric probing', to 'penetration weapons' and 'the deep-down effect'. This penetration of American integrity, for Packard, also took the form of ingestion of foods 'loaded with hidden meaning'.[33] As with brainwashing, advertising manifested the quintessential inversion and confusion of inside and outside. The external motivation became internalised as the disguised – impenetrably disguised – expression of the self.

Thus the first half of the book, 'Persuading Us as Consumers', concludes with the cautionary sentence: 'The aim now is nothing less than to influence the state of our mind and to channel our behavior as citizens.'[34] In the second part of the book, 'Persuading Us as Citizens', as the word 'channel' may suggest, the media become the hidden persuaders, such that merely talking about media strategies becomes synonymous with the persuasive subversion of character and consciousness that undermines the notion of (American) citizenship. By 1957, only one decade into the television era, the television set had morphed into the formulator of reality. As a result, the citizen too had morphed into the simulator of that televisual reality, lacking independent will or inner direction. According to Cold War criteria, in other words, television had succeeded in perfecting the dark science that Pavlov initiated, the Russians developed and the Red Chinese implemented (with limited success) in Korea. As such, television rendered the triumph of American technology and the subversion of American character as inextricable strands in the fabric of Cold War reality.

NOTES

1. See Erik Barnouw, *A Tube of Plenty* (New York: Oxford University Press, 1982) and *The Golden Web: A History of Broadcasting in the United States*, vol. 2: *1933–1953* (New York: Oxford University Press, 1968); William Boddy, *Fifties Television: The Industry and its Critics* (Urbana: University of Illinois Press, 1990); and Lynn Spigel, *Make Room for Television* (Chicago: University of Chicago Press, 1992).
2. Raymond Williams, *Television: Technology and Cultural Form* (Hanover, NH: Wesleyan University Press, 1992).
3. Nina C. Leibman, *Living Room Lectures: The Fifties Family in Film and Television* (Austin: University of Texas Press, 1995).
4. Edward Hunter, *Brainwashing in Red China: The Calculated Destruction of Men's Minds* (New York: Copp Clark, 1951).
5. Edward Hunter, *Brainwashing: The Story of the Men Who Defied It* (New York: Farrar Straus and Cuhday, 1956), p. 38.
6. Ibid. p. 39.
7. Ibid. p. 44.
8. Ibid. p. 44.
9. Alan Nadel, *Containment Culture: American Narratives, Postmodernism, and the Atomic Age* (Durham, NC, and London: Duke University Press, 1995), p. 23.
10. H. G. Christensen, 'Long Shots and Close-ups', *Television: The Magazine of Video Fact*, 3/2 (February 1946), p. 29.
11. Orin E. Dunlap, Jr, *The Future of Television* (New York: Harper and Bros, 1942), pp. 349–50.
12. Gilbert Seldes, 'Television: The Golden Hope', *Atlantic*, 3 (1949), p. 36.
13. Cited in J. Fred MacDonald, *One Nation under Television: The Rise and Decline of Network TV* (New York: Pantheon, 1990), p. 54.
14. James Caddigan, 'Station Operations: Setting up a Special Events Department', *Television: The Magazine of Video Fact*, 2/10 (December 1945), p. 12.
15. Jeanne Allen, 'The Social Matrix of Television: Invention in the United States', in E. Ann Kaplan (ed.), *Regarding Television: Critical Approaches – An Anthology* (Los Angeles: American Film Institute, 1983), p. 112.
16. Caddigan, 'Station Operations', p. 13.
17. David Marc, 'Beginning to Begin Again', in Horace Newcomb (ed.), *Television: The Critical View*, 4th edn (New York: Oxford University Press, 1987), p. 326.

18. Dunlap, *The Future of Television*, p. 15.
19. Ibid. p. 16.
20. Hunter, *Brainwashing*, p. 3.
21. Ibid. p. 3.
22. Ibid. pp 3–4.
23. David Reisman, *The Lonely Crowd* (Yale Paperbound Edition); (New Haven: Yale University Press, 1961), p. 4.
24. Ibid. p. 4.
25. Ibid. p. 3.
26. Ibid. p. 24.
27. Ibid. p. 25.
28. Ibid. p. 25.
29. Ibid. p. 25.
30. Don Siegel, Dir. Allied Artists (1955).
31. Reisman, *The Lonely Crowd*, p. 79.
32. Vance Packard, *The Hidden Persuaders* (New York: David Mckay, 1957), p. 3.
33. Ibid. p. 100.
34. Ibid. p. 178.

CHAPTER NINE

Poetry

Confession, Autobiography and Resistance: Robert Lowell and the Politics of Privacy

Hugh Stevens

After the Second World War, mainstream American poetry shied away from direct representations of the political world; this was in part a reaction against the highly politicised generation of poets prominent in the 1930s, in particular W. H. Auden. Lyric poetry traditionally represents private experience, taking as its subject matter topics such as love, jealousy, loss, grief, death and mourning. Yet, just as the Cold War saw the lines between public and private being continually remade, and surveillance became a major aspect of American life because of desires to safeguard the nation against the (imagined or real) threat posed by communism, throughout the 1950s and 1960s American poetry began more and more to represent private domestic space as highly inflected with public and political anxieties. This chapter discusses the career of Robert Lowell, one of the most well-known American poets writing during the Cold War, and shows how changes in his poetic practice enabled him to develop new modes of poetic writing, in which vivid representations of the poet's private world, portraits of his present life and memories of his past describe the climate of the Cold War with urgency and immediacy.

The chapter discusses various political positions taken by Lowell: his refusal to serve in the Second World War, because of his disgust with the Allies' aggressive bombing of German cities; his involvement with a Cold War 'witch hunt' at the writers' colony in Yaddo, New York, in 1949; and his very public protest of American involvement in the Vietnam War. What is the relationship between Lowell's political poetry and these public inter-ventions? As Lowell's poetry in two key volumes, *Life Studies* (1959) and *For the Union Dead* (1964), comes increasingly to represent the present, it also registers dissent. It portrays the negative effects of American foreign policy, not in terms of the damage done in foreign lands, but in terms of the troubled and anxious domestic landscape created by reckless military aggression. Lowell could be a vocal opponent of communism, but in his poetic world threats to stability come from America itself. The most prominent threat portrayed in his poetry is that of nuclear war, but Lowell's political poetry, rather than focusing single-mindedly on this issue, provides a wide-ranging critique of state power and an exploration of the possibilities of resistance. Lowell's poetry is often pessimistic in its appraisal of the ability of the private citizen to effect political change. Its strengths include, nevertheless, a profound representation of political feelings, and a vivid portrayal of the psychology of everyday life that resulted from the ambiguities of the Cold War.

The poetry explored in this article is most effective first in its portrayals of a private realm that has been invaded by political anxieties, and secondly in its pervasive resistance of 'victory culture'. An exploration of Lowell's poem 'Memories of West Street and Lepke' takes account of the influence of Allen Ginsberg on Lowell's writing, and maps out connections between Lowell's depiction of lobotomy and capital punishment and the use of psychiatry as a means of social control. In other poems the 'hawks' of war are responsible for disruptions to domestic tranquillity and security, whether because of their carelessness with the possibility of nuclear apocalypse (as in 'Fall 1961'), their endless waging of 'small wars' ('Waking Early Sunday Morning') or the demands made by the state of its citizens and its surveillance of their private lives ('Eye and Tooth'). The proud nationalism continually reiterated by Cold War policy as a justification for aggression is subjected to a thoroughly critical eye in Lowell's poems, which take the most central symbols of American triumphalism and present them as hollow, false and corrupted. A detailed reading of 'For the Union Dead' shows how Lowell takes a proud symbol of America's past – the 'Shaw Memorial', the monument to Colonel Shaw's African-American Civil War Regiment by Augustus St Gaudens, which faces the Massachusetts State House across Boston Common – and shows this heroic past to be a sorry contrast to a present characterised by a 'savage servility', in which the nation is still torn by its inability to confront its legacy of racial problems. Lowell's political poetry typically works not by directly exhorting the reader to protest and resistance, but by undermining the nationalism and patriotism that make resistance seem impossible.

America I feel sentimental about the Wobblies.
America I used to be a communist when I was a kid I'm not sorry.
I smoke marijuana every chance I get.

(Allen Ginsberg, 'America', 1956)[1]

These are the tranquillized *Fifties*,
and I am forty. Ought I to regret my seedtime?
I was a fire-breathing Catholic C.O.,
and made my manic statement,
telling off the state and president, and then
sat waiting sentence in the bull pen
beside a Negro boy with curlicues
of marijuana in his hair.

> (Robert Lowell, 'Memories of
> West Street and Lepke', 1957)[2]

DRIFTING TOWARDS RUIN, MAKING NO DIFFERENCE

In 1971 Ian Hamilton asked the poet Robert Lowell, 'what do you think literature can do – anything or nothing?' Lowell replied: 'Auden says poetry makes nothing happen. In the teeth of this, Flaubert wrote that his *education sentimentale* might, if read, have prevented the bloodshed of the Paris Commune. I do think being in something makes a difference.'[3] Lowell's ambivalent answer shows the tensions not only of his own career but of American poetry more generally in the post-war period. Auden's claim that 'poetry makes nothing happen' is made in his poem 'In Memory of W. B. Yeats', written soon after Yeats's death in January 1939: 'For poetry makes nothing happen . . . it survives, / A way of happening, a mouth.'[4] The lines can be seen as an epitaph to the highly politicised poetry of the 1930s. In the late 1950s, however, American poetry was again beginning to take political subjects, challenging the tidy formalism of the 'well-constructed poem' of the early 1950s produced in accordance with New Critical ideals, in particular the valorisation of irony as that literary feature that can resolve the apparent contradictions of the poem into an organic whole.[5] Lowell wants to believe – even if his 'I do think' indicates that this belief is tentative, a mere hope – that poetry might prevent bloodshed.

If 'being in something makes a difference', it is not clear what this difference might be. Lowell's career shows a continuing negotiation with the poet's relationship to the public and private spheres. If lyric poetry traditionally represents private experience, in doing so it also brings the private into the public domain. Lowell's poetry develops and refines an awareness of the political implications of representations of the private realm, and demonstrates how the relationship between private and public is always able to be reconstructed, reconceived. Its deployments of private experience exist alongside a range of public references, and, if he is often regarded as one of the founders of the 'confessional' school of poetry, he is also acutely aware of the political potential of confession. The 'self' confessed in Lowell's poetry is not a transparent and faithful translation of private life; rather it is constructed with a continual awareness of the impact made by 'confession' and autobiography, and of the power of writing to portray relationships between the individual and a larger social structure. In Lowell's conception of democratic politics, the 'individual' must always be aware of responsibilities in a wider political field. If democracy is ideally a politics of consensus, this consensus must allow for the possibility of dissent.

Lowell's political beliefs often led him to take public stances, with varying degrees of effectiveness. His refusal to serve in the Second World War, because of his abhorrence of the devastating bombings of German cities at a time when the Allies had already gained a military advantage, might not have prevented bloodshed, but it did give publicity to an unpopular stance of resistance. Early in 1949, Lowell was a key figure in what has been called 'one of the many "witch hunts" of the Cold War period'.[6] In the writers' colony at remote and serene Yaddo, of upstate New York, a Cold War in miniature was fought. Four writers – Lowell, the novelist Elizabeth Hardwick, the short-story writer Flannery O'Connor and Edward Maisel – banded together as freedom fighters of sorts, attempting a coup against the supposedly hardline Marxist regime run by executive director Elizabeth Ames. In this New England pastoral, an American version of George Orwell's *Animal Farm: A Fairy Story*, first published four years earlier, the self-righteous, rightist writers played the part of the pigs. According to the US Army (as reported in the *New York Times* on 11 February 1949), Agnes Smedley – a former Yaddo resident whose political activities of several decades included agitation against British rule in India, campaigning with Margaret Sanger to legalise birth control, campaigning against the Jim Crow laws and extensive involvement with the Chinese Revolution – had been acting as a contact for a Soviet spy ring.[7] On 19 February the army admitted that it had no evidence against Smedley, but this did nothing to dampen the rebels' fervour. Under Lowell's leadership, they asked the board of the Yaddo corporation to fire Ames, charging that 'Mrs Ames is somehow deeply and mysteriously involved in Mrs Smedley's political activities'. In a statement to the Yaddo board of directors, Lowell identified Yaddo as a 'body' and Mrs Ames as 'a diseased organ, chronically poisoning the whole system'; Bacon comments on this outburst that Lowell is using 'the Cold War language of disease'.[8]

This unpleasant attack on Ames and Smedley, the Missouri-born daughter of a Native American labourer, prefigured two dominant trends in American letters in the subsequent decade: the brisk sprint rightwards best exemplified by the volte-face of the editorial board of the once left-wing

Partisan Review, and the paranoiac harassment of writers and intellectuals who resisted cultural pressures to abandon left-wing causes.[9] Lowell's seemingly odd combination of pacifism and communist witch-hunting belies the equation made by the House Un-American Activities Commission (HUAC) of political resistance (and especially resistance to US imperialist objectives) and left-wing political beliefs.

Lowell's intervention at Yaddo might have been ineffectual and misguided, but his skills and instincts as a political activist were to develop impressively. At the end of May 1965, Lowell accepted an invitation from President Johnson to read at a White House Festival of the Arts. He then changed his mind because of his concern over the Vietnam War, and sent a copy of the letter explaining his position to the *New York Times*. *The Times* broke the story on 3 June, and followed it the next day with a report headed 'Twenty Writers and Artists Endorse Poet's Rebuff of President'; the figures included Hannah Arendt, John Berryman, Stanley Kunitz, Mark Rothko, Louis Simpson, W. D. Snodgrass and Robert Penn Warren. Lowell's gesture gained a great deal of publicity for anti-war sentiment at a time when opposition to the Vietnam War in the USA was not widespread.

Lowell's letter to Johnson was civil but firm. He wrote:

Although I am very enthusiastic about most of your domestic legislation and intentions, I nevertheless can only follow our present foreign policy with the greatest dismay and distrust. What we will do and what we ought to do as a sovereign nation facing other sovereign nations seem now to hang in the balance between the better and the worse possibilities. We are in danger of imperceptibly becoming an explosive and suddenly chauvinistic nation, and may even be drifting on our way to the last nuclear ruin.[10]

Lowell's confident public statement shows him as an accomplished activist, able to cause the government considerable embarrassment. His increasing skills as an activist matched certain developments in his poetry, and his letter to Johnson is a condensed summary of the political anxieties voiced in many key poems from the late 1950s and early 1960s, from two of his most successful books, *Life Studies* (1959) and *For the Union Dead* (1964). In these collections he develops a more accessible poetic language and style, a more direct representation of the private and the everyday, without sacrificing complexity. The poems register the pressure of public events on private existence, and in turn use the private to register political concerns.

In a 1952 editorial entitled 'Our Country and Our Culture', the editors of the *Partisan Review* claimed that 'Most writers no longer accept alienation as the artist's fate in America . . . More and more writers have ceased to think of themselves as rebels and exiles.'[11] A poem Lowell wrote in 1953 shows him directly at odds with the *Partisan Review*'s position. 'Inauguration Day: January 1953' is one of his earliest poems to register the effects of the Cold War, and anticipates a long series of political poems to follow. Lowell acts as an unelected and irreverent poet laureate, penning an occasional poem for the day of Eisenhower's inauguration, 20 January. Eisenhower and the nation are associated with ice, stasis, paralysis, death and nuclear destruction:

> Ice, ice. Our wheels no longer move.
> Look, the fixed stars, all just alike
> as lack-land atoms, split apart,
> and the Republic summons Ike,
> the mausoleum in her heart.[12]

Michael Thurston, in his superb commentary on this poem, points out that 'Ike' is the 'latest in [the US's] long line of martial heroes who hoped to heal and lead the country' and was also involved in the planning of the carpet bombing of German cities, the policy that led Lowell to become a conscientious objector in the Second World War. Thurston writes that, in Lowell's vision, 'the nation, dead as its monuments, looks to instal death at the helm', and suggests that 'the cold here refers to the Cold War more broadly'.[13]

The poetic persona in 'Inauguration Day: January 1953' is impersonal. The 'I' observing the scene is placed in public space, and is barely characterised. Lowell's subsequent political poetry, however, has close affiliations with autobiography. His poem 'Fall 1961', from *For the Union Dead*, shows his ability to move dynamically between private domestic space and the political world. Written at a time of extensive nuclear testing and enormous anxiety about the threat of nuclear war, the poem shows the writer in his 'studio', listening as

> Back and forth, back and forth
> goes the tock, tock, tock
> of the orange, bland, ambassadorial
> face of the moon
> on the grandfather clock.

'Fall 1961' is a narrative poem of sorts, but the narrative is made up of a stream of consciousness, registering the poet's thoughts. This enables it to make dramatic leaps from stanza to stanza, leaps seemingly dictated by associations in the poet's mind. This poetic method enables Lowell to record the complexity of his experience in a way that is intimate for the reader, but that does not dictate any positions: the reader is free to interpret. The 'tock tock tock' obviously suggests time passing, but also a countdown to a final moment (as in the ticking of a bomb). In 1961 this back-and-forth movement (the phrase 'back and forth' occurs five times in the poem) might suggest to the reader the movement 'back and forth' of the hands on the 'Bulletin clock', also known as the 'Doomsday clock', the famous symbol used on covers of the *Bulletin of the Atomic Scientists* since 1947, showing various times before midnight, the time of the impending apocalypse (the clock has moved seventeen times since its first appearance, showing times between seventeen minutes and two minutes before midnight).[14] Such associations appear to be in the mind of the poet, as the next stanza tells us bluntly

> All autumn, the chafe and jar
> of nuclear war;
> we have talked our extinction to death.
> I swim like a minnow
> behind my studio window.[15]

The poem may be implicitly political, but, rather than engaging in direct protest, it registers the poet's feelings of helplessness. Lowell's office has become an aquarium; he can be seen through the glass, but is powerless to influence what is beyond it. 'Our end drifts nearer', the next stanza begins (imagining the clock hands moving towards midnight?). In an image that links the state to the private self, the poet worries that 'The state / is a diver under a glass bell'.[16] One's time under a glass bell is limited by the amount of air the bell contains: this is an image of extreme vulnerability.

The poem continues to bring together the private and the public with its statement, 'A father's no shield / for his child'.[17] The shield, like the clock's 'tock tock', brings Cold War rhetoric into a domestic setting, as 'The North American Air Defense Command engaged in an exercise called "Sky Shield II" against a simulated Russian nuclear attack on October 14, 1961'.[18] The father wanting to shield his child shows a masculine role radically different from the military prowess the state demands of its soldier-citizens. Men, as fathers, might work to protect their children rather than sending them to war. The state, which causes wars instead of saving its citizens from them, cannot protect its children: Lowell expresses this in a sentimental, moving domestic tableau.

TRANQUILLIZED RESISTANCE

In the two quotations I have chosen as epigraphs for this chapter, Allen Ginsberg and Robert Lowell fuse defiant confession and political statement, and bring their own personal histories into the public domain. Lowell first drafted 'Memories of West Street and Lepke' in November of 1957; it became one of the best-known poems in his 1959 collection, *Life Studies*. In March 1957 he had given a three-week poetry-reading tour of the west coast, and his contact with the Beats, and Ginsberg in particular, had a decisive influence on his writing.[19]

In interviews Lowell recalls that 'poetry reading was sublimated by the practice of Allen Ginsberg'; he found, when reading what he called 'my old New Criticism religious, symbolic poems', that 'audiences just didn't understand, and I didn't always understand myself while reading'.[20] As a result, 'more and more I found that I was simplifying my poems . . . That seemed to improve the reading.'[21] While not aligning his own poetic practice with that of the Beats, Lowell shared with them the desire to communicate experience directly, and to establish a more intimate relationship with his readership. This involved a distancing from the formally intricate poetry praised by the New Critics. In 1961 Lowell complained that 'we've gotten into a sort of Alexandrian age. Poets of my generation and particularly younger ones have gotten terribly proficient at these forms. They write a very musical, difficult poem with tremendous skill . . . Yet the writing seems divorced from the culture.' Lowell thought that his poetry would need to take some of the qualities of prose, because, 'on the whole, prose is less cut off from life than poetry is . . . I couldn't get my experience into tight metrical forms'.[22]

Allen Ginsberg wrote 'America' on 17 January 1956, so it is likely that Lowell heard this poem during his west-coast tour. Despite the differences between the two poets' work, 'Memories of West Street and Lepke' and 'America' have many shared qualities. Both poems use 'autobiography and reminiscence' not only to represent the past but also to critique the present. In both poems the personal recollections record a stance of political dissent. Ginsberg recalls that 'when I was seven momma took me to Communist Cell meetings' while demanding in 'manic', indecorous terms:

> America when will we end the human war?
> Go fuck yourself with your atom bomb.[23]

Both poets position themselves as individuals in opposition to the power of the state: Ginsberg aggressively berates the American nation, just as Lowell recalls 'telling off the state and president'. There is an important difference, however. Whereas Ginsberg's poem *is* the protest, Lowell's poem remembers a moment of protest located in the past. It appears to follow Wordsworth's recipe for 'all good poetry' in that 'it takes its origin from emotion recollected in tranquillity'.[24] Lowell's caustic reference to the 'tranquillized *Fifties*' puts a negative spin on tranquillity, however. 'Ought I to regret my seedtime?' he asks. The poem is uncertain whether Lowell's tranquillized present is to be preferred to his fire-breathing past. Yet its representation of the present, of the 'Fifties' (a word that Lowell italicises, drawing the reader's attention to it), is implicitly just as negative as Ginsberg's.

Before *Life Studies*, Lowell's politics and poetry can be seen as separate spheres of activity. Lowell had written to President Roosevelt on 7 September 1943, politely refusing 'the opportunity you offer me in your communication of August 6, 1943, for service in the Armed Forces'. His accompanying 'Declaration of Personal Responsibility' protested 'the staggering civilian casualties that had resulted from the mining of the Ruhr Dams' and 'the razing of Hamburg, where 200,000 non-combatants are reported dead, after an almost apocalyptic series of all-out air-raids'.[25] Although in 'Memories of West Street and Lepke' Lowell characterises his statement as 'manic', it was in fact measured in tone, even if its content was radical and uncompromising. Its argument is important for the relationship it envisages between the individual and the nation. The 'Declaration of Personal Responsibility' (a title that Lowell, ever the poet mindful of words' associations, seems to have chosen to echo America's 'Declaration of Independence') argues that the individual is as responsible as the State for moral and political questions:

> It is a fundamental principle of our American Democracy, one that distinguishes it from the demagoguery and herd hypnosis of the totalitarian tyrannies, that with us each individual citizen is called upon to make voluntary and responsible decisions on issues which concern the national welfare . . . No matter how expedient I might find it to entrust my moral responsibility to the State, I realize that it is not permissible under a form of government which derives its sanctions from the rational assent of the governed.[26]

Lowell resists state authority in terms that carefully differentiate his position from a collective or socialist politics. Such differences in modes of resistance were to become tremendously important in the 1950s, when state suppression of communism was used as a pretext for the suppression of a wide range of political positions viewed as 'subversive'.[27] Lowell's affirmation of the importance of the individual conscience represents a highly politicised New England puritanism (Lowell preserved a puritan temperament even when he was a converted Catholic).

Lowell was punished for his refusal to serve. On 13 October 1943 he was sentenced for a year and a day in prison, and spent a few days in Manhattan's West Street Jail before being moved to the Federal Correction Centre at Danbury, Connecticut. He ended up spending 'only five and a half months in jail, then six and a half on parole in a Catholic cadet nurses' dormitory, mopping corridors and toilets'.[28] 'Memories of West Street and Lepke' contrasts Lowell's (relatively) stable professional present with his time in West Street Jail, where he met Louis 'Lepke' Buchalter, the notorious head of 'Murder Incorporated', a 'murder for hire' syndicate. Many commentators have noted how Lowell recalls his imprisonment through the lens of the Cold War. For Philip Metres, Lowell's 'odd caricature of his younger, objecting self' can be seen in relation to America's 'larger containment culture': 'Lowell's poem projects onto the past the atomism of the 1950s; all the figures in prison are "others", ciphers of disconnection, separation, and alienation from the mainstream.'[29]

Yet Lowell's positioning of himself in relation to Cold War authority is ambiguous, to say the least. Metres comments, 'It is as if Lowell were answering HUAC's question, "Are you now, or have you ever been, a Communist?" with a half-embarrassed, half-bragging, "No, I was a fire-breathing Catholic C.O."' and goes on to argue: 'If one reads Lowell's "confession" as ironic, these lines have a subversive quality, because they answer the question with self-caricature. At the same time, Lowell's irony here is a strategy of defeatism, insofar as the self-caricature replicates dominant stereotypes of dissent.'[30] Yet the irony in the poem, deriving from its sardonic redeployment of Cold War tropes, makes the poem seriously disturbing, and much more than a self-defeating caricature. Although in 1957 Lowell was a lapsed Catholic (or a lapsed convert to Catholicism, which is something different), there is no evidence that his opposition to war had lessened, and in the poem his younger self, the 'fire-breathing Catholic C.O.', despite his humorous zeal, is not subject to ridicule. In 1971 Lowell affirmed that he still maintained his position of opposition:

I became an objector of the saturation bombing of Hamburg and the proclamation of unconditional surrender . . . in 1943, when we'd conquered Sicily, and won the war, in a sense, I refused to report to the Army, and sent a rather humorless bombastic statement to President Roosevelt. I still stand on it.

Asked by Hamilton, 'And you'd take a similar position now, on Vietnam', Lowell replied: 'I would on Vietnam . . . I pray that I'd take the position of the draft evader, not leave the country but go to jail.'[31]

Even if Lowell represents his fellow-inmates – 'Abramowitz, / a jaundice-yellow . . . / and fly-weight pacifist', 'Bioff and Brown, / the Hollywood pimps' and Lepke himself – as Other, he shares with them a sense of 'alienation from the mainstream', and this alienation is not merely a part of his past. Lowell's language shows a pleasure in popular culture (the gangster movie), but his use of popular culture is not always approving. The language of advertising surrounding his daughter, who 'Like the sun . . . rises in her flame-flamingo infants' wear', suggests a commercial cheapening of the present; domesticity has been 'incorporated' by American industry no less than Czar Lepke incorporated murder. The poem's famous closing lines, with their frightening representation of state brutality, are as resonant for the Fifties as they are for 1943:

> Flabby, bald, lobotomized,
> he drifted in a sheepish calm,
> where no agonizing reappraisal
> jarred his concentration on the electric chair–
> hanging like an oasis in his air
> of lost connections . . .[32]

Conspiracy theory thrives on finding lost connections (difficult to do when lobotomised), and we should not resist these lines' invitation to concentration and enquiry. Lepke's sheepish calm echoes the 'tranquillised' condition of the Fifties, which find Lowell employed by the university, 'book-worming / in pajamas fresh from the washer' and 'hog[ging] a whole house on Boston's / "hardly passionate Marlborough Street"', wearing laundered clothes rather than doing the laundry or cleaning toilets, unlike 'Czar Lepke, / there piling towels on a rack'.[33] Has the tranquillised Cold War public lost its ability to make connections? The poem takes a negative stance on the use of psychiatry as a means of social control and opposes capital punishment; it depicts the 'containment' of Louis Buchalter, but by no means approves it. The 1950s reader might also connect mention of the 'electric chair' with two other Jews accused of criminal behaviour, Julius and Ethel Rosenberg; Buchalter was executed in Sing Sing Prison in 1944, the fate of the Rosenbergs seven years later.[34]

Like some of Ginsberg's poems and Sylvia Plath's *The Bell Jar*, the poem makes connections between lobotomy, the use of psychiatry, the use of the electric chair and state control.[35] Plath's novel begins with a chilling depiction of the Rosenbergs' execution, and this depiction is echoed by the narrator, Esther Greenwood's, descriptions of her experiences of electro-shock therapy. Ginsberg brings a similar set of associations into play in his poem 'Television Was a Baby Crawling Toward that Deathchamber', in which he describes conservative radio commentator Fulton Lewis 'making an evil suggestion that entered my mouth':

> that Julius and Ethel Rosenberg smelled bad & shd die, he sent to kill them with personal electricity, his power station is the spirit of generation leaving him thru his asshole by Error, that very electric entered Ethel's eye[36]

'Memories of West Street and Lepke' does not spell out such connections quite as explicitly as Ginsberg, but shares with Ginsberg's work the power to make the reader uneasy about the social conditions it portrays. It achieves this power through its astringent irony, most evident in the words used by Eisenhower's Secretary of State John Foster Dulles at the end of 1953, when announcing that France's failure to ratify the European Defence Community would result in 'an agonizing reappraisal of basic United States policy' towards France and Europe. 'Agonizing reappraisal' and another phrase used by Dulles, 'massive retaliation', became well known in association with US foreign policy.[37]

The use of Dulles's phrase in association with the 'lobotomised' Lepke hints at another 'lost connection', that of Dulles's younger brother, Allen Dulles, director of the CIA from 1953 to 1961.[38] Allen Dulles oversaw the CIA's promotion of research into dubious uses of psychiatry as a means of social control. This included the programme with the code name MKUL-TRA, authorised in April 1953 by Dulles, who was concerned about rumours alleging that brainwashing techniques had been used by the communists in the Korean War. MKULTRA used patients in psychiatric hospitals and other unwitting subjects, such as prisoners, to develop mind-control techniques. The programme's experiments included the use of electro-convulsive treatment, sensory deprivation and the use of a variety of drugs, most notoriously LSD.[39]

The subliminal presence of John Foster Dulles and Allen Dulles in the poem's close connects the taming of the notorious Lepke with the tranquillisation of the American public. HUAC and the CIA, like the authorities in charge of Lepke's fate, practised a 'massive retaliation' not only on communists in foreign countries, but also on dissidents within. If 'Memories of West Street and Lepke' does not make the kind of angry and direct statements to be found in Ginsberg's 'America', it nevertheless subtly depicts a diseased social organ, in which the absence of resistance is in itself a cause of alarm.

PRIVACY, PROPHECY AND SENTIMENT

'Thirsting for / the hierarchic privacy / of Queen Victoria's century', the 'hermit heiress' of Lowell's 'Skunk Hour' (written in 1957) 'buys up all / the eyesores facing her shore / and lets them fall'.[40] Only great wealth, it seems, can buy privacy in the 1950s. Lowell often depicts the individual as if on display in a compromised private space. The 'minnow / behind [his] studio window' in 'Fall 1961' can be seen by those outside the house better than he can see out; he is like the suffering poet of 'Eye and Tooth' (also written in 1961) who tells us:

> My whole eye was sunset red.
> The old cut cornea throbbed,
> I saw things darkly,
> As through an unwashed goldfish globe.[41]

Lowell's poems in this period, with their eyesores and sore eyes, depict the act of seeing as fraught with tension, difficulty, pain, even trauma. A footnote to 'Eye and Tooth' in the *Collected Poems* tells us that Lowell 'had suffered a corneal abrasion from a contact lens', but the associations mapped out in the poem make other 'connections'.[42] Lowell's 'dark sight' alludes to 1 Corinthians 13 ('For now we see through a glass, darkly; but then face to face'), with its contrast between seeing the divine or being trapped in a murky container – the goldfish globe is like a dirty prison, or cage. These associations are made elsewhere in Lowell's poetry, suggesting that America is far from the divine, and has lost touch with the key precept of Christianity (as famously expressed in the same biblical chapter), 'charity' or 'love': 'Though I speak with the tongues of men and of angels, but have not love, I have become sounding brass or a clanging cymbal.' Lowell again refers to 1 Corinthians 13 in 'Waking Early Sunday Morning' (1965), where he asks: 'When will we see Him face to face? / Each day, He shines through darker glass.'[43] Cold War America might be a state that encourages surveillance and vigilance, but true sight, the vision of love, suffers as the glass through which we might see God darkens.

'Eye and Tooth' suggests that eyes suffer when they spy – 'No ease for the boy at the keyhole, / his telescope'. The eyes have other threats in the poem, however. The title, 'Eye and Tooth', refers to the biblical verse 'eye for eye, tooth for tooth' (Exodus 21), the most well-known example of the *lex talionis*, the law of retaliation (Latin *lex* 'law', *talo* 'retaliation'), or what John Foster Dulles might call the law of 'massive retaliation'. Lowell's poetic mind links *talionis* with the *talons* of the hawks of war (*talionis* with the 'i's plucked out?), and in this poem private trauma is inseparable from the anxieties resulting from the behaviour of vengeful nations:

> No ease from the eye
> of the sharp-shinned hawk in the bird book there,
> with reddish brown buffalo hair
> on its shanks, one ascetic talon
>
> clasping the abstract imperial sky.
> It says:
> *an eye for an eye,*
> *a tooth for a tooth.*[44]

This sharp-shinned hawk gives private citizens 'no ease', threatening to clasp them with its talons, chew them up, leaving behind only traces, hair on its shanks. In this poem Lowell turns an instance of private suffering into a meditation on the ills of the United States in the Cold War, suggesting the collapse of privacy, the culture of surveillance, and the demands made on the individual by an imperialist state. (In our twenty-first century, we have already had a surfeit of the *lex talionis* and its hawks.)

The minnow's studio habitat and the state's glass bell of 'Fall 1961' and the 'goldfish globe' in 'Eye and Tooth' resonate poetically with the fish tanks of another of Lowell's most celebrated 'public poems' (although by now it should be clear how blurred the lines between public and private become in his poetry), 'For the Union Dead' (1960). Here, however, the tanks are empty. The fish, once 'cowed, compliant' (like calm, 'sheepish' Lepke: note the mixed animal and human metaphors in Lowell's language of degradation), are gone; 'The Aquarium is gone'; 'The airy tanks are dry'. 'For the Union Dead' has the adult poet remembering childhood visits to the 'old South Boston Aquarium', which, like the 'buried' statue of Stuyvesant in 'Inauguration Day: January 1953' 'stands / in a Sahara of snow now'.[45] From mourning the loss of the South Boston Aquarium, which was demolished in the 1950s, the poem describes the 'goug[ing] of the Boston Common to construct an 'underworld garage' (a car park), before beginning a sustained meditation on Augustus St Gaudens' 'Shaw

Memorial', a bronze relief opposite the Boston State House commemorating Colonel Robert Gould Shaw's 54th Massachusetts Volunteer Infantry Regiment, the first regiment of African-American soldiers organised in the North in the American Civil War.

'For the Union Dead' describes threats to cherished things. Just as the aquarium stands in a 'Sahara of snow', an odd apocalyptic landscape merging heat and cold, fire and ice, and the fish are gone God knows where, the Boston Statehouse and Shaw memorial are 'shaking', threatened with the same fate of undignified burial suffered by the men it honours, a threat posed by a man-made earthquake:

> A girdle of orange, Puritan-pumpkin colored girders
> braces the tingling Statehouse,
>
> shaking over the excavations, as it faces Colonel Shaw
> and his bell-cheeked Negro infantry
> on St. Gaudens' shaking Civil War relief,
> propped by a plank splint against the garage's earthquake.[46]

Although Lowell's poem is reverent towards the monument itself, its portrayal of the relationship between the monument and contemporary America is extremely pessimistic. After a stanza that tells us that

> Shaw's father wanted no monument
> except the ditch,
> where his son's body was thrown
> and lost with his 'niggers'

the poem goes on to describe present-day Boston in terms that negate any possibility of hope about the monument's legacy:

> The ditch is nearer.
> There are no statues for the last war here;
> on Boylston Street, a commercial photograph
> shows Hiroshima boiling
>
> over a Mosler safe, the 'Rock of Ages'
> that suvived the blast. Space is nearer.
> When I crouch to my television set,
> the drained faces of Negro school-children rise like balloons.[47]

The image of Hiroshima 'boiling / over a Mosler safe' works retroactively to account for the preceding apocalyptic landscape of the poem. The common is being dug by 'yellow dinosaur steamshovels', strange fusions of machine and prehistoric animals that, like the advertised Mosler safe, might survive the blast. This landscape is hostile to human beings and creatures of the sea, but 'Parking spaces luxuriate like civic / sandpiles in the heart of Boston'; the only preserved civic space in the poem is devoted to automobiles, which occupy the sandpiles in which children might play.[48] The fish cannot survive in the 'airy tanks', and the 'bronze weathervane cod' of the Aquarium 'has lost half its scales'. (The cod is a famous symbol of Massachusetts and Boston.)[49] Colonel Shaw, we are told in the penultimate stanza, 'is riding on his bubble, / he waits / for the blessèd break'. His bubble is as fragile as the bubbles the poet as a child observed 'drifting from the noses' of the fish in the aquarium, or the faces of the African-American children seen by the poet on television, presumably from coverage of the forced integration of schools and universities. In this dehumanised landscape, human beings are disembodied. 'Balloons' are not connected to bodies but float, or, like the fish bubbles, 'drift' aimlessly. Through repetition, the word 'drift' in Lowell's writing accretes ominous meanings. In his letter to President Johnson, he claims we are 'drifting on our way to the last nuclear ruin'; in 'Fall 1961', he worries that 'Our end drifts nearer'; in 'Memories of West Street and Lepke', Lepke 'drifted in a sheepish calm'. Drifting suggests a movement devoid of agency and purpose, a kind of passive surrender to contingency; and Lowell's writing expresses anxieties that the American public is 'drifting' in just this way. In the crashing ending of 'For the Union Dead' we are told that

> Everywhere,
> giant finned cars nose forward like fish
> a savage servility
> slides by on grease.[50]

Those lovely proud finned cars of the 1950s, now objects of nostalgia, with dreamy, romantic names like the Chevy Bel Air, the Plymouth Fury and the Ford Fairlane, have no romance here, but, mutating between machine and fish, have become dark mechanical symbols of the technologies that threaten to destroy us. Instead of the noble human aspirations expressed in St Gaudens' idealistic monument, we have only a 'savage servility' that 'slides by', a movement with the same absence of purpose as 'drifting'. The poet 'crouches' to his television set, and Webster's *Dictionary of the American Language* illuminates the significance of this word: 'to crouch' is 'to bend down; to stoop low' or 'to bend servilely; to stoop meanly; to fawn; to cringe'. Lowell does not exempt himself from the 'savage servility'; he too, crouching to the tube, is subject to the power of the media – just as Hiroshima has become mere advertising fodder – and his poem is not optimistic that his voice can 'make a difference'. Can a poetic voice be heard amid the flotsam and jetsam of media saturation? Can some political purpose be discerned in this atmosphere of drifting and servility? The poem's power, like most of Lowell's Cold War poems I have discussed here, lies not in a confident articulation of protest but in its refusal to celebrate America or to accede to what has been termed 'victory culture'. Lowell's poetry does not naively expect that its very existence will make a difference; rather that difference can be made only by readers, by the heightening of consciousness reading can make. If this consciousness includes an awareness of the difficulty of 'making a difference', then Lowell's 'protest poems' avoid a naive triumphalism, a smug pleasure in their own acts of dissent. Lowell is a reluctant prophet, one of those prophets like Jonah, Isaiah and Jeremiah who were sought out in their privacy, summoned to a vocation they wanted to hide from. Like these reluctant prophets, Lowell does not believe his thunderings will be effective. Death and destruction will continue, regardless. It might seem pessimistic to avoid feeling pride in refusing to assent, but this is a pessimism grounded in Lowell's awareness of the limits of his own political effectiveness. He can write to the President, but the President won't listen and will not write back.[51] His protest might make the press, but it will be just more news to sell safes or television sets. The television brings political events into the privacy of the home, but not in any way that makes meaningful critique possible. Gone, it seems, are the heroic possibilities expressed by Colonel Shaw and the 54th Regiment. Shaw 'seems to wince at pleasure / and suffocate for privacy', unlike the America of Lowell's present, whose media encourage the pleasures of consumption while they rob citizens of their privacy.[52]

'For the Union Dead', despite its mention of Hiroshima, focuses most intently on the internal construction of the USA, rather than on the USA's relations with the rest of the world. Lowell is attempting to hold up a glass in which the USA might see itself not darkly but clearly. As Tom Engelhardt writes in *The End of Victory Culture: Cold War America and the Disillusioning of a Generation*, 'it proved impossible to fashion a narrative of triumph' from the history of the American Civil War.[53] Lowell's representation of the difficulties of integration questions how liberal America likes to see itself. Rather than seeing these problems as confined to the American South, he chides Boston's pride in its monument to Colonel Shaw 'and his bell-cheeked Negro infantry': 'Their monument sticks like a fishbone / in the city's throat.' Civic space, the Boston Common itself, is torn apart and set off by a 'barbed and galvanized / fence'.[54] Lowell's refusal to celebrate the American nation and his questioning of the effectiveness of its monuments are heard in an ambiguity in the poem's title: is he writing for those who died for the union, or is he writing about a union that is dead, a union with a mausoleum in its heart?

These ambiguities and hesitations mean that Lowell is not replacing the authority of the state with another set of hollow certainties. Rather he captures the texture of feeling and foregrounds the difficulty of construing oneself as a political agent. And this uncertainty makes his poetry resonate; it is not merely dated, confident but ineffectual protest from the American past. Its power can be seen in the famous conclusion of 'Waking Early Sunday Morning', lines whose power is still as haunting and germane as when they were written:

> No weekends for the gods now. Wars
> flicker, earth licks its open sores,
> fresh breakage, fresh promotions, chance
> assassinations, no advance.
> Only man thinning out his kind
> sounds through the Sabbath noon, the blind
> swipe of the pruner and his knife
> busy about the tree of life . . .

> Pity the planet, all joy gone
> from this sweet volcanic cone;
> peace to our children when they fall
> in small war on the heels of small
> war – until the end of time
> to police the earth, a ghost
> orbiting forever lost
> in our monotonous sublime.[55]

How bleak to end with this orbiting lost ghost, the ghost of politics past that has no effectiveness in the sublime dehumanisation of postmodernism. Yet note the beauty of the human voice, the 'still small voice', that precedes the apparition of the ghost. This voice registers pain, and is not confident that it can make things happen. The landscape it describes, of 'open sores', 'breakage' and 'assassinations', is one of terrible violence, characterised by the 'blind / swipe of the pruner and his knife' savaging God's tree, the tree of life, on a Sunday. [56] The Second World War (the war for which, Lowell writes in

'For the Union Dead', 'there are no statues . . . here') was a 'big' war. The wars since then, the Korean War and the Vietnam War, are (only comparatively) 'small', but they have a 'domino effect', and in Lowell's vision, the USA is stacking and toppling the dominos. His vision of a succession of 'small' wars following on each other's heels is a powerful supplement to his fear of one great nuclear apocalypse. 'Waking Early Sunday Morning', a poem for the Sabbath, suggests that more small wars will follow, a suggestion that is heart-breakingly poignant and dishearteningly accurate as I write this essay in 2004. Lowell's language, with its talk of 'small wars' and peace, takes on a moving childishness, and its rhythms – 'Pity the planet, all joy gone' – are briefly the rhythms of a hymn or a prayer. A father is no shield for his child, and 'our children' will continue to fall in wars – unless, that is, we stop waging them. Peace to our children? This is a frail but worthy hope, and, despite Lowell's turmoil, he never gave up on it.

NOTES

1. Allen Ginsberg, 'America', in *Collected Poems, 1947–1980* (New York: Harper and Row, 1984), p. 146.
2. Robert Lowell, 'Memories of West Street and Lepke', in *Collected Poems*, ed. Frank Bidart and David Gewante (London: Faber and Faber, 2003), p. 187.
3. 'A Conversation with Ian Hamilton' (1971), reprinted in Robert Lowell, *Collected Prose*, ed. Robert Giroux (London: Faber and Faber, 1987), p. 285.
4. W. H. Auden, *Another Time: Poems* (London: Faber and Faber, 1940), p. 108.
5. For a famous example of New Critical practice, see Cleanth Brooks, *The Well-Wrought Urn: Studies in the Structure of Poetry* (London: D. Dobson, 1949). See Mark Jancovich, *The Cultural Politics of the New Criticism* (Cambridge: Cambridge University Press, 1993) for an overview of the New Critics.
6. Jon Lance Bacon, *Flannery O'Connor and Cold War Culture* (New York and Cambridge: Cambridge University Press, 1993), p. 58.
7. Smedley's publications include the novel *Daughter of Earth* (London: Virago, [1929] 1977), *China's Red Army Marches* (New York: Vanguard Press, 1934) and *Battle Hymn of China* (New York: Knopf, 1943). An account of her life and career can be found in Ruth Price, *The Lives of Agnes Smedley* (Oxford: Oxford University Press, 2004).
8. Ian Hamilton, *Robert Lowell: A Biography* (London: Faber and Faber, 1983), p. 146. For a description of this incident, see pp. 142–56; Bacon, *Flannery O'Connor and Cold War Culture*, p. 58.
9. On such harassment, see William E. Cain, *F. O. Matthiessen and the Politics of Criticism* (Madison: University of Wisconsin Press, 1988), and David Caute, *The Great Fear: The Anti-Communist Purge under Truman and Eisenhower* (New York: Simon and Schuster, 1978).
10. Letter to President Lyndon Johnson, reprinted in Robert Lowell, *Collected Prose*, p. 371.
11. Anon., 'Editorial Statement: Our Country and Our Culture', *Partisan Review*, 19 (1952), p. 284.
12. Lowell, 'Inauguration Day: January 1953', in *Collected Poems*, p. 117.
13. Michael Thurston, 'Robert Lowell's Monumental Vision: History, Form, and the Cultural Work of the Postwar American Lyric', *American Literary History*, 12/1 (2000), p. 92.

14. My thanks to Douglas Field for suggesting the relevance of the *Bulletin* clock. See the introduction to Jacqueline Foertsch, *Enemies Within: The Cold War and the AIDS Crisis in Literature, Film, and Culture* (Urbana and Chicago: University of Illinois Press, 2001) for a discussion of the clock's importance.
15. Lowell, 'Fall 1961', in *Collected Poems*, p. 329.
16. Ibid. p. 329.
17. Ibid. p. 329.
18. From a note in *Collected Poems*, p. 1058. For a fuller discussion of the Cold War context of 'Fall 1961', see Steven Axelrod, 'Robert Lowell and the Cold War', *New England Quarterly*, 72 (1999), pp. 339–61.
19. See Hamilton, *Robert Lowell*, pp. 231–3; Paul Mariani, *Lost Puritan: A Life of Robert Lowell* (New York: W. W. Norton, 1994), p. 251.
20. 'A Conversation with Ian Hamilton', p. 284.
21. 'An Interview with Frederick Seidel' (1961), reprinted in *Collected Prose*, p. 243.
22. Ibid. p. 244.
23. Ginsberg, 'America', pp. 146–7.
24. Wordsworth's preface to the *Lyrical Ballads*, 2nd edn (London, Longman 1800).
25. Robert Lowell, *Collected Prose*, pp. 367–9.
26. Ibid. p. 369.
27. For a detailed account of Diana Trilling's efforts to distinguish liberal anti-communism from McCarthyism, see Ronald Radosh, 'The Legacy of the Anti-Communist Liberal Intellectuals', *Partisan Review*, 47/4 (2000), pp. 550–67.
28. 'A Conversation with Ian Hamilton', p. 279.
29. Philip Metres, 'Confusing a Naive Robert Lowell and Lowell Naeve: "Lost Connections" in 1940s War Resistance at West Street Jail and Danbury Prison', *Contemporary Literature*, 41/4 (2000), pp. 673, 675.
30. Ibid. p. 673.
31. 'A Conversation with Ian Hamilton', p. 280.
32. Lowell, 'Memories of West Street and Lepke', p. 188.
33. Ibid. p. 187.
34. See Virginia Carmichael, *Framing History: The Rosenberg Story and the Cold War* (Minneapolis: University of Minnesota Press, 1993), for an excellent discussion of literary representations of the Rosenbergs.
35. Sylvia Plath, *The Bell Jar* (London: Faber, 1966). *The Bell Jar* was first published in 1963 by Heinemann under the pseudonym Victoria Lucas.
36. Ginsberg, *Collected Poems, 1947–1980*, p. 278.
37. The expression 'massive retaliation' can be found in John Foster Dulles, 'The Evolution of Foreign Policy', *Department of State Bulletin*, 30, 25 January 1962, p. 110.
38. Many commentators on the poem point out the reference to John Foster Dulles, but no reading that I have seen has suggested that Allen Dulles may also be hinted at here.
39. For details of the MKULTRA programme, see John D. Marks, *The Search for the 'Manchurian Candidate': The CIA and Mind Control* (New York: Times Books, 1979), and Harvey M. Weinstein, *Psychiatry and the Central Intelligence Agency: Victims of Mind Control* (Washington: American Psychiatric Press, 1990).
40. Lowell, 'Skunk Hour', in *Collected Poems*, p. 191.
41. Lowell, 'Eye and Tooth', in *Collected Poems*, pp. 334–5.
42. Lowell, *Collected Poems*, p. 1059.
43. Lowell, 'Eye and Tooth', p. 385.
44. Ibid. p. 334.
45. Lowell, 'For the Union Dead', in *Collected Poems*, pp. 376–8.
46. Ibid. p. 376.
47. Ibid. p. 377.
48. Ibid. p. 376.

49. For this information I am indebted to the outstanding website devoted to 'For the Union Dead' compiled by Sarah Luria of the English Department of the College of the Holy Cross of Worcester, MA. See http://www.holycross.edu/departments/english/sluria/Poem.htm

50. Lowell, 'For the Union Dead', p. 378.

51. Instead of writing back to Lowell, Johnson instructed his 'special consultant' Eric F. Goldman to reply to Lowell with 'just an acknowledgement' (Hamilton, *Robert Lowell*, pp. 320–2).

52. Lowell, 'For the Union Dead', p. 377.

53. Tom Engelhardt, *The End of Victory Culture: Cold War America and the Disillusioning of a Generation*, 2nd edn (Amherst, MA: University of Massachusetts Press, 1995), p. 29.

54. Lowell, 'For the Union Dead', p. 376.

55. Lowell, 'Waking Early Sunday Morning', in *Collected Poems*, p. 386.

56. Ibid. pp. 383–6.

Bibliography

(*References to magazine articles cited in Jacqueline Foertsch's chapter are listed at the end of Chapter 1.*)

Abrams, Nathan and Julie Hughes (eds), *Containing America: Cultural Production and Consumption in 50s America* (Birmingham: Birmingham University Press, 2000).

Algren, Nelson, (review of *Giovanni's Room*, by James Baldwin), 'Lost Men', *Nation*, 1 December 1956, p. 484.

All about Eve, Joseph L. Mankiewicz, Dir., 20th Century Fox (1950).

Allen, Jeanne, 'The Social Matrix of Television: Invention in the United States', in E. Ann Kaplan (ed.) *Regarding Television: Critical Approaches – An Anthology* (Los Angeles: American Film Institute, 1983).

Anderson, Carol, *Eyes off the Prize: The United Nations and the African American Struggle for Human Rights, 1944–1955* (Cambridge: Cambridge University Press, 2003).

Anderson, Perry, 'A Ripple of the Polonaise', *London Review of Books*, 21, 25 November 1999, pp. 3, 5–10.

Anon., *Cold War Chronology* (1939–55), http://www.people.memphis.edu/sherman/chrono ColdWar.htm

Anon., 'White Regrets Film', *New York Times*, 28 November 1946, p. 40.

Anon., 'Editorial Statement: Our Country and our Culture', *Partisan Review*, 19 (1952), pp. 282–6.

Anon., 'Trailerite as Typical American', *Mobile Life Magazine* (yearbook) (1954), p. 13.

Anon., 'War on the Home Front', *Daily Telegraph*, 10 March 2003, http://www.telegraph.co.uk/opinion/main.jhtml?xml=%2Fopinion%2F2003%2F03%2F10%2Fdl1001.xml&secureRefresh=true&_requestid=9649

Anon., 'Orwell's List', *The Guardian*, 21 June 2003, Review, p. 7.

Appleby, Joyce, Lynn Hunt and Margaret Jacob, *Telling the Truth about History* (New York: W. W. Norton, 1994).

Appy, Christian G. (ed.), *Cold War Constructions: The Political Culture of the United States Imperialism, 1945–1966* (Amherst, MA: University of Massachusetts Press, 2000).

Arendt, Hannah, *The Origins of Totalitarianism* (New York: Harcourt Brace, 1951).

Atkins, John, *George Orwell* (London: Calder and Boyars, 1945).

Auden, W. H., *Another Time: Poems* (London: Faber and Faber, 1940).

Axelrod, Steven, 'Robert Lowell and the Cold War', *New England Quarterly*, 72 (1999), pp. 339–61.

Baard, Erik, 'Buying Trouble', *Village Voice*, 24–30 July 2002, http://villagevoice.com/issues/0230/baard.php

Babson, Roger W., 'We'll Soon Be Living on Wheels', *Trailer Travel* (January–February 1936), pp. 10–12, 26.

Bacon, Jon Lance, *Flannery O'Connor and Cold War Culture* (New York and Cambridge: Cambridge University Press, 1993).

Baker, Houston A., Jr, *Blues, Ideology, and Afro-American Literature: A Vernacular Theory* (Chicago and London: University of Chicago Press, 1984).

Baldwin, James, 'Preservation of Innocence', *Zero*, 1 (Summer 1949), pp. 14–22.

Baldwin, James, *Notes of a Native Son* (London: Penguin, [1955] 1995).

Baldwin, James, *Giovanni's Room* (London: Penguin, [1956] 1990).

Baldwin, James, *Just above my Head* (London: Penguin, [1979] 1994).

Baldwin, James, *Jimmy's Blues: Selected Poems* (London: Michael Joseph, 1983).

Baldwin, James, *The Price of the Ticket: Collected Nonfiction, 1948–1985* (New York: St Martin's/ Marek, 1985).

Banham, Reyner, 'A Home is Not a House', in Penny Sparke (ed.), *Design by Choice* (New York: Rizzoli, 1981), pp. 56–60.

Barkan, Joann, '"My Mother, Drunk or Sober": George Orwell on Nationalism and Patriotism', *Dissent* (Winter 2003), http://www.dissentmagazine.org/menutest/archives/2003/wi03/barkan.htm

Barnouw, Erik, *The Golden Web: A History of Broadcasting in the United States*, vol. 2: *1933–1953* (New York: Oxford University Press, 1968).

Barnouw, Erik, *A Tube of Plenty* (New York: Oxford University Press, 1982).

Barrios, Richard, *Screened Out: Playing Gay in Hollywood from Edison to Stonewall* (New York: Routledge, 2002).

Bartley, Numan V., *The Rise of Massive Resistance: Race and Politics in the South during the 1950s* (Baton Rouge, LA: Louisiana State University Press, 1969).

Bataan, Tay Garnett, Dir., Metro-Goldwyn-Mayer (1943).

Bell, Daniel, *The End of Ideology: On the Exhaustion of Political Ideas in the Fifties* (New York: Free Press, 1962).

Ben-Hur, Willam Wyler, Dir., Metro-Goldwyn-Mayer (1959).

Benshoff, Harry M., *Monsters in the Closet: Homosexuality and the Horror Film* (Manchester and New York: Manchester University Press, 1997).

Berlet, Chip and Matthew N. Lyons, *Right-Wing Populism in America: Too Close for Comfort* (New York and London: Guilford Press, 2000).

Bernstein, Matthew, 'Needed: A Negro Legion of Decency', *Ebony* (February 1947), p. 36.

Birth of a Nation, D.W. Griffith, Dir., David W. Griffith Corp. (1915).

Blair, Tony, 'The Left should not Weep if Saddam is Toppled', *The Guardian*, 10 February 2003, http://www.guardian.co.uk/comment/story/0,3604,892331,00.html

Blum, William, *The CIA – A Forgotten History: US Global Interventions since World War Two* (London: Zed, 1996).

Boddy, William, *Fifties Television: The Industry and its Critics* (Urbana: University of Illinois Press, 1990).

Bone, Robert A., *The Negro Novel in America* (1958), rev. edn (New Haven: Yale University Press, 1965).

Borstelmann, Thomas, *The Cold War and the Color Line: American Race Relations in the Global Arena* (Cambridge, MA: Harvard University Press, 2001).

Bowker, Gordon, *George Orwell* (London: Little, Brown, 2003).

Brands, H. W., *What America Owes the World: The Struggle for the Soul of Foreign Policy* (Cambridge: Cambridge University Press, 1998).

Brooks, Cleanth, *The Well-Wrought Urn: Studies in the Structure of Poetry* (London: D. Dobson, 1949).

Brooks, Richard, 'Orwell's Room 101 to be Work of Art', *Sunday Times*, 23 March 2003, p. 14.

Brown, Sterling, *The Negro in American Fiction*, published with *Negro Poetry and Drama*, with a preface by Robert Bone (New York: Atheneum, 1969).

Brown, Sterling A., Arthur P. Davis and Ulysses Lee (eds), *The Negro Caravan: Writings by American Negroes*, introduced by Julius Lester (New York: Arno Press and the *New York Times*, [1941] 1970).

Bush, George W., address to Congress, 20 September 2001, reprinted at http://www.whitehouse.gov/news/releases/ 2001/09/print/20010920-8.html

Bush, George W., *We will Prevail: George Bush on War, Terrorism, and Freedom*, foreword by Peggy Noonan, introduction by Jay Nordlinger (New York and London: Continuum International Publishing Group, 2003).

Cabin in the Sky, Vincente Minnelli, Dir., Metro-Goldwyn-Mayer (1943).

Caddigan, James, 'Station Operations: Setting up a Special Events Department', *Television: The Magazine of Video Fact*, 2/10 (December 1945), pp. 11–14.

Cain, William E., *F. O. Mathiessen and the Politics of Criticism* (Madison: University of Wisconsin Press, 1988).

Campbell, James, *Exiled in Paris: Richard Wright, James Baldwin, Samuel Beckett, and Others on the Left Bank* (New York and London: Scribner's, 1995).

Campbell, James, 'I Heard it through the Grapevine', *Granta*, 73 (Spring 2001), pp. 153–82.

Carey, John, 'The Invisible Man', *Sunday Times*, 18 May 2003, Culture, p. 35.

Carmichael, Virginia, *Framing History: The Rosenberg Story and the Cold War* (Minneapolis: University of Minnesota Press, 1993).

Caute, David, *The Great Fear: The Anti-Communist Purge under Truman and Eisenhower* (New York: Simon and Schuster, 1978).

Cesarani, David, *Arthur Koestler: The Homeless Mind* (London: William Heinemann, 1998).

Chauncey, George, 'From Sexual Inversion to Homosexuality: The Changing Medical Conceptualization of Female "Deviance"', in Kathy Piess and Christina Simmons (eds), *Passion and Power: Sexuality in History* (Philadelphia: Temple University Press, 1989), pp. 87–117.

Chauncey, George, *Gay New York: Gender, Urban Culture, and the Making of the Gay Male World, 1890–1940* (New York: Basic Books, 1994).

Chester, Eric Thomas, *Covert Network: Progressives, the International Rescue Committee, and the CIA* (Armonk, NY: M. E. Sharpe, 1995).

Chomsky, Noam, 'Objectivity and Liberal Scholarship', in *American Power and the New Mandarins* (London: Chatto and Windus, 1969), pp. 65–98.

Christensen, H. G., 'Long Shots and Close-ups', *Television: the Magazine of Video Fact*, 3/2 (February 1946), pp. 28–9.

Cockburn, Alexander, 'Orwell and Koestler', *The Nation* (April 1998), p. 7.

Cockburn, Alexander, 'Hitch the Snitch', *Counterpunch* (February 1999), http://www.counterpunch.org/snitch.html

Condon, Richard, *The Manchurian Candidate* (New York: New American Library, 1959).

Corber, Robert J., *In the Name of National Security: Hitchcock, Homophobia and the Political Construction of Gender in Postwar America* (Durham, NC, and London: Duke University Press, 1993).

Corber, Robert J., *Homosexuality in Cold War America: Resistance and the Crisis of Masculinity* (Durham, NC, and London: Duke University Press, 1997).

Corey, Donald Webster, *The Homosexual in America: A Subjective Approach* (New York: Greenberg, 1951).

Cousins, Paul M., *Joel Chandler Harris* (Baton Rouge, LA: Louisiana State University Press, 1968).

Crick, Bernard, *George Orwell: A Life* (Harmondsworth: Penguin, 1982).

Crick, Bernard, 'Blair vs. the Left', *The Guardian*, 12 July 1996, p. 14.

Crick, Bernard, 'Orwell's "Premature Anti-Stalinism"', *The Guardian*, 24 June 2003, http://www.guardian.co.uk/letters/story/0,3604,983788,00.html

Crowther, Bosley, 'Spanking Disney', *New York Times*, 8 December 1946, p. 5.

David, Arthur P., 'Integration and Race Literature' (1956), in Angelyn Mitchell (ed.), *Within the Circle: An Anthology of African American Literary Criticism from the Harlem Renaissance to the Present* (Durham, NC, and London: Duke University Press, 1994), pp. 156–61.

Davis, James F., *Who is Black? One Nation's Definition* (Pennsylvania: Pennsylvania State University Press, 1991).

Davis, Mike, 'Fortress Los Angeles: The Militarization of Urban Space', in Michael Sorkin (ed.), *Variations on a Theme Park: The New American City and the End of Public Space* (New York: Hill and Wang, 1992), pp. 154–80.

Debord, Guy, '"Situationists": International Manifesto', in Ulrich Conrads (ed.), *Programs and Manifestoes on Twentieth-Century Architecture* (Cambridge, MA: MIT Press, 2002), pp. 172–4.

D'Emilio, John, *Sexual Politics, Sexual Communities: The Making of a Homosexual Minority in the United States, 1940–1970* (Chicago and London: University of Chicago Press, 1983).

D'Emilio, John and Estelle B. Freedman, *Intimate Matters: A History of Sexuality in America* (New York and Cambridge: Harper and Row, 1988).

Deutscher, Isaac, '1984–The Mysticism of Cruelty', in *Russia in Transition and Other Essays* (London: Hamish Hamilton, 1957), pp. 230–45.

Dickstein, Morris, *Gates of Eden: American Culture in the Sixties* (New York: Basic Books, 1977).

Doremus, Thomas (ed.), *Frank Lloyd Wright and Le Corbusier: The Great Dialogue* (New York: Van Nostrand, 1985).

Dowd, Maureen, 'Streetcar Named Betrayal', *New York Times*, 24 February 1999, http://www.nytimes.com/library/opinion/dowd/022499dowd.html

Drury, Margaret J., *Mobile Homes: The Unrecognized Revolution in American Housing* (New York: Praeger Publishers, 1972).

Dudziak, Mary L., *Cold War Civil Rights: Race and the Image of American Democracy* (Princeton: Princeton University Press, 2000).

Dulles, John Foster, 'The Evolution of Foreign Policy', *Department of State Bulletin*, 30, 25 January 1962, pp. 107–10.

Dunlap, Orin E., Jr, *The Future of Television* (New York: Harper and Bros, 1942).

Edwards, Carl M., *Homes for Travel and Living: The History and Development of the Recreational Vehicle and Mobile Home Industries* (East Lansing, MI: C. Edwards, 1977).

Elgrably, John and George Plimpton, 'The Art of Fiction 1984: James Baldwin' (1984), in Fred L. Standley and Louis H. Pratt (eds), *Conversations with Baldwin* (Jackson and London: University of Mississippi Press, 1989), pp. 232–54.

Ellis, Havelock, *Studies in the Psychology of Sex: Sexual Inversion* (Honolulu, HI: University Press of the Pacific, [1906] 2001).

Engelhardt, Tom, *The End of Victory Culture: Cold War America and the Disillusioning of a Generation*, 2nd edn (Amherst, MA: University of Massachusetts Press, 1995).

Evans, Malcolm, 'Text Theory, Criticism: 20 Things You Never Knew about George Orwell', in Christopher Norris (ed.), *Inside the Myth – Orwell: Views from the Left* (London: Fontana, 1984), pp. 12–38.

Ezard, John, 'Blair's Babe', *The Guardian*, 21 June 2003, http://www.guardian.co.uk/uk_news/story/0,3604,982159,00.html

Fanon, Frantz, *Black Skin, White Masks* (1952), trans. Charles Lam Markmann (New York: Grove Weidenfeld, 1967; London: Pluto Press, 1986).

Farber, Manny, 'Movies: Dixie Corn', *New Republic*, 115, 23 December 1946, p. 879.

Fernandez-Armesto, Filipe, *Millennium* (London: Bantam, 1995).

Fiedler, Leslie, 'Come Back to the Raft Ag'in, Huck Honey!' (1948), in *The Collected Essays of Leslie Fiedler*, vol. 1 (New York: Stein and Day, 1971), pp. 142–51; reprinted in Gerald Graff and James Phelan (eds), *The Adventures of Huckleberry Finn*, by Mark Twain (Boston: Bedford Books, 1995), pp. 528–34.

Fiedler, Leslie, 'A Homosexual Dilemma', *New Leader*, 39/10 (1956), p. 17.

Fiedler, Leslie, *Love and Death in the American Novel* (New York: Dell, 1960).

Fiedler, Leslie, *The Return of the Vanishing American* (London: Jonathan Cape, 1968).

Fishman, Robert, *Bourgeois Utopias* (New York: Basic Books, 1987).

Foertsch, Jacqueline, *Enemies Within: The Cold War and the AIDs Crisis in Literature, Film, and Culture* (Urbana and Chicago: University of Illinois Press, 2001).

Foster, Jack, 'Mrs Mobile Homemaker of 1959', *Mobile Life Magazine* (yearbook) (1959), pp. 11–13.

Franklin, John Hope, 'A Brief History', in Mabel M. Smythe (ed.), *The Black American Reference Book* (Englewood Cliffs: Prentice-Hall, 1976), pp. 1–90.

Fraser Hart, John, John T. Morgan and Michelle J. Rhodes, *The Unknown World of the Mobile Home* (Baltimore: Johns Hopkins University Press, 2002).

Freedland, Richard, *The Truman Doctrine and the Origins of McCarthyism* (New York: Knopf, 1971).

Freud, Sigmund, *On Metapsychology* (1915), trans. James Strachey, Penguin Freud Library, vol. 11 (London: Penguin, 1984).

Fukuyama, Francis, *The End of History and the Last Man* (London: Penguin, 1992).

Fuss, Diana, 'Fashion and the Homospectatorial Look', *Critical Inquiry*, 18/2 (Summer 1992), pp. 713–37.

Gaddis, John Lewis, *The United States and the Origins of the Cold War, 1941–1947* (New York: Columbia University Press, 1972).

Gardner, Lloyd C., *Spheres of Influence: The Partition of Europe from Munich to Yalta* (London: John Murray, 1993).

Garton Ash, Timothy, 'Orwell for our Time', *The Guardian*, 5 May 2001, http://www.guardian.co.uk/saturday_review/story/0,3605,485972,00.html.

Garton Ash, Timothy, 'Love, Death, and Treachery', *The Guardian*, 21 June 2003, Review, pp. 4–7.

Garton Ash, Timothy, 'Orwell's List', *New York Review of Books*, 25 September 2003, http://www.nybooks.com/articles/16550

Gayle, Addison, Jr (ed.), *The Black Aesthetic* (New York: Doubleday and Company, 1971).

Geertz, Clifford, *The Interpretation of Cultures* (London: Fontana, 1993).

Geist, Kenneth L., *Pictures Will Talk: The Life and Films of Joseph L. Mankiewicz* (New York: Scribner's, 1978).

Gerstle, Gary, *American Crucible: Race and Nation in the Twentieth Century* (Princeton: Princeton University Press, 2001).

Gienow-Hecht, Jessica C. E., 'Shame on US? Academics, Cultural Transfer, and the Cold War – A Critical Review', *Diplomatic History*, 24/3 (Summer 2000), pp. 465–94.

Ginsberg, Allen, *Collected Poems, 1947–1980* (New York: Harper and Row, 1984).

Ginsberg, Elaine K. (ed.), *Passing and the Fictions of Identity* (Durham, NC, and London: Duke University Press, 1996).

Gleason, Abbot, *Totalitarianism: The Inner History of the Cold War* (New York: Oxford University Press, 1995).

Graff, Gerald and James Phelan (eds), *The Adventures of Huckleberry Finn*, by Mark Twain (Boston: Bedford Books, 1995).

Gress, David, *From Plato to NATO: The Idea of the West and its Opponents* (New York: Free Press, 1998).

Halberstam, Judith, *Female Masculinity* (Durham, NC: Duke University Press, 1998).

Hamilton, Ian, *Robert Lowell: A Biography* (London: Faber and Faber, 1983).

Harris, Joel Chandler, *Uncle Remus: His Songs and His Sayings* (New York: Penguin Classics, [1880] 1986).

Harris, Joel Chandler, *The Complete Tales of Uncle Remus*, compiled by Richard Chase (Boston: Houghton Mifflin Company, 1955).

Hartz, Louis, *The Liberal Tradition in America* (New York: Harcourt, Brace and Company, 1955).

Harvey, David, *The Condition of Postmodernity* (Cambridge, MA: Blackwell, 1989).

Haynes, John E., *Red Scare or Red Menace? American Communism and Anticommunism in the Cold War Era* (Chicago: Ivan R. Dee, 1986).

Hemenway, Robert , 'Introduction: Author, Teller and Hero' (1982), in Joel Chandler Harris, *Uncle Remus: His Songs and His Sayings* ([1880] 1982; New York: Penguin Classics, 1986), pp. 7–31.

Hencke, David and Rob Evans, 'How Big Brothers Used Orwell to Fight the Cold War', *The Guardian* (30 June 2000), http://www.guardian.co.uk/international/story/0,3604, 338230,00.html

Henrikson, Alan K., 'Mental Maps', in Michael J. Hogan and Thomas G. Paterson (eds), *Explaining the History of American Foreign Relations* (Cambridge: Cambridge University Press, 1992), pp. 177–92.

Herman, Arthur, *Joseph McCarthy: Reexamining the Life and Legacy of America's Most Hated Senator* (New York: Free Press, 2000).

Hicks, Granville, 'Tormented Triangle' (review of *Giovanni's Room*, by James Baldwin), *New York Times Book Review*, 14 October 1956, p. 5.

Hinman, Chauncey T., 'How You Can Help the FBI', *Travel Trailer Magazine* (March 1953), pp. 24, 50–51, 61.

Hitchens, Christopher, 'Orwell – A Snitch?', *The Nation* (February 1998), p. 3.

Hitchens, Christopher, *Orwell's Victory* (London: Allen Lane, 2002).

Hixson, Walter L., *Parting the Curtain: Propaganda, Culture and the Cold War, 1945–1961* (London: Macmillan, 1997).

Hofstadter, Richard, *The American Political Tradition and the Men Who Made it* (New York: Knopf, 1948).

Hofstadter, Richard, *The Age of Reform* (New York: Knopf, 1955).

Hogan, Michael J., *A Cross of Iron: Harry S. Truman and the Origins of the National Security State, 1945–1954* (Cambridge: Cambridge University Press, 1998).

Hoover, J. Edgar with Courtney Ryley Cooper, 'Camps of Crime', in Todd B. Kimmell and Kristin P. Kimmel (eds), *Lost Highways* (Philadelphia: Lost Highways, the Classic Trailer and Mobile Home Club, 1940), pp. 22–8.

Hunter, Edward, *Brainwashing in Red China: The Calculated Destruction of Men's Minds* (New York: Copp Clark, 1951).

Hunter, Edward, *Brainwashing: The Story of the Men Who Defied It* (New York: Farrar Straus and Cuhday, 1956).

I Was a Communist for the FBI, Gordon Douglas, Dir., Warner Brothers (1951).

Independence Day, Roland Emmerich, Dir., 20th Century Fox (1996).

Invasion of the Body Snatchers, Don Siegel, Dir., Allied Artists (1955).

Ivie, Robert L., 'Fire, Flood, and Red Fever: Motivating Metaphors of Global Emergency in the Truman Doctrine Speech', *Presidential Studies Quarterly*, 29/3 (September 1999), pp. 570–91.

Jackson, Rosemary, *Fantasy: The Literature of Subversion* (London and New York: Routledge, 1995).

Jancovich, Mark, *The Cultural Politics of the New Criticism* (Cambridge: Cambridge University Press, 1993).

Johnson, Frank, 'Orwell Was Right to Spy for Britain', *Daily Telegraph*, 12 July 1996, p. 26.

Jones, Mervyn, 'Fears that Made Orwell Sneak on his Friends', *The Guardian*, 13 July 1996, p. 26.

Just Around the Corner, Irving Cummings, Dir., 20th Century Fox (1938).

Kammen, Michael, *Mystic Chords of Memory: The Transformation of Tradition in American Culture* (New York: Vintage Books, 1993).

Kaplan, Ann (ed.), *Regarding Television: Critical Approaches – An Anthology* (Los Angeles: American Film Institute, 1983), pp. 109–19.

Kaplan, Amy, ' "Left Alone with America": The Absence of Empire in the Study of American Culture', in Amy Kaplan and Donald E. Pease (eds), *Cultures of United States Imperialism* (Durham, NC: Duke University Press, 1993), pp. 3–21.

Kelly, Michael, 'Phony Pacifists', *Washington Post*, 3 October 2001, p. 31.

Kennan, George, telegram to Secretary of State, Washington (The Long Telegram), 22 February 1946, http://www.gwu.edu/nsarchiv/coldwar/documents/episode-/kennan.htm

Kennan, George/Mr X, 'The Sources of Soviet Conduct', *Foreign Affairs*, 25/4 (July 1947), pp. 566–82; reprinted in George F. Kennan, *American Diplomacy, 1900–1950* (Chicago: University of Chicago Press, 1951), pp. 89–106.

Kent, Eleanor, 'Now comes the age of the . . . Dream House on Wheels', *Mobile Life Magazine* (yearbook) (1963), 35–41.

Kiesler, Frederick, 'Space City Architecture', in Ulrich Conrads (ed.), *Programs and Manifestoes on Twentieth-Century Architecture* (Cambridge, MA: MIT Press, 2002), p. 98.

Kinsey, Alfred, *Sexual Behavior in the Human Male* (Philadelphia and London: W. B. Saunders Company, 1948).

Koestler, Arthur, *Darkness at Noon*, trans. Daphne Hardy (London: Vintage, [1940] 1994).

Kolko, Gabriel, *Century of War: Politics, Conflict, and Society since 1914* (New York: New Press, 1994).

Kolko, Joyce and Gabriel Kolko, *The Limits of Power: The World and United States Foreign Policy, 1945–1954* (New York: Harper and Row, 1972).

Kroes, Rob, 'American Empire and Cultural Imperialism: A View from the Receiving End', *Diplomatic History*, 23/3 (Summer 1999), pp. 463–77.

LaFeber, Walter, *America, Russia and the Cold War, 1945–1990* (New York: McGraw-Hill, 1991).

Lapovsky Kennedy, Elizabeth and Madeline Davis, *Boots of Leather and Slippers of Gold: The History of a Lesbian Community* (New York: Penguin Books, 1994).

Le Corbusier, *Towards a New Architecture*, trans. Frederick Etchells (London: Architectural Press, 1946).

Lears, Jackson, 'A Matter of Taste: Corporate Cultural Hegemony in a Mass-Consumption Society', in Lary May (ed.), *Recasting America: Culture and Politics in the Age of Cold War* (Chicago and London: University of Chicago Press, 1989), pp. 38–57.

Lee, A. Robert, *Multicultural American Literature: Comparative Black, Latino/a and Asian American Fictions* (Edinburgh: Edinburgh University Press, 2003).

Leeming, David, *James Baldwin: A Biography* (New York: Alfred A. Knopf, 1994).

Leeming, David, 'The White Problem', in 'Home and Away: Twentieth Century Masters Tribute to James Baldwin', in M. Mark (ed.), *Pen America: A Journal for Writers and Readers*, 1/2 (Fall 2001), pp. 18–23.

Leffler, Melvyn P., *A Preponderance of Power: National Security, the Truman Administration, and the Cold War* (Stanford, CA: Stanford University Press, 1992).

Leffler, Melvyn P., 'Inside Enemy Archives: The Cold War Reopened', *Foreign Affairs*, 75/4 (July – August 1996), pp. 120–34.

Lehman, Susan (1999), 'Et Tu, Christopher?', *Salon*, 11 February 1999, http://archive.salon.com/media/lehm/1999/02/11lehm2.html

Leibman, Nina C., *Living Room Lectures: The Fifties Family in Film and Television* (Austin: University of Texas Press, 1995).

Leland, John, 'Trying to Stay Put in Florida Mobile Homes', *New York Times*, 22 June 2003, pp. 1–3.

Leuchtenberg, William, *A Troubled Feast: American Society since 1945* (Boston: Little, Brown and Company, 1973).

Lipschutz, Ronnie D., *Cold War Fantasies: Film, Fiction, and Foreign Policy* (Lanham, MD: Rowman and Littlefield, 2001).

The Long, Long Trailer, Vincente Minnelli, Dir., Loew's Inc. (1954).

Looby, Christopher, ' "Innocent Homosexuality": The Fiedler Thesis in Retrospect', in Gerald Graff and James Phelan (eds), *The Adventures of Huckleberry Finn*, by Mark Twain (Boston: Bedford Books,1995), pp. 535–50.

Lott, Eric, *Love and Theft: Blackface Minstrelsy and the American Working Class* (New York: Oxford University Press, 1995).

Lowell, Robert, *Collected Prose*, ed. Robert Giroux (London: Faber and Faber, 1987).

Lowell, Robert, *Collected Poems*, ed. Frank Bidart and David Gewanter (London: Faber and Faber, 2003).

Lucas, Scott and C. J. Morris, 'A Very British Crusade: The Information Research Department and the Cold War', in Richard Aldrich (ed.), *British Intelligence, Strategy, and the Cold War* (London: Routledge, 1992), pp. 85–111.

Lucas, Scott, *Freedom's War: The US Crusade against the Soviet Union, 1945–56* (New York: New York University Press, 1999).

Lucas, Scott, 'Afterword: Considering Cultures: How to Make Sense of our Cold War', in Nathan Abrams and Julie Hughes (eds), *Containing America: Cultural Production and Consumption in 50s America* (Birmingham: Birmingham University Press, 2000), pp. 187–99.

Lucas, Scott, 'Mobilizing Culture: The CIA and the State–Private Networks in the Early Cold War', in Dale Carter and Robin Clifton (eds), *War and Cold War in American Foreign Policy 1942–62* (London: Palgrave, 2002), pp. 83–107.

McAlister, Melani, *Epic Encounters: Culture, Media, and US Interests in the Middle East, 1945–2000* (Berkeley and Los Angeles: University of California Press, 2001).

MacDonald, J. Fred, *One Nation under Television: The Rise and Decline of Network TV* (New York: Pantheon, 1990).

McKinstry, Leo, 'Why isn't CND cheering Bush?', *Daily Telegraph*, 11 January 2004, http://www.telegraph.co.uk/opinion/main.jhtml?xml=%2Fopinion%2F2004%2F01%2F11%2Fdo1102.xml&secure Refresh=true&_requestid=6212

McNeill, William H., 'The Changing Shape of World History', *History and Theory*, 34/2 (1995), pp. 8–26.

Mailer, Norman, 'Sixth Advertisement for Myself', in Mailer, *Advertisements for Myself* (New York: G. P. Putnam's Sons, 1959), pp. 331–6.

Mailer, Norman, 'The White Negro: Superficial Reflections on the Hipster', in Mailer, *Advertisements for Myself* (New York: G. P. Putnam's Sons, 1959), pp. 337–58.

Mailer, Norman, *The Presidential Papers* (London: André Deutsch, 1964).

Marc, David, 'Beginning to Begin Again', in Horace Newcomb (ed.), *Television: The Critical View*, 4th edn (New York: Oxford University Press, 1987), pp. 323–60.

Marcuse, Herbert, *One-Dimensional Man: Studies in the Ideology of Advanced Industrial Society* (London: Routledge, [1964] 1991).

Mariani, Paul, *Lost Puritan: A Life of Robert Lowell* (New York: W. W. Norton, 1994).

Marks, John D., *The Search for the 'Manchurian Candidate': The CIA and Mind Control* (New York: Times Books, 1979).

Martin, Emily, *Flexible Bodies: Tracking Immunity in American Culture – From the Days of Polio to the Age of AIDS* (Boston: Beacon Press, 1994).

Matthews, John T., 'How Remus Frames Race' (forthcoming).

May, Lary, 'Movie Star Politics: The Screen Actors' Guild, Cultural Conversion, and the Hollywood Red Scare', in Lary May (ed.), *Recasting America: Culture and Politics in the Age of Cold War* (Chicago and London: the University of Chicago Press, 1989), pp. 125–53.

Medovoi, Leerom, 'Reading the Blackboard: Youth, Masculinity, and Racial Cross-Identification', in Harry Stecopoulos and Michael Uebel (eds), *Race and the Subject of Masculinities* (Durham, NC, and London: Duke University Press, 1997), pp. 138–69.

Mengay, Donald H., 'The Failed Copy: *Giovanni's Room* and the (Re) Contextualisation of Difference', *Genders*, 17 (Fall 1993), pp. 59–70.

Metres, Philip, 'Confusing a Naive Robert Lowell and Lowell Naeve: "Lost Connections" in 1940s War Resistance at West Street Jail and Danbury Prison', *Contemporary Literature*, 41/4 (2000), pp. 661–92.

Mezzrow, Mezz and Bernard Wolfe, *Really the Blues*, with an introduction by Barry Gifford (New York: Citadel Underground, [1946] 1990).

Miller, Arthur, *The Crucible* (London: Penguin, [1953] 2000).

Moylan, Tom, *Demand the Impossible: Science Fiction and the Utopian Imagination* (New York: Methuen, 1986).

Munslow, Alun, *Deconstructing History* (London: Routledge, 1997).

Muse, Benjamin, *Ten Years of Prelude: The Story of Integration since the Supreme Court's 1954 Decision* (Beaconsfield: Darwen Finlayson, 1964).

My Son John, Leo McCarey, Dir., Paramount (1952).

Myrdal, Gunnar, *An American Dilemma: The Negro Problem and Modern Democracy* (New York: Harper, 1944).

Nadel, Alan, *Containment Culture: American Narratives, Postmodernism and the Atomic Age* (Durham, NC, and London: Duke University Press, 1995).

National Security Council, US Policy toward Africa South of the Sahara Prior to Calendar Year 1960, NSC 5719, 31 July 1957, Record Group 273, pp. 9–10.

Newton, Esther, 'The Mythic Mannish Lesbian: Radclyffe Hall and the New Woman', *Signs*, 9/4 (Summer 1984), pp. 557–75.

Niebuhr, Reinhold, *The Irony of American History* (New York: Charles Scribner's Sons, 1952).

Noakes, John A., 'Racializing Subversion: The FBI and the Depiction of Race in Early Cold War Movies', *Ethnic and Racial Studies*, 26/4 (July 2003), pp. 728–49.

Noble, David W., 'The Reconstruction of Progress: Charles Beard, Richard Hofstadter and Postwar Historical Thought', in Lary May (ed.), *Recasting America: Culture and Politics in the Age of Cold War* (Chicago: University of Chicago Press, 1989), pp. 61–75.

North, Barry, *Something to Lean On: The First Sixty Years of the British Polio Fellowship* (South Ruislip: BPF, 1999).

Norton-Taylor, Richard and Seamus Milne, *The Guardian*, 11 July 1996, http://www.guardian.co.uk/international/story/0,3604,338230,00.html

Novik, Peter, *That Noble Dream: The 'Objectivity Question' and the American Historical Profession* (Cambridge: Cambridge University Press, 1988).

NSC-68, 'United States Objectives and Programs for National Security', 14 April 1950, reprinted at http://www.fas.org/irp/offdocs/nsc-hst/nsc-68.htm

O'Reilly, Kenneth, 'Racial Integration: The Battle General Eisenhower Chose Not to Fight', *Journal of Blacks in Higher Education*, 0/18 (Winter 1997-8), pp. 110–19.

Orwell, George, *The Road to Wigan Pier* (London: Penguin, [1937] 1962).

Orwell, George, *Homage to Catalonia* (Harmondsworth: Penguin, [1938] 1989),

Orwell, George, *The Lion and the Unicorn* (London: Secker and Warburg, 1941).

Orwell, George, 'As I Please', *Tribune*, 1 September 1944, in *The Collected Essays, Journalism and Letters of George Orwell*, ed. Ian Angus and Sonia Orwell, vol. 3: *As I Please, 1943–1945* (London: Secker and Warburg, 1968), p. 224.

Orwell, George, *The Collected Essays, Journalism and Letters of George Orwell*, ed. Ian Angus and Sonia Orwell, vol. 1: *An Age Like This, 1920–1940* (London: Secker and Warburg, 1968).

Orwell, George, *The Collected Essays, Journalism and Letters of George Orwell*, ed. Ian Angus and Sonia Orwell, vol. 2: *My Country Right or Left, 1940–1943* (London: Secker and Warburg, 1968).

Orwell, George, *The Collected Essays, Journalism and Letters of George Orwell*, ed. Ian Angus and Sonia Orwell, vol. 3: *As I Please, 1943–1945* (London: Secker and Warburg, 1968).

Orwell, George, *The Collected Essays, Journalism and Letters of George Orwell*, ed. Ian Angus and Sonia Orwell Par, vol. 4: *In Front of your Nose, 1945–1950* (London: Secker and Warburg, 1968).

Orwell, George, *The Complete Works of George Orwell*, ed. Peter Davison, vol. 20: *Our Job is to Make Life Worth Living* (London: Secker and Warburg, 1998).

Packard, Vance, *The Hidden Persuaders* (New York: David McKay, 1957).

Patterson, James, *Grand Expectations: The United States, 1945–1974* (New York: Oxford University Press, 1996).

Pick Up on South Street, Samuel Fuller, Dir., 20th Century Fox (1953).

Plath, Sylvia, *The Bell Jar* (London: Faber, [1963] 1966).

Podhoretz, Norman, 'If Orwell were Alive Today, He'd be a Neo-Conservative', *Harper's* (January 1983), pp. 30–7.

Porter, Horace, *Stealing the Fire: The Art and Protest of James Baldwin* (Middletown: Wesleyan University Press, 1989).

Price, Ruth, *The Lives of Agnes Smedley* (Oxford: Oxford University Press, 2004).

Pryce-Jones, David, 'Orwell's Reputation', in Miriam Gross (ed.), *The World of George Orwell* (London: Weidenfeld and Nicolson, 1971), pp. 144–52.

Pynchon, Thomas, 'The Road to 1984', *The Guardian*, 3 May 2003, http://books.guardian.co.uk/review/story/0,12084,948203,00.html

Quo Vadis, Mervyn LeRoy, Dir., Metro-Goldwyn-Mayer (1951).

Radosh, Ronald, 'The Legacy of the Anti-Communist Liberal Intellectuals', *Partisan Review*, 47/4 (2000), pp. 550–67.

Rahv, Philip, 'The Unfuture of Utopia', *Partisan Review* (July 1949), reprinted in Jeffrey Meyers (ed.), *George Orwell: The Critical Heritage* (London: Routledge and Kegan Paul, 1975), pp. 267–73.

Rampersad, Arnold, *The Life of Langston Hughes*, vol. 2: *1941–1967 I Dream a World* (New York: Oxford University Press, 1988).

Rebecca, Alfred Hitchcock, Dir., Selznick International Pictures (1940).

Rees, Richard, *George Orwell: Fugitive from the Camp of Victory* (London: Secker and Warburg, 1961).

Reisley, Roland and John Timpane (2001), *Usonia, New York: Building a Community with Frank Lloyd Wright*, foreword by Martin Filler (New York: Princeton Architectural Press, 2001).

Reisman, David, *The Lonely Crowd* (Yale Paperbound Edition; New Haven: Yale University Press, 1961).

Rella, Franco, *The Myth of the Other: Lacan, Foucault, Deleuze, Bataille*, trans. Nelson Moe (Washington: Maisonneuve Press, 1994).

Report by the Policy Planning Staff, PPS/23, Review of Current Trends in US Foreign Policy, 24 February 1948, *Foreign Relations of the United States*, vol. 1 (1948), pp. 510–29.

Rodden, John, 'Orwell and the London Left Intelligentsia', in Graham Holderness, Bryan Loughrey, and Nahem Yousaf (eds), *George Orwell* (London: Macmillan, 1998), pp. 161–81.

Rogin, Michael, *Ronald Reagan, the Movie: And Other Episodes of Political Demonology* (Berkeley and Los Angeles: University of California Press, 1987).

Rolo, Charles, 'Other Voices, Other Rooms' (review of *Giovanni's Room*, by James Baldwin), *Atlantic Monthly*, 198/6 (December 1956), p. 98.

Rosenberg, Emily, *Spreading the American Dream: American Economic and Cultural Expansion, 1890–1945* (New York: Hill and Wang, 1982).

Rosenberg, Emily, 'Rosenberg's Commentary', in Ernest R. May (ed.), *American Cold War Strategy: Interpreting NSC-68* (Boston: Bedford Books, 1993), pp. 160–4.

Ross, Andrew, *No Respect: Intellectuals and Popular Culture* (New York and London: Routledge, 1989).

Russo, Vito, *The Celluloid Closet: Homosexuality in the Movies* (New York: Harper and Row, 1987).

Ryan, Alan (ed.), *After the End of History* (London: Collins and Brown, 1992).

Ryan, David, *US Foreign Policy in World History* (London: Routledge, 2000).

Sahara, Zoltan Korda, Dir., Columbia Pictures (1943).

Said, Edward, *Culture and Imperialism* (London: Chatto and Windus, 1993).

Savran, David, *Communists, Cowboys and Queers: The Politics of Masculinity in the Work of Arthur Miller and Tennessee Williams* (London and Minneapolis: University of Minneapolis Press, 1992).

Sealander, Judith , 'Families, World War II, and the Baby Boom (1940–1955)', in Joseph M. Hawes and Elizabeth I. Nybakken (eds), *American Families: A Research Guide and Historical Handbook* (New York: Greenwood Press, 1991), pp. 157–81.

Sedley, Stephen, 'An Immodest Proposal: *Animal Farm*', in Christopher Norris (ed.), *Inside the Myth – Orwell: Views from the Left* (London: Fontana, 1984), pp. 155–62.

Seed, David, *American Science Fiction and the Cold War* (Edinburgh: Edinburgh University Press, 1999).

Segal, Charlene, 'Young Marrieds Salute Mobile Life', *Mobile Life Magazine* (yearbook) (1953), pp. 6–9.

Seldes, Gilbert, 'Television: The Golden Hope', *Atlantic*, 3 (1949), pp. 34–7.

Shannon, Christopher, *A World Made Safe for Differences: Cold War Intellectuals and the Politics of Identity* (Lanham, MD: Rowman and Littlefield, 2001).

Skolnick, Arlene, *Embattled Paradise: The American Family in an Age of Uncertainty* (New York: Basic Books, 1991).

Smedley, Agnes, *Daughter of Earth* (London: Virago, [1929] 1977).

Smedley, Agnes, *China's Red Army Marches* (New York: Vanguard Press, 1934).

Smedley, Agnes, *Battle Hymn of China* (New York: Knopf, 1943).

Smith, Jane S., *Patenting the Sun: Polio and the Salk Vaccine* (New York: Anchor Books, 1990).

Smythe, Mabel M. (ed.), *The Black American Reference Book* (Englewood Cliffs: Prentice-Hall, Inc., 1976).

Snead, James, 'Trimming Uncle Remus's Tales: Narrative Revisions in Walt Disney's *Song of the South*', in Colin MacCabe and Cornel West (eds), *White Screens, Black Images: Hollywood from the Dark Side* (New York: Routledge, 1994), pp. 81–99.

Song of the South, Harve Foster and Wilfred Jackson, Dir., Walt Disney Pictures (1946).

'Southern Declaration on Integration', *New York Times*, 12 March 1956; reprinted in Anthony Cooper (ed.), *The Black Experience, 1865–1978* (Dartford: Greenwich University Press, 1995), pp. 239–40.

Spigel, Lynn, *Make Room for Television* (Chicago: University of Chicago Press, 1992).

Stacey, Jackie, 'Desperately Seeking Difference', *Screen*, 18/1 (Winter 1987), pp. 48–61.

Stacey, Jackie, 'Feminine Fascinations: Forms of Identification in Star – Audience Relations', in Christine Gledhill (ed.), *Stardom: Industry of Desire* (London: Routledge, 1991), pp. 141–63.

Staggs, Sam, *All about 'All about Eve'* (New York: St Martin's Griffin, 2000).

Standley, Fred L. and Louis H. Pratt (eds), *Conversations with Baldwin* (Jackson and London: University of Mississippi Press, 1989).

Stecopoulos, Harry and Michael Uebel (eds), *Race and the Subject of Masculinities* (Durham, NC: Duke University Press, 1997).

Stilgoe, John, *Borderland: Origins of the American Suburb, 1820–1939* (New Haven: Yale University Press, 1990).

Stonor Saunders, Frances, *Who Paid the Piper? The CIA and the Cultural Cold War* (London: Granta, 1999).

Stormy Weather, Andrew L. Stone, Dir., 20th Century Fox (1943).

Straw, Jack, 'Blame the Left, Not the British', *The Observer*, 15 October 2000, http://observer.guardian.co.uk/comment/story/0,6903,382758,00.html

Stripes, Ivan Reitman, Dir., Columbia Pictures (1981).

Sullivan, Andrew, 'The E-Mails Pour In', *AndrewSullivan.com*, 30 October 2002, http://www.andrewsullivan.com/book__club.php?book__num=book__club__blog.html

Susman, Warren (with the assistance of Edward Griffin), 'Did Success Spoil the United States? Dual Representations in Postwar America', in Lary May (ed.), *Recasting America: Culture and Politics in the Age of the Cold War* (Chicago and London: University of Chicago Press, 1989), pp. 19–37.

Taylor, D. J., *Orwell* (London: Chatto and Windus, 2003).

The Ten Commandments, Cecil B. DeMille, Dir., Motion Picture Associates (1956).

Thurston, Michael, 'Robert Lowell's Monumental Vision: History, Form, and the Cultural Work of Postwar American Lyric', *American Literary History*, 12/1 (2000), pp. 79–112.

Tiffany, Daniel, *Toy Medium: Materialism and Modern Lyric* (Berkeley and Los Angeles: University of California Press, 2000).

Tomes, Robert R., *Apocalypse Then: American Intellectuals and the Vietnam War, 1954–1975* (New York: New York University Press, 1998).

Tools, Story, 'Trailer Park Makes LA Historic Monument List', *Associated Press*, 8 November 2002, pp. 1–2.

Trilling, Lionel, 'George Orwell and the Politics of Truth', in Trilling, *The Opposing Self* (London: Secker and Warburg, 1955), pp. 151–72.

Truman, President, address to a Joint Session of Congress, 12 March 1947, in Raymond Dennett and Robert K. Turner (eds), *Documents on American Foreign Relations*, vol. 9 (Princeton: Princeton University Press, 1949), pp. 6–7.

Tyler May, Elaine, *Homeward Bound: American Families in the Cold War Era* (New York: Basic Books, 1988).

US Senate, 81st Cong., 2nd sess., Committee on Expenditures in Executive Departments, *The Employment of Homosexuals and Other Sex Perverts in Government* (Washington: Government Printing Office, 1950).

Vallely, Paul, 'On the Road Again', *The Independent*, 30 April 2003, http://news.independent.co.uk/uk/this__britain/story.jsp?story=401640

Van Vechten, Carl, *Nigger Heaven*, introduction by Kathleen Pfeiffer (Urbana and Chicago: University of Illinois Press, [1926] 2000).

Vicinus, Martha, ' "They Wonder to Which Sex I Belong": The Historical Roots of the Modern Lesbian Identity', in Martha Vicinus (ed.), *Lesbian Subjects: A Feminist Studies Reader* (Bloomington, IN: Indiana University Press, 1996), pp. 233–60.

Vidal, Gore, *The City and the Pillar* (1949); reprint, with a new preface by Gore Vidal (London: Abacus, 1994).

Wald, Gayle, *Crossing the Line: Racial Passing in Twentieth-Century US Literature and Culture* (Durham, NC, and London: Duke University Press, 2000).

Walk on the Wild Side, Edward Dmytryk, Dir., Columbia Pictures (1962).

Wall, Wendy L., 'Italian Americans and the 1948 Letters to Italy Campaign', in Christian G. Appy (ed.), *Cold War Constructions: The Political Culture of the United States Imperialism, 1945–1966* (Amherst, MA: University of Massachusetts Press, 2000), pp. 89–109.

Wallace, Maurice, ' "I'm Not Entirely What I Look Like": Richard Wright, James Baldwin, and the Hegemony of Vision; or, Jimmy's FBEye Blues', in Dwight A. McBride (ed.), *James Baldwin Now* (New York and London: New York University Press, 1999), pp. 289–306.

Wallis, Alan, *Wheel Estate: The Rise and Decline of Mobile Homes* (New York: Oxford University Press, 1991).

Wassermann, Elizabeth, 'The Power of Facing', *Atlantic Unbound*, 23 October 2002, http://www.theatlantic.com/unbound/interviews/int2002-10-23.htm

Weatherby, W. J., *James Baldwin: Artist on Fire* (London: Michael Joseph, 1990).

Weinstein, Harvey M., *Psychiatry and the Central Intelligence Agency: Victims of Mind Control* (Washington: American Psychiatric Press, 1990).

Weiss, Andrea, *Vampires and Violets: Lesbians in Film* (Harmondsworth: Penguin Books, 1993).

Wellington, Alexander C., 'Trailer Camp Slums', *The Survey* (October 1951), pp. 418–22.

Wheatcroft, Geoffrey, 'Big Brother with a Moral Sense', *Independent on Sunday*, 28 June 1998, reprinted at http://www.netcharles.com/orwell/ctc/docs/defence.htm

White, Patricia, *Uninvited: Classical Hollywood Cinema and Lesbian Representability* (Bloomington, IN: Indiana University Press, 1999).

Whitfield, Stephen J., *The Culture of the Cold War* (1991), 2nd edn (Baltimore: Johns Hopkins University Press, 1996).

Wiegman, Robyn, 'Fiedler and Sons', in Harry Stecopoulos and Michael Uebel (eds), *Race and the Subject of Masculinities* (Durham, NC, and London: Duke University Press, 1997), pp. 45–68.

Wilson, Edward L., 'Housing Dollar: Lowest Cost', *Mobile Life Magazine* (yearbook) (1954), pp. 4–5.

Williams, Raymond, *Orwell* (London: Fontana, 1971).

Williams, Raymond, *Television: Technology and Cultural Form* (Hanover, NH: Wesleyan University Press, 1992).

Wolfe, Bernard, 'Uncle Remus and the Malevolent Rabbit', *Commentary*, 8/1 (July 1949), pp. 31–41.

Wood, Robert E., 'From the Marshall Plan to the Third World', in Melvyn P. Leffler and David S. Painter (eds), *The Origins of the Cold War: An International History* (London: Routledge, 1994), pp. 201–14.

Woodhouse, C. M., 'Animal Farm', *Times Literary Supplement*, 6 August 1945, pp. xxx–xxxi.

Woodhouse, C. M., *Something Ventured* (London: Granada, 1982).

Wordsworth, William, *Lyrical Ballads*, 2nd edn (London: Longman, 1800).

Wright, Richard, *White Man, Listen!* (Westport, CT: Greenwood Press, 1957).

Wylie, Philip, *Generation of Vipers* (Normal, IL: Dalkey Archive Press, [1942] 1996).

Zuk, William and Roger H. Clark, *Kinetic Architecture* (New York: Van Nostrand Reinhold Company, 1970).

Further Reading

Altman, Dennis, *Homosexual: Oppression and Liberation* (New York: New York University Press, [1971] 1993).

The American Writer and his Roots: Selected Papers from the First Conference of Negro Writers, March 1959 (New York: American Society of African Culture, 1960).

Anisfield, Nancy (ed.), *The Nightmare Considered: Critical Essays on Nuclear War Literature* (Bowling Green, OH: Popular Press, 1991).

Barson, Michael, *'Better Dead than Red!' A Nostalgic Look at the Golden Years of Russiaphobia, Red-Baiting, and Other Commie Madness* (New York: Hyperion, 1992).

Beckett, Francis, *Enemies Within: The Rise and Fall of the British Communist Party* (Woodbridge: Merlin Press, 1998).

Bell, Daniel (ed.), *The Radical Right* (Garden City, NY: Doubleday and Co., Anchor Books, 1964).

Bergler, Edmund, *Homosexuality: Disease or Way of Life?* (New York: Hill and Wang, 1956).

Bernhard, Nancy E., *US Television News and Cold War Propaganda, 1947–1960* (Cambridge: Cambridge University Press, 2003).

Biskind, Peter, *Seeing is Believing: How Hollywood Taught us to Stop Worrying and Love the Bomb* (London: Bloomsbury, 1983).

Boyd Hinds, Lynn and Theodore Otto Windt, *The Cold War as Rhetoric: The Beginnings, 1945–1950* (New York: Praeger, 1991).

Boyer, Paul, *By the Bomb's Early Light: American Thought and Culture at the Dawn of the Atomic Age* (New York: Pantheon, 1985).

Brands, H. W., *The Devil We Knew: Americans and the Cold War* (New York: Oxford University Press, 1993).

Brown, Howard, *Familiar Faces, Hidden Lives: The Story of Homosexual Men in America Today* (New York and London: Harcourt Brace Jovanovich, 1976).

Burley, Dan, 'Whites "Pass" for Negroes', *New York Age*, 24 September 1949, p. 17.

Byars, Jackie, *All That Hollywood Allows: Re-Reading Gender in 1950s Melodrama* (Chapel Hill, NC: University of North Carolina Press, 1991).

Campbell, James, *This is the Beat Generation: New York – San Francisco – Paris* (London: Secker and Warburg, 1999).

Campbell, Neil, *American Youth Cultures* (Edinburgh: Edinburgh University Press, 2004).

Campbell, Neil, Jude Davies and George Mackay (eds), *Issues in Americanisation and Culture: A Handbook* (Edinburgh: Edinburgh University Press, 2004).

Ceplair, Larry and Steven Englund, *The Inquisition in Hollywood: Politics in the Film Community, 1930–1960* (Berkeley and Los Angeles: University of California Press, 1979).

Chomsky, Noam, *Hegemony or Survival: America's Quest for Global Domination* (New York: Owl Books, 2004).

Chomsky, Noam, R. C. Lewontin, Ira Katzuelson, Laura Nader, Richard Ohmann, David Montgomery, Immanuel Wallerstein, Ray Siever and Howard Zinn, *The Cold War and the University: Toward an Intellectual History of the Postwar Years* (New York: New Press, 1997).

Cohan, Steven, *Masked Men: Masculinity and the Movies in the Fifties* (Bloomington, IN: Indiana University Press, 1997).

Cohan, Steven, 'Masquerading as the American Male in the Fifties: *Picnic*, William Holden and the Spectacle of Masculinity in the Hollywood Film', in Constance Penley and Sharon Willis (eds), *Male Trouble* (Minneapolis: University of Minneapolis Press, 1993), pp. 203–33.

Condon, Richard, *The Manchurian Candidate* (New York: New American Library, 1959).

Coover, Robert, *The Public Burning* (New York: Viking Press, 1977).

Corkin, Stanley, *Cowboys as Cold Warriors: The Western and US History* (Philadephia: Temple University Press, 2004).

Cornis-Pope, Marcel, *Narrative Innovation and Cultural Rewriting in the Cold War Era and After* (New York: Palgrave, 2001).

Cuordileone, Kyle, *Manhood and American Political Culture in the Cold War* (New York, Routledge, 2004).

Davis, Mike, *Prisoners of the American Dream: Politics and Economy in the History of the US Working Class* (London: Verso, 1986).

Dean, Robert D., *Imperial Brotherhood: Gender and the Making of Cold War Foreign Policy* (Amherst, MA: University of Massachusetts Press, 2003).

D'Emilio, John, 'The Homosexual Menace: The Politics of Sexuality in Cold War America', in K. Peiss and C. Simmons (eds), *Passion and Power: Sexuality in History* (Philadelphia: Temple University Press, 1989), pp. 225–40.

Derrida, Jacques, 'No Apocalypse, Not Now (Full Speed Ahead, Seven Missiles, Seven Missives)', *Diacritics*, 14/2 (1984), pp. 20–31.

Dickstein, Morris, *Leopards in the Temple: The Transformation of American Fiction, 1945–1970* (Cambridge, MA: Harvard University Press, 2002).

Diggins, John Patrick, *The Proud Decades: America in War and Peace, 1941–1960* (New York: W. W. Norton, 1988).

Doane, Mary Ann, *The Desire to Desire: The Woman's Film of the 1940s* (Bloomington, IN: Indiana University Press, 1987).

Doctorow, E. L., *The Book of Daniel* (London: Pan Books, 1973).

Doherty, Thomas, *Teenagers and Teenpics: The Juvenilization of American Movies in the 1950s* (Winchester: Unwin Hyman, 1988).

Doherty, Thomas, *Cold War, Cool Medium: Television, McCarthyism, and American Culture* (New York: Columbia University Press, 2003).

Donner, Frank, *The Age of Surveillance: The Aims and Methods of America's Political Intelligence System* (New York: Alfred A. Knopf, 1980).

Douglas, Susan J., *Where the Girls Are: Growing up Female with the Mass Media* (New York: Crown, 1994).

Duberman, Martin B., *Paul Robeson* (New York, Knopf, 1988).

Ehrenreich, Barbara, *Fear of Falling: The Inner Life of the Middle Class* (New York: Pantheon Books, 1989).

Fiedler, Leslie, *Waiting for the End: The American Literary Scene from Hemingway to Baldwin* (Harmondsworth: Penguin Books, [1964] 1967).

Field, Hermann and Kate Field, *Trapped in the Cold War: The Ordeal of an American Family* (Stanford, CA: Stanford University Press, 1999).

Finney, Jack, *The Invasion of the Body Snatchers* (New York: Dell, 1955).

Fitzgibbon, Constantine, *Secret Intelligence in the Twentieth Century* (London: Hart-Davis MacGibbon, 1976).

Foreman, Joel, *The Other Fifties: Interrogating Midcentury American Icons* (Urbana and Chicago: University of Illinois Press, 1997).

Fousek, John, *To Lead the Free World: American Nationalism and the Cultural Roots of the Cold War* (Chapel Hill, NC: University of North Carolina Press, 2000).

Fried, Richard M., *Nightmare in Red: The McCarthy Era in Perspective* (New York: Oxford University Press, 1990).

Gaddis, John Lewis, *We Now Know: Rethinking Cold War History* (New York: Oxford University Press, 1997).

Garber, Majorie and Rebecca L. Walkowitz (eds), *Secret Agents: The Rosenberg Case, McCarthyism, and Fifties America* (New York: Routledge, 1995).

Garrow, David, *The FBI and Martin Luther King* (New York: W. W. Norton, 1981).

George, Nelson, *The Death of Rhythm & Blues* (New York: Dutton, 1989).

Gilbert, James, *A Cycle of Outrage: America's Reaction to the Juvenile Delinquent in the 1950s* (New York: Oxford University Press, 1988).

Harris, Oliver, 'Can You See a Virus? The Queer Cold War of William Burroughs', *Journal of American Studies*, 33/2 (August 1999), pp. 243–66.

Haut, Woody, *Pulp Culture: Hardboiled Fiction and the Cold War* (London: Serpent's Tail, 1996).

Hendershot, Cyndy, 'The Bear and the Dragon: Representations of Communism in Early Sixties American Culture', *Journal of American and Comparative Cultures*, 23/44 (Winter 2000), pp. 67–74.

Hendershot, Cyndy, *Anti-Communism and Popular Culture in Mid-Century America* (Jefferson, NC: McFarland, 2003).

Henriksen, Margot A., *Strangelove's America: Society and Culture in the Atomic Age* (Berkeley and Los Angeles: University of California Press, 1997).

Henry, Charles, *Ralph Bunche: Model Negro or American Other?* (New York: New York University Press, 1999).

Hogan, Michael J. (ed.), *The End of the Cold War: Its Meaning and Implications* (New York: Cambridge University Press, 1992).

Horowitz, Daniel, *Betty Friedan and the Making of the Feminine Mystique: The American Left, the Cold War, and Modern Feminism* (Amherst, MA: University of Massachusetts Press, 2001).

Houen, Alex, *Terrorism and Modern Literature: From Joseph Conrad to Ciaran Carson* (Oxford: Oxford University Press, 2002).

Hunter, Allen (ed.), *Rethinking the Cold War: Critical Perspectives on the Past* (Philadelphia: Temple University Press, 1998).

Jancovich, Mark, *Rational Fears: American Horror in the 1950s* (Manchester: Manchester University Press, 1996).

Kinkead, Eugene, *Why They Collaborated* (London: Longman, Green and Co., Ltd, 1959).

Kinsey, Alfred C., *Sexual Behavior in the Human Female* (Philadelphia: Saunders, 1953).

Knight, Peter, *Conspiracy Culture: American Paranoia from Kennedy to the X-Files* (London: Routledge, 2001).

Kodat, Catherine Gunther, 'Dancing through the Cold War: The Case of *The Nutcracker*', *Mosaic*, 33/3 (September 2000), pp. 1–17.

Krabbendam, Hans and Giles Scott-Smith (eds.), *The Cultural Cold War in Western Europe, 1945–1960* (London: Frank Cass, 2003).

Kramer, Hilton, *The Twilight of the Intellectuals: Culture and Politics in the Era of the Cold War* (Chicago: I.R. Dee, 1999).

Kuznick, Peter J. and James Gilbert (eds), *Rethinking Cold War Culture* (Washington: Smithsonian Institution Press, 2001).

Leffler, Melvyn P., 'New Approaches, Old Interpretations, and Prospective Reconfigurations', *Diplomatic History*, 19/2 (Spring 1995), pp. 173–96.

Leonard, Heil, *Jazz and the White Americans* (Chicago: University of Chicago Press, 1962).

Lindey, Christine, *Art in the Cold War: From Vladivostok to Kalamazoo, 1945–1962* (London: Herbert Press Ltd, 1990).

Lippman, Walter, *The Cold War: A Study in US Foreign Policy* (New York: Harper & Row, 1947).

Lipsitz, George, *Class and Culture in Cold War America: 'A Rainbow at Midnight'* (New York: Praeger, 1981).

Lucas, Scott, *George Orwell: Life and Times* (London: Haus, 2003).

Lucas, Scott, *The Betrayal of Dissent: Beyond Orwell, Hitchens, and the New American Century* (London: Pluto, 2004).

Luciano, Patrick, *Them or Us: Archetypal Interpretations of Fifties Alien Invasion* (Bloomington, IN: Indiana University Press, 1987).

McCarthy, Joseph, *McCarthyism: The Fight for America* (New York: Devin-Adair, 1952).

McClarnand, Elaine and Steve Goodson (eds), *The Impact of the Cold War on American Popular Culture* (Carrollton, GA: State University of West Georgia, 1999).

McClintock, Michael, *Instruments of Statecraft: US Guerilla Warfare, Counter-Insurgency, and Counter-Terrorism, 1940–1990* (New York: Pantheon Books, 1992).

McConachie, Bruce A., *American Theater in the Culture of the Cold War: Producing and Contesting Containment, 1947–1962* (Iowa City: University of Iowa Press, 2003).

McDonald, Dwight, *Masscult and Midcult* (New York: Random House, 1961).

McDonald, Dwight, *Against the American Grain* (London: Victor Gollancz, 1963).

MacDonald, J. Fried, *Television and the Red Menace: The Video Road to Vietnam* (New York, Praeger, 1985).

Maier, Charles S. (ed.), *The Cold War in Europe* (New York: M. Wiener, 1991).

Marchetti, Victor and John D. Marks, *The CIA and the Cult of Intelligence* (New York: Knopf, 1974).

Marling, Karal Ann, *As Seen on TV: The Visual Culture of Everyday Life in the 1950s* (Cambridge, MA: Harvard University Press, 1996).

Marotta, Toby, *The Politics of Homosexuality: How Lesbians and Gay Men Have Made Themselves a Political and Social Force in Modern America* (Boston: Houghton Mifflin, 1981).

Martin, Lind and Kerry Segrave, *Anti-Rock: The Opposition to Rock 'n' Roll* (New York: Da Capo Press, 1993).

May, Ernest R. (ed.), *American Cold War Strategy: Interpreting NSC-68* (New York: St Martin's Press, 1993).

Medhurst, Martin J., Robert L. Ivie, Robert L. Scott and Philip Wander, *Cold War Rhetoric: Strategy, Metaphor, and Ideology* (Westport, CT: Greenwood Press, 1990).

Millar, Mark, illustrated by Dave Johnson and Kilian Plunkett, *Superman: Red Son* (London: Titan Books, 2004).

Monteiro, George, 'Frost's Politics and the Cold War', in Robert Faggen (ed.), *The Cambridge Companion to Robert Frost* (Cambridge and New York: Cambridge University Press, 2001), pp. 221–39.

Morgan, Ted, *Reds: McCarthyism in Twentieth Century America* (New York: Random House, 2004).

Nadel, Alan, 'A Whole New (Disney) World Order: Aladdin, Atomic Power, and the Muslim Middle East', in Matthew Bernstein and Gaylyn Studlar (eds), *Visions of the East: Orientalism in Film* (New Brunswick, NJ: Rutgers University Press, 1997), pp. 184–204.

Nadel, Alan, *Flatlining on the Field of Dreams: Cultural Narratives in the Films of President Reagan's America* (New Brunswick, NJ: Rutgers University Press, 1997).

Nadel, Alan, 'The New Frontier, the Old West, and the Free World: The Cultural Politics of "Adult Western TV Dramas"', *American Drama* (Spring 1998), pp. 1–23.

Nadel, Alan, 'American Fiction and Televisual Consciousness' (review essay), *Contemporary Literature* (Summer 1998), pp. 303–16.

Nadel, Alan, '"Johnny Yuma Was a Rebel; He Roamed through the West": Television, Race, and the Real West', in James Friedman (ed.), *Reality Squared: Televisual Discourse on the Real* (New Brunswick, NJ: Rutgers University Press, 2002), pp. 50–73.

Nelson, Deborah, *Pursuing Privacy in the Cold War* (New York: Columbia University Press, 2002).

O'Reilly, Kenneth, *Black Americans: The FBI Files* (New York, Carroll & Graf, 1994).

Packard, Vance, *The Status Seekers: An Exploration of Class Behavior in America* (Harmondsworth: Penguin, 1959).

Paterson, Thomas G., *The Origins of the Cold War* (Lexington, MA: D. C. Heath, 1970).

Patton, Cyndy, *Sex and Germs: The Politics of AIDS* (Boston: South End Press, 1985).

Pease, Donald E., 'Leslie Fiedler, the Rosenberg Trial, and the Formulation of an American Canon', *boundary*, 2/17 (1990), pp. 155–98.

Pells, Richard, *The Liberal Mind in a Conservative Age: American Intellectuals in the 1940s and 1950s* (New York: Harper Row, 1985).

Pessen, Edward, *Losing Our Souls: The American Experience in the Cold War* (Chicago: Ivan R. Dee, 1995).

Polenberg, Richard, *One Nation Divisible: Class, Race, and Ethnicity in the United States since 1938* (New York: Viking, 1980).

Record, Wilson, *Race and Radicalism: The NAACP and the Communist Party in Conflict* (Ithaca, NY: Cornell University Press, 1964).

Rees, David, *The Age of Containment: The Cold War, 1945–1965* (London: Macmillan, 1967).

Rodriguez, Robert, *The 1950s' Most Wanted: The Top 10 Book of Rock & Roll Rebels, Cold War Crises, and All-American Oddities* (Dulles, VA: Brassey's, 2004).

Rogin, Michael Paul, *The Intellectuals and McCarthy: The Radical Specter* (Cambridge, MA: MIT Press, 1967).

Rose, Kenneth D., *One Nation Underground: The Fallout Shelter in American Culture* (New York: New York University Press, 2001).

Ruthven, Ken, *Nuclear Criticism* (Carlton: Melbourne University Press, 1993).

Ryan, David, *US Foreign Policy in World History* (London: Routledge, 2000).

Ryan, David, *The United States and Europe in the Twentieth Century* (London: Longman, 2003).

Savage, William W., Jr, *Comic Books and America, 1945–54* (Norman: University of Oklahoma Press, 1990).

Sayre, Nora, *Running Time: Films of the Cold War* (New York: Dial Press, 1982).

Schaub, Thomas Hill, *American Fiction in the Cold War* (Wisconsin: University of Wisconsin Press, 1991).

Schlesinger, Arthur M., Jr, *The Vital Center: The Politics of Freedom* (Boston: Houghton Mifflin, 1949).

Siebers, Tobin, *Cold War Criticism and the Politics of Scepticism* (New York: Oxford University Press, 1993).

Simpson, Caroline-Chung, *An Absent Presence: Japanese Americans in Postwar American Culture, 1945–1960* (Durham, NC: Duke University Press, 2001).

Sinfield, Alan, 'Un-American Activities', in *Cultural Politics – Queer Reading* (London: Routledge, 1994), pp. 40–59.

Smith, Dina, 'Global Cinderella: *Sabrina* (1954), Hollywood and Postwar Internationalism', *Cinema Journal*, 41/4 (2002), pp. 27–51.

Smith, Dina, 'The Narrative Limits of the Global Guggenheim', *Mosaic*, 35/4 (December 2002), pp. 85–101.

Smith, Dina, 'Lost Trailer Utopias: *The Long, Long Trailer* (1954) and Fifties America', *Utopian Studies*, 14/1 (2003), pp. 112–131.

Smith, Geoffrey S., 'National Security and Personal Isolation: Sex, Gender, and Disease in the Cold-War United States', *International History Review*, 14 (1992), pp. 307–37.

Southern, David W., *Gunnar Myrdal and Black – White Relations: The Use and Abuse of 'An American Dilemma', 1944–1969* (Baton Rouge: Louisiana State University Press, 1987).

Theoharris, Athan G. and John Stuart Cox, *The Boss: Edgar J. Hoover and the Great American Inquisition* (Philadelphia: Temple University Press, 1988).

Trilling, Lionel, *The Liberal Imagination: Essays on Literature and Society* (New York: Viking, 1950).

Wagnleitner, Reinhold and Elaine Tyler May (eds), *Here, There and Everywhere: The Foreign Politics of American Popular Culture* (Hanover, NH: University Press of New England, 2000).

Weber, Cynthia, *Moral America: Contemporary Politics and Film from 9/11 to Gulf War II* (Edinburgh: Edinburgh University Press, 2005).

Weinstein, Allen, *Perjury: the Hiss-Chambers Case* (New York, Knopf, 1978).

Whyte, William, *The Organization Man* (Harmondsworth: Penguin, 1956).

Winkler, Allan M., *Life under a Cloud: American Anxiety about the Atom* (New York: Oxford University Press, 1993).

Index